P9-DYP-809

HURON COUNTY LIBRARY

3 6492 00526202

DiscCookery

641.5 Got

Gothe, J.
Jurgen Gothe presents
DiscCookery.

PRICE: $22.95 (3559/go   )

Jurgen Gothe presents

DiscCookery

The DiscDrive 20th Anniversary Cookbook

whitecap

This one is for everybody who's worked up an
appetite listening to the radio this afternoon.

And for the two great eaters:
Herbie the cat and Benson the dog.

Go ahead, chow down.

Copyright © 2005 by CBC

Whitecap Books

All rights reserved. No part of this publication may be reproduced, stored in a retrieval system, or transmitted in any form or by any means, electronic, mechanical, photocopying, recording or otherwise, without the prior written permission of the publisher. All recommendations are made without guarantee on the part of the author or Whitecap Books Ltd. The author and publisher disclaim any liability in connection with the use of this information. For additional information, please contact Whitecap Books, 351 Lynn Avenue, North Vancouver, British Columbia, Canada V7J 2C4. Visit our website at www.whitecap.ca.

Edited by Elizabeth Wilson / Marial Shea
Copy-edited by Ben D'Andrea
Proofread by Joan Templeton
Artwork by Wil Rafuse
Cover and interior design by Jacqui Thomas
Photo of Jurgen Gothe's pets (p. 241) by Kate Williams

Printed and bound in Canada by Friesens

LIBRARY AND ARCHIVES CANADA CATALOGUING IN PUBLICATION

Gothe, Jurgen, 1944–
    DiscCookery : Jurgen Gothe presents the DiscDrive 20th anniversary
cookbook / Jurgen Gothe.

Includes index.
ISBN 1-55285-756-5

    1. Cookery. 2. DiscDrive (radio program) I. Title.

TX714.G679 2005   641.5   C2005-903036-4

The publisher acknowledges the financial support of the Government of Canada through the Book Publishing Industry Development Program for our publishing activities.

Contents

Foreword...vi
Acknowledgments................................vii
Introduction..ix
Abbreviations.....................................xii

CHAPTER 1 .... Starters 1

CHAPTER 2 .... Soups & Salads 13

CHAPTER 3 .... Snacks & Sides 35

CHAPTER 4 .... Pastas 47

CHAPTER 5 .... Fish 65

CHAPTER 6 .... Chicken Et Cetera 81

CHAPTER 7 .... Meats 101

CHAPTER 8 .... Vegetables 131

CHAPTER 9 .... Stews 149

CHAPTER 10 .... A Small Handful of 165
Large Extravaganzas

CHAPTER 11 .... Drinks 189

CHAPTER 12 .... Desserts 209

Index 233
About the Author 240

Foreword

I first became acquainted with Jurgen Gothe while listening to his popular afternoon "DiscDrive" show on CBC Radio 2 (what used to be called "Stereo" then) and have been a faithful program follower over the years.

A few years ago Jurgen took his Vancouver-based "DiscDrive" clear across the country to broadcast from St. John's, Newfoundland. Since I'd been fortunate to visit the Rock many times, I decided to let him know of some good eating establishments I had "taste tested" there. That conversation revealed several things we have in common.

I told him how much I enjoyed his show and his wide, appealing choice of tasteful music. He, in turn, surprised me by saying that he was a big fan of our television show ("The Tommy Hunter Show") and that his career began with emceeing some country music shows in Medicine Hat, Alberta. I later found out that he'd also played drums in a country band in rural Manitoba!

Once, when the show was on tour, I stopped by the CBC studios in Vancouver to say hello. It was our first face-to-face meeting and served to cement a mutual respect. We discovered we're of one mind—whether the music is country, jazz, opera, blue or classical, if it's well performed and recorded, it should be recognized for what it is.

The many recipes in *DiscCookery* are different from each other, but once the chef has mixed the ingredients, the result is a culinary delight. This cookbook celebrates 20 years of good listening and honours "DiscDrive" listeners for sharing their recipes. Many of the recipes, of course, reflect Jurgen's own culinary experiences.

For years a multitude of listeners have waited daily for Jurgen to skillfully weave together delicious, relaxing afternoons of musical enjoyment, and now *DiscCookery* offers a practical and delightful potpourri for the palate as well.

It may come as a surprise to you that during the years of hosting "The Tommy Hunter Show," I learned to love classical music as a change of pace and method of relaxation. Jurgen's calm and knowledgeable way of introducing selections was just what I needed as we prepared for the next segment of the show.

With the help of the right musical selections, the chef behind the microphone has a masterful way of preparing a gourmet meal that has his listeners coming back again and again. It takes a special talent to accomplish this, and Jurgen Gothe dishes it up on "DiscDrive," five days a week, without fail.

I, along with many thousands of fans across Canada and elsewhere, continue to enjoy Jurgen's "DiscDrive" on a daily basis. It's a habit, some say, like eating! Jurgen never fails to feed us just the right musical nourishment that leaves us wanting more.

Tommy Hunter, CM, O. Ont.
May 2005

Acknowledgments

This is it—the toughest part of the book.

All the rest just took time and energy; this takes brains, memory. The "thanks to" section is critical not because of what goes in but what's—frequently, inadvertently—left out.

I hope, nothing and no one, but just in case—the mind being far more fallible than the metric system—I'll start with a blanket apology and take it up from there.

So many people worked so long and hard, so creatively and efficiently on the assembly of this book that it actually made the whole thing pretty much a breeze. So if there's someone whose name isn't in the list below, forgive me and consider yourself doubly thanked, deeply appreciated, in perpetuity, or till the next one comes along, whichever be greater, to the power of ten, as Spike Milligan would have said.

First, Kate Williams, for all the pix and all the laughs and all the rest, all these years. Who'd have imagined it?

Now then—the role of the Big Bang was played by Grant Rowledge, producer extraordinaire, who paused only a split second when I said, "We should do a 'DiscDrive' cookbook for our 20th," before saying, "Sure," and then did the kickoff.

Catching the ball—a superb display of sporty skill—was publisher Robert McCullough, whose future is secure in the world of cuisine should he ever decide to give up words in favour of copper pots.

The word "brilliant" is probably overused, so I'll use it only once in these pages to describe the skills and good graces of Elizabeth Wilson, who rose to the increasing technological challenges, as they befell the prime author, as well as the predictably syntactic ones, which she'll recall from the last book, one more time—for the hat trick. Could we make it four, some time?

Canada's Country Gentleman, my friend Tommy Hunter, deserves a long round of applause for his good counsel about where to eat, his abiding sense of humour and his unerring understanding of what makes good music. I'd like nothing better than to bring them all together in a new network series one of these days.

Friends, colleagues far and wide—particularly Lucy Waverman and James Chatto; Tony Aspler and Canada's own Iron Chef Rob Feenie; the great Diana Krall (sorry there aren't more oyster dishes in this one), for all the wonderful things you do, and the good words you said.

All of the editors, designers, marketers—the whole marvellous Whitecap production team— I want you all flying my 747s, handling any future surgeries, being on call in case a tree falls on the house, whatever takes expertise and teamwork—Marial Shea, AnnMarie MacKinnon, Jacqui Thomas, Sophie Hunter, Alicia Schlag and Aydin Virani—plus the boys and girls in the backrooms and warehouses across the country.

The listeners, twenty years on, still tuning in, in numbers bigger than ever; the readers and viewers; the contributors of recipes and the chefs and cooks who over the years have let me mess with theirs—go ahead, feel free to reciprocate.

Will Rafuse for great art; Kent Kallberg for two decades of postcards and other pictures. (How many photographers *does* it take to change a lightbulb?)

Tom Deacon for the Very Beginning, shrouded in the mists of time and a haze of *langos*, fuelled by Egri Bikaver or was it Tokaj? Whatever it was, there probably wasn't enough of it at that lunch.

Janet Lea, for a longer season together than either of us would have anticipated, and all of it a delight. Barbara Brown, Manager of CBC Merchandising, for her drive and organizing.

The current "DiscDrive" Crew—Ede Wolk and Neil Ritchie for cheerful daily company, an unending supply of old movie material and obscure new music (The Vienna *Vegetable* Orchestra???) and a preponderance of chocolate, dispensed with a sardonic world view. Sundry other CBC colleagues—for a more comprehensive list, see the "DiscDrive" 20th anniversary CD.

The booksellers, naturally—big and, especially, small.

The Cats of all the years; the occasional doglet.

All the dinner guests. And salty old ABC for the barbecues, Craig for the rocket fuel, D.B. for the [yt] and, as we used to say about Radio 2, beyond. And hundreds more.

You rock.

Jurgen Gothe
Mayne Island, British Columbia
Summer 2005

Introduction

Let me tell you
how I do it and
then we can
compare notes …

Let me tell you how I do it and then we can compare notes: first time out, with an unfamiliar recipe, I follow it to the letter. This makes for considerable overrun of, let's say, french-fried *lutefisk*, if it's the recipe for 20. But it's the only way to test the thing: see if it's all there and find out where the chef and I differ.

The next time—except maybe in the case of *lutefisk*, in which case I might like to move right along to something else—I do it my way, substituting, adding more pepper (almost always), less salt (ditto), extra garlic (double ditto).

So feel free to do the same. A recipe isn't much more than a set of guidelines; the result has to be something you're going to be happy to serve and eat. So improvise—it's more fun that way.

You won't find a lot of basic instruction here; it's assumed you know how to steam, sauté, julienne, and what a *bain-marie* is. If not, there are lots of books out there with the answers—the best one being *The Food Lover's Companion* by Sharon Tyler Herbst, which is the only food and cooking dictionary you'll ever need. Might as well get *The Wine Lover's Companion* (Ron Herbst and Sharon Tyler Herbst) as well.

What I'm saying is—you want leeway, room to move, use what's in the refrigerator. My darling editors want everything spelled out carefully, which is why they're the editors—God love 'em!—and I'm the cook God help me! Substitutions? As you like it. Them.

If it doesn't work out, blame (a) yourself, (b) me—not the aforementioned darling eds.

Despite rigorous scrutinizing and proofing, there are bound to be errors. They're all mine and I'm proud of them; as the weavers of Paisley put it, when they always deliberately put a small mistake into their patterns: only God should be perfect. Hard for a German-born guy to accept, sure, but I've been working on it.

Next: butter always means unsalted butter. Cream always means whipping cream. What else is there?

Be creative. Use the recipe as your point of departure and take flight from there.

Herbs and spices are wonderful; most recipes are wimpily cautious with them. I fling them about with great abandon. Seasonings should be tasteable, so be liberal. Any recipes I've created or adapted already tend to be, so you might want to bring your own personal hot or tart or bitter or spicy scale into the picture right at the start.

Creativity is what cooking is all about. Be creative. Use the recipe as your point of departure and take flight from there. If you come up with something that really soars, let me know.

How the wine choices were made: easy. There's no great mystery about that whole matching thing; wasn't, even before the red-wine-with-fish guys came along and liberated us. You drink what you like, when you eat what you like.

There are some suggestions, guidelines, sure—for some curious reason, Gewürztraminer really hangs in there for spicy stir-fries; Riesling rocks with sauerkraut; Pinot Noir with seared lamb carpaccio is a heavenly combo; rich Banyuls with Roquefort makes me roll over; oysters and steely Pinot Blanc go great; boerewors sausage and shiraz—hoo, boy!

But in the end, when you're sitting at the table, a robust pot of short ribs steaming away, and you really fancy Chardonnay—fill your glass. Because who's going to tell the wine police? Not me; I've got a tumbler full of Late Harvest Kerner going with my merguez sausage and Miss Vickie's sour cream and red chili chips!

How the music choices were made: not so easy. I've been resisting this concept ever since the last cookbook, even longer, but finally I gave in—it's the "DiscDrive" 20th anniversary cookbook after all. Cerebral choices rarely work—there's nothing particularly complementary about the Coffee Cantata with a double latte; no logical reason to hear the Trout Quintet with a piece of poached fish.

So, the musical selections, while not arbitrary, are heart-and-soul things, gut selections, not head trips. I happen to think Prawns with Sugar and Garlic Snap Peas go well with the sound of four bassoons; the "Neurology Edition" of the Goldberg Variations with a Moroccan b'stillah. Oh, all right, in a couple of cases I went regional—Alphorn Concertos with a fondue, Kim Darwin with the Mayne Island Oyster Stew, tournedos with a Rossini overture, Ken Hyder's Talisker with the Drambuie Salmon, that sort of thing.

Here too, as in everything else I try to do, it's got to be fun. And—substitute: if you want Callas with your *tonno tonnato*, as Jack Lemmon used to say: *avanti!*

This book has been a labour of love—believe me, one doesn't come to the Corporation for the money or the glory. It's all just a voyage—a "trip" we'd have said in the 60s—so thanks for coming along, and enjoy the journey. At least you won't be hungry any time soon.

Abbreviations of Countries / Regions

The following abbreviations appear in the lists of wine pairings that accompany each recipe.

AG	Argentina	NF	Newfoundland
AU	Australia	NL	Netherlands
BC	British Columbia	NJ	New Jersey
BL	Belgium	NM	New Mexico
BU	Bulgaria	NY	New York
CH	Chile	NZ	New Zealand
CY	Cypress	ON	Ontario
CZ	Czech Republic	OR	Oregon
DK	Denmark	PL	Poland
FR	France	PO	Portugal
GR	Greece	QC	Québec
GY	Germany	SA	South Africa
HU	Hungary	SC	Scotland
IR	Ireland	SP	Spain
IT	Italy	SW	Switzerland
JP	Japan	TA	Tahiti
KY	Kentucky	TX	Texas
LB	Lebanon	UK	United Kingdom
MB	Manitoba	WA	Washington
MX	Mexico		

starters

Prawns with Sugar Snap Peas & Garlic 2

Japanese Eggplant Baked with Apricots 3

Fiery Prawns in Orange Juice 4

Shrimp & Mango Ceviche 5

Beef Tartare with Avocado, Papaya & Lime 6

Entrée de Tête Fromagée Maison (Homemade Head Cheese) 8

Passion Pâté 9

Antipasto of Roasted Red Peppers 10

Three-Alarm Black Bean "Caviar" 11

Niku-Miso 12

The first recipe in
this book is also
the newest in my
kitchen …

The first recipe in this book is also the newest in my kitchen, born out of seren-dipity one day when I was having a little weekend wind-down on Mayne Island and found all the ingredients for this at the market, where it's not always easy to get fresh prawns, fresh snap peas and fine Shanti-McDougall-grown garlic at the same time. It all came together with a big yum! and takes no time at all. Finish prepping the main course for your dinner and then start this one as the guests are sitting down.

Prawns with Sugar Snap Peas *&* Garlic

serves 2

for stir-frying	vegetable or olive oil
3 cloves	garlic, thinly sliced
small handful	whole red and black peppercorns, mixed
1	dried serrano or similar hot dried pepper, whole
½ lb (250 g)	fresh prawns (shells on or off, your call)
½ lb (250 g)	fresh, plump sugar snap peas, strings removed
½	onion, halved and thinly sliced
splash	dry white wine

WINE PAIRINGS

Hearty pinks:

Gray Monk Rotberger [BC]

Sumac Ridge
Okanagan Blush [BC]

Cilento Renaissance Rosé
Riesling [ON]

MUSIC TO COOK WITH

Caliban Quartet: *Bassoonatics*
[CBC]

Heat oil in a frying pan or wok until it starts to smoke. Add the garlic, pepper-corns and dried pepper and stir-fry for 1 minute. (Take out the dried pepper if you don't like a lot of heat.) Add the prawns and sugar snap peas. Stir-fry for 1–2 minutes, till the prawns take on some colour. Splash in a little white wine and stir everything all around. Serve at once with dipping bread, lemon wedges, sliced onion and sea salt on the side.

I love eggplant in all its configurations ... if you can't find the long ones, the small globular ones work just as well; you just need to use more of them. Sometimes you can find the sour dried apricots, which also work in this dish, but you might want to add a little sweetening to them before you put them on the eggplant. *Piano, piano* with the sesame oil, though, okay?

I love eggplant in all its configurations ...

Japanese Eggplant Baked with Apricots

4 long	purple Japanese eggplants	
to taste	salt and pepper	
½ tsp (2 mL)	ground cumin	
1 tsp (5 mL)	dark sesame oil (more or less)*	
½ lb (250 g)	dried apricots	
2 Tbsp (25 mL)	vegetable oil (more or less)*	
¼ cup (50 mL)	chicken stock	
1	lemon, juice of (more or less)*	
1 Tbsp (15 mL)	chopped parsley	

serves 4

WINE PAIRINGS

chilled Momokawa
Sapphire sake [JP]

Selbach Dry Riesling [GY]

*Liquid measurements are to taste. Sesame oil can be very strong so I like to use a bit less; if you prefer the dish to taste a little more tart, the vegetable oil can be lessened and the fresh lemon juice increased.

Preheat the oven to 325°F (160°C).

Cut the eggplants in half the long way and put them in a shallow baking pan. Sprinkle with salt, pepper and cumin. Drizzle the sesame oil over top. Cover the eggplants with the apricots.

Mix together the vegetable oil, chicken stock and lemon juice and pour over the eggplants.

Bake for 1 hour, more or less, depending on the size of the apricots; make sure they don't blacken.

Serve sprinkled with chopped parsley.

MUSIC TO COOK WITH

Modern Jazz Quartet:
Concorde [PRESTIGE]

MJQ: *Blues at Carnegie Hall*
[ATLANTIC]

This is a recipe
given to me
by LA chef
Michael Roberts
many years ago …

This is a recipe given to me by LA chef Michael Roberts many years ago during a summer I did some on-air work on KUSC. He signed my copy of his cookbook: "Eating well is the best revenge," and I've been resoundingly vengeful ever since, especially with this excellent party appetizer. If you're doubling quantities, don't double the amount of sesame oil.

Fiery Prawns in Orange Juice

serves 4
Needs to sit overnight.

WINE PAIRINGS

Iced Essensia Orange
Muscat [CA]

**or a chubby but
unoaked Chardonnay:**

Crowsnest "Stahltank" [BC]

Banrock Station "Unwooded" [AU]

Peninsula Ridge "Inox" [ON]

MUSIC TO COOK WITH

Los Angeles Guitar Quartet:
Pachelbel's (Loose) Canon [DELOS]

MARINADE

1	good-looking fresh orange, grated zest of
1 cup (250 mL)	fresh orange juice, without the pulp
2 Tbsp (25 mL)	fresh lemon juice
1 or 2	cinnamon sticks, broken in pieces
½ tsp (2 mL)	cayenne (more or less, to taste)
1 tsp (5 mL)	salt
1 tsp (5 mL)	dark sesame oil (more or less, to taste)
20	prawns (or those oxymoronic "jumbo shrimp") peeled and deveined but with the tails left on
for garnish	tomato slices, ripe avocado wedges, chopped parsley

Combine the marinade ingredients in a medium pot over high heat. Bring to the boil, cover and cook 2 minutes.

Put the prawns in a glass bowl and pour the boiling marinade over. Cover and let cool to room temperature. Take out the cinnamon sticks if you want just a hint of that flavour, otherwise leave them in. Refrigerate overnight.

Just before serving, arrange tomatoes and avocados on a platter, put the prawns artfully on or around and spoon the cold marinade over everything. Sprinkle with parsley. The tails are your pick-up utensils.

This was one of the side dishes for my True North Chili extravaganza, the one with muskox and caribou in it (it can be found further along in this book). Sorry to saddle you with volume for a dozen, but that's just the way it came together; it divides up easily. When I say "light" extra virgin olive oil I mean one that you've tasted and found to be lighter in flavour, not one of those artificially "lightened" aberrations. A little sauce made with plain yogurt, orange or lemon juice and a dab of honey goes nicely on the side.

This was one of the side dishes for my True North Chili extravaganza, the one with muskox and caribou in it …

Shrimp & Mango Ceviche

2 lb (1 kg)	fresh shrimp (or prawns, halved lengthwise)
1½ cups (375 mL)	fresh lime juice (at least 12 limes)
½ cup (125 mL)	light extra virgin olive oil
1 medium	red onion, thinly sliced
2	habanero or jalapeño peppers, seeded, thinly sliced
handful	black peppercorns
1 tsp (5 mL)	coarse salt (*fleur de sel* is nice)
1 medium	mango, ripe but still firm, peeled and thinly sliced
	fresh greens
for garnish	cilantro, mint sprigs, lime wedges

serves 10–12
Needs to sit for 6 hours or more.

Cover the shrimp/prawns with lime juice and marinate in the refrigerator for 5–6 hours. Then, either proceed with the recipe or drain, re-cover and refrigerate overnight, or till ready, stirring occasionally.

Combine the olive oil, onion, peppers, black peppercorns and salt in a big bowl about an hour before serving.

Just before serving, add the sliced mango, and serve in (sturdy!) stemware with escarole or mustard greens for colour, and herb sprigs and lime wedges as garnish.

WINE PAIRINGS

Le Brasserie Nouvelle-France's "La Messagère" [QC] gluten-free beer

St Peter's Lemon & Ginger Ale [UK]

frozen Hendrick's Gin [SC]

MUSIC TO COOK WITH

Handel: *Harp Concertos* [DGG]

This winds up
a sort of beef
ceviche and it's
fabulous if you
love meat.

This winds up a sort of beef ceviche and it's fabulous if you love meat. As an unrepentant carnivore I keep it in my basic rep regardless of what scares come down the pike. I do check with the guests, and the papaya and avocado on their own are pretty good, too.

Beef Tartare with Avocado, Papaya & Lime

serves 4
Two marinations required,
so this needs to sit
overnight.

WINE PAIRINGS

cool
Georges Duboeuf St. Amour
[FR]

Le Mât Blanc Banyuls [FR]

MUSIC TO COOK WITH

Praetorius:
Dances from Terpsichore [ARCHIV]

½ lb (250 g)	super-lean beef sirloin, no fat in it, cut into small pieces, then minced with a sharp knife till the texture is like coarse ground beef
½ cup (125 mL)	fresh lime juice (5–6 limes)
¼ cup (50 mL)	avocado oil (or good-quality olive oil)
one 398-mL (14-oz) can	Italian diced tomatoes, drained (or use 3 or 4 fresh medium tomatoes, peeled and chopped—a lot of work)
½ cup (125 mL)	chopped red onion
2 Tbsp (25 mL)	minced cilantro (optional)
2 Tbsp (25 mL)	chopped fresh Italian parsley
to taste	salt and pepper
2	ripe avocados (without browning inside)
1	papaya
1 bunch	green onions

Put the chopped beef in a glass or porcelain bowl, add ⅓ cup (75 mL) of the lime juice and mix well. Cover with a tight lid or some cling wrap and refrigerate overnight.

At least 3 hours before you plan to serve, stir in the avocado or olive oil, tomatoes, onion, cilantro (if you're using it—I find it a little too soapy tasting in this dish) and the Italian parsley, plus salt and pepper to taste. Cover again (use a different piece of cling wrap, if that's what you started with) and refrigerate for another 3 hours or so.

Just before serving, taste for salt and pepper. Cut the avocados in half, remove the stones and slice into 4 or 5 slices. Cut the papaya in half, scoop out the seeds and slice into 8 thin slices. Arrange the avocado and papaya slices on 4 serving plates and pour the remaining lime juice on top. Divide the meat into 4 equal portions and mound on the plates. Garnish with chopped green onions (or leave the onions whole and have a little mound of sea salt on each plate for dipping). Serve while still well chilled.

If you want to gild the lily, serve a fresh, raw, free-range egg yolk in an egg cup with each plate.

**This was
the third-place
winner in the draw
that kicked off our
recipe contest.**

This was the third-place winner in the draw that kicked off our recipe contest. Yvan and Louise Choquette of Sherwood Park, Alberta, have been making this for years, even longer than they've been listening to "DiscDrive." Don't worry, there's no head in it.

Entrée de Tête Fromagée Maison (Homemade Head Cheese)

serves 8

3 lb (1.5 kg)	pork shoulder butt
2	veal shanks
8 cups (2 L)	salted water
1 medium	onion, coarsely chopped
3 cloves	garlic
½ cup (125 mL)	loosely packed fresh parsley
1 tsp (5 mL)	freshly ground pepper
1 Tbsp (15 mL)	ground dried marjoram
¾ tsp (4 mL)	ground allspice
¾ tsp (4 mL)	ground thyme
¾ tsp (4 mL)	ground bay leaf
pinch	saffron

WINE PAIRINGS

Serego Alighieri Valpolicella [IT]

Joseph Drouhin Rully [FR]

MUSIC TO COOK WITH

Canteloube:
Songs of the Auvergne [CBC]

Place the pork shoulder butt and veal shanks in a large pot with the salted water. Bring to a boil and cook the meat until it comes easily off the bone, about 1 hour. Remove the meat and let it cool.

Continue boiling the remaining liquid to reduce it by about half. Strain.

Separate the meat from the bones and fat. In a blender, process the meat with the onion, garlic and parsley until it has the texture of ground meat.

Once processed, return the meat to a clean pot and pour in the strained bouillon. Add the pepper, ground marjoram, ground allspice, ground thyme, ground bay leaf and saffron, adjusting the quantities to taste. Bring to a boil and simmer for an hour or so. When the mixture looks jellied (it will wobble when shaken) pour 1 cup (250 mL) in each of eight 10-ounce (300-mL) frosted ramekins and refrigerate.

When ready, unmould this delicacy and serve it on lettuce with a dab of a mixture of mayo and horseradish. The rest of the decoration is left to your imagination.

According to Wanda Mae Anderson of Vancouver, this pâté sends diehard vegetarians over the moon. I don't know if she means that's a good thing or not! The recipe makes about two pounds (one kilogram) and you'll wonder where it went.

According to Wanda Mae Anderson of Vancouver, this pâté sends diehard vegetarians over the moon.

Passion Pâté

for bath	milk
½ lb (250 g)	smoked bacon, diced
1½ lb (750 g)	chicken livers
½ cup (125 mL)	butter
2	onions
2 cloves	garlic
2	apples
1 cup (250 mL)	pecans, toasted
⅓ cup (75 mL)	brandy
½ lb (250 g)	cream cheese
2 tsp (10 mL)	tarragon
1 tsp (5 mL)	thyme
1 tsp (5 mL)	allspice

serves 6

WINE PAIRINGS

Tavel Rosé [FR]

Beringer White Zinfandel [CA]

MUSIC TO COOK WITH

Philip Glass: *Piano Pieces* [SONY]

Sauté the bacon and chicken livers (after they have had a little milk bath, of course). Set aside.

In a separate pan, heat the butter and sauté the onions, garlic and apples until transparent.

Grind toasted pecans in a food processor. Add the brandy, cream cheese, tarragon, thyme and allspice and combine. With the processor going, alternately add the above ingredients until the texture is to your liking.

Serve with Bretons Original crackers or with chunks of French bread.

Emilie Berger-
Semko grew up on
a Fraser Valley farm,
where she developed
a passion for
homegrown
vegetables ...

Emilie Berger-Semko grew up on a Fraser Valley farm, where she developed a passion for homegrown vegetables, particularly red peppers. She suggests adding some of this to a sandwich.

Antipasto of Roasted Red Peppers

**serves 8
as an appetizer**

4 large	red sweet bell peppers
2	anchovy fillets, drained, rinsed and minced
2 cloves	garlic, minced
¼ cup (50 mL)	extra virgin olive oil
1 Tbsp (15 mL)	drained capers
to taste	salt and freshly ground black pepper
2 Tbsp (25 mL)	slivered fresh basil or parsley leaves

To roast the peppers, place the whole peppers directly over a gas burner and roast, turning frequently with tongs—about 10 minutes OR until blackened and blistered all over. Alternatively, grill or broil, turning frequently, for 15–20 minutes. Place in a paper bag and set aside for 15 minutes. Slip off the skin, discard seeds and membrane and rinse under cold water.

Cut peppers into thin strips. Place in a bowl and add the anchovies, garlic, olive oil and capers. Toss well, seasoning with salt and pepper to taste.

Garnish with basil or parsley.

WINE PAIRINGS

Yellow Tail Shiraz [AU]

Nichol Vineyards Pinot Gris [BC]

Vineland Estates Pinot Gris [ON]

**(both are really
pinots pink)**

MUSIC TO COOK WITH

Annie Whitehead: *Home/Naked*
[VOICEPRINT]

David Lyon and Elizabeth Heon of Warkworth, Ontario, claim that this version of "caviar" from the *American Medical Association Family Health Cookbook* tastes every bit as good as the high-priced delicacy. In true Texas style, this dish is hot enough to make your lips sting, so tame it down with a bit less cayenne pepper if you like. Serve the caviar with chips or use it as a piquant relish for cold meats.

David Lyon and Elizabeth Heon of Warkworth, Ontario, claim that this version of "caviar"…

Three-Alarm Black Bean "Caviar"

one 14-oz (398-mL) can	black beans, rinsed and drained, or 1¾ cups (425 mL) cooked black beans
1 medium	onion, chopped
1 small	red bell pepper, seeded and chopped
1	pickled jalapeño pepper, finely chopped
1 clove	garlic, finely chopped
¼ cup (50 mL)	red wine vinegar
2 Tbsp (25 mL)	sugar
1 tsp (5 mL)	chili powder
½ tsp (2 mL)	dried savory
½ tsp (2 mL)	ground cumin
½ tsp (2 mL)	salt
¼ tsp (1 mL)	black pepper
¼ tsp (1 mL)	cayenne pepper
¼ tsp (1 mL)	white pepper
⅛ tsp (0.5 mL)	fresh lemon juice

makes 2½ cups/625 mL
—about 8 servings

WINE PAIRINGS

Las Rocas de San Alejandro Calatayud Garnacha [SP]

Fraoch Heather Ale [SC]

MUSIC TO COOK WITH

Monty Alexander & Ernest Ranglin: *Rocksteady* [TELARC]

In a large mixing bowl, combine the beans, onion, red pepper, jalapeño and garlic.

In a medium saucepan, combine the vinegar, sugar, chili powder, savory, cumin, salt, black pepper, cayenne and white pepper. Bring to a boil, stirring until the sugar is dissolved. Add the beans, return the mixture to a boil, and simmer for 1 minute. Using the back of a spoon, mash about a quarter of the beans against the side of the saucepan. (This will help thicken the mixture.) Remove from the heat and stir in the lemon juice. Transfer to a bowl, cool to room temperature, and refrigerate for at least 1 hour (up to 5 days).

Return to room temperature before serving. Serve in a bowl, accompanied by chips for scooping.

Margaret Sadler of Edmonton learned this dish "from our friend Masako, sitting in her little house in Nayoro ..."

Margaret Sadler of Edmonton learned this dish "from our friend Masako, sitting in her little house in Nayoro, Hokkaido, Japan. Fortunately, Masako's son (who spoke English) was visiting at Christmas that year, since Masako and I had few words in common. Outside, it snowed and snowed and snowed. Inside, we were warm; we laughed a lot; and we were well fed."

Niku-Miso

serves 8–10

WINE PAIRINGS

13th Street "Sandstone" Gamay [ON]

Hillebrand Gamay Noir [ON]

MUSIC TO COOK WITH

Takemitsu: *Beatles Songs for Guitar* [SONY]

2 Tbsp (25 mL)	dark sesame oil
¾ lb (375 g)	ground pork, preferably lean
1	leek, white part sliced
1 Tbsp (15 mL)	grated ginger
1 clove	garlic, crushed
1	dried chili, or 1 tsp dried hot pepper flakes (to taste)
1 cup (250 mL)	water
1 cube	chicken or vegetable bouillon
7 oz (200 g)	miso (low sodium, if possible)
¼ tsp (1 mL)	hot pepper oil (layu) (optional: if not available, increase hot pepper flakes)
4 Tbsp (60 mL)	sesame seeds, crushed
4 Tbsp (60 mL)	soy sauce
2 Tbsp (25 mL)	sugar
for wrapping	lettuce leaves
	carrot sticks, cucumber sticks, radish sprouts and other fresh vegetables cut in matchsticks

Heat the sesame oil in a pan. Sauté the meat, leek, ginger, garlic and chili or hot pepper flakes until the meat is cooked. Drain fat, as needed.

Add the water and bring to a boil. Dissolve the bouillon cube in the hot mixture and stir in the miso, oil, sesame seeds, soy sauce and sugar. Bring to a boil and simmer for 10 minutes. Remove the hot pepper, if you have used a whole one. Adjust the ingredients to suit your taste, recognizing that it's a salty mix intended to be balanced with all the fresh veggies.

Place a heaping teaspoon of the meat mixture in a lettuce leaf, add fresh vegetables and roll up.

soups & salads

Caldo Verde 14

Prawn & Peanut Soup with Lime & Coconut 15

Escarole & Tomato Soup with Lemon & Mint 16

Fennel & Orange Salad with Black Olives 17

Sharon's Caesar Salad & Diane's State-of-the-Art Croutons 18

Raspberry Crab Salad 20

Mexican-Style Chicken Salad 22

Jicama & Green Papaya Slaw with Water Chestnuts 24

Italian Sausage, Eggplant & Dill Winter Soup 25

Uncle John's Nostalgic Carrot Bisque & Sweet Variation 26

Sauerkraut Soup 28

Spicy Sweet Potato, Roasted Corn & Chipotle Bisque 29

Ribollita 30

Minestronska 32

Quintessential comfort food, this one, with various ways of preparing it.

Quintessential comfort food, this one, with various ways of preparing it. But the variations lie in the add-ons rather than the basics, those being kale, potatoes and olive oil. If you can get Portuguese olive oil, so much the better; it has a distinctive, fruity-green edge that brings out all the best in the other ingredients. A mid-range extra virgin olive oil is fine, but not one of those 50-dollar designer deals in the garage-sale bottle. Sometimes chicken stock instead of water is nice—makes it richer. Delete the sausage and heavy-up on the oil and there's a lovely, full vegetarian version—the flavour no less intense for the lack of the sausage. It reheats nicely, although it thickens up; you may want to add more water or stock the second time around.

Caldo Verde

for a big table as a starter, for 4–6 as a main course

WINE PAIRINGS

Gazela Vinho Verde [PO]

2 or 3	Portuguese sausages (chouriço or linguica)
5–6 large	potatoes, peeled and cut into chunks
6–7 cups (1.5–1.75 L)	cold salted water (or chicken stock, or a combination)
to taste	salt and pepper
½ cup (125 mL)	olive oil, more or less (Portuguese, if possible)
5–6 cups (1.25–1.5 L)	finely shredded kale, stems trimmed, well washed in several changes of water

Simmer the sausages in water to cover for 10–12 minutes, then slice them. Set aside.

In a big pot, bring the potatoes to a boil in the salted water, then simmer with the lid off for 15 minutes or so. Take the potatoes out with a slotted spoon; do not pour out the cooking water!

Mash the potatoes in a bowl and beat in the salt, pepper and oil. (Don't mash the potatoes too fine; a few mini-chunks are nice).

Now stir the mush back into the hot potato water. Bring the soup to a boil again and stir in the kale. Boil 5–7 minutes more (some like the kale crunchy; not me, so I tend to cook it a little longer.) Add the sausage slices and let soup bubble another 2–3 minutes.

Eat as soon as you can without burning your tongue. Toasted Portuguese cornbread is nice on the side, with lots of butter.

MUSIC TO COOK WITH

Sara Marreiros Trio
[SYNTONIC ARTS]

Portuguese Baroque Harpsichord Music [NAXOS]

Maria João Pires:
Mozart Piano Sonatas [DGG]

Great flavours come together here: ginger and chili and garlic and onion, plus cilantro and on and on. The easy way of doing this is to buy the prawns already shelled and cleaned—although it makes the soup a little lighter in flavour. Otherwise, you can cook the prawn shells together with the spices for about 10 minutes, then take the shells out and cook with the chicken stock. The danger here is that if you're talking to all the people who've come to congregate in the kitchen, you might, as I did more than once, pour the lovely, shelly broth down the sink by mistake. You need lots of crusty bread with this. You need lots of crusty bread (and butter) with just about anything, I figure.

Great flavours come together here: ginger and chili and garlic and onion ...

Prawn & Peanut Soup with Lime & Coconut

2 Tbsp (25 mL)	unsalted butter
1½ lb (750 g) medium	prawns
1 large	onion, chopped
6–8 cloves	garlic, minced
2–3	hot chilies, minced
2–3 Tbsp (25–45 mL)	minced fresh ginger
4 cups (1 L)	chicken stock or water, or combination
two or three 14-oz (398-mL) cans	Italian diced tomatoes
one 14-oz (398-mL) can	unsweetened coconut milk
½ cup (125 mL)	peanut butter (creamy is better than chunky)
½ cup (125 mL)	fresh lime juice (5 or 6 limes)
to taste	chopped cilantro
to taste	salt and pepper
for garnish	more cilantro and lime slices

serves 6 as a generous first course

WINE PAIRINGS

Unibroue "La Fringante" [QC]

Henschke Semillon-Chardonnay [AU]

MUSIC TO COOK WITH

Yo-Yo Ma: *Obrigado Brasil* [SONY]

Melt the butter in a good-sized soup kettle or pot. Add the prawns, onion, garlic, chilies and ginger and cook for 2 minutes.

Take out the prawns with a slotted spoon. Add the chicken stock or water and simmer for 10 minutes. Stir in the tomatoes and simmer 10 minutes more.

Mix together the coconut milk and peanut butter until smooth (use a hand-mixer, whisk or food processor). Stir this mixture into the broth.

Add the prawns, lime juice and cilantro. Simmer gently to heat through, 2–3 minutes.

Season with salt and pepper and serve with chopped cilantro and slices of lime on top.

This is one
of my all-time
favourite soups …

This is one of my all-time favourite soups, going back to the days I spent in the wine country of Lebanon. For all its heartiness, it's relatively fast and easy to put together.

Escarole & Tomato Soup with Lemon & Mint

**serves 4,
if they're hungry**

WINE PAIRINGS

Growers Nectarine Dry Cider
[BC]

Unibroue "Eau Benite" [QC]

white wine spritzer

MUSIC TO COOK WITH

Rabih Abou-Khalil:
Oud Music [ENJA]
—pick any one
of his 12 CDs

2 Tbsp (25 mL)	unsalted butter
2 Tbsp (25 mL)	olive oil
1 large	onion, coarsely chopped
2 cloves	garlic, minced
to taste	salt and pepper (if you use canned beef stock, cut back on the salt)
two 14-oz (398-mL) cans	Italian tomatoes, crushed or diced (maybe a little more)
1 cup (250 mL)	hot water
2–3 cups (500–750 mL)	hot beef stock (depending on how thick you like your soup)
2 cups (500 mL)	packed escarole, shredded (romaine lettuce will do in a pinch but it's worth the effort to find escarole)
2/3 cup (150 mL)	tiny soup pasta (stelline, acini di pepe, nothing bigger than orzo)
2	lemons, juice of
2–3 Tbsp (25–45 mL)	chopped fresh mint leaves, or 1 tsp (5 mL) dried, crushed in the palm of your hand

Heat the butter and oil together in a soup pot on medium heat. Add the onion, garlic, salt and pepper. Cook till the onion is soft, but don't let the garlic brown.

Stir in the tomatoes and cook 5 minutes. Pour in the water and stock, stir and bring to simmer. Simmer for 10 minutes. Add the escarole and cook 5 minutes more.

Add the pasta and cook until done (depending on the size, 5 minutes is usually plenty).

Add the lemon juice and mint leaves and simmer a minute or two till everything's blended.

Serve hot, remembering to scoop up the pasta from the bottom.

Cool, fresh and crunchy, so just the thing to accompany a spicy TNC (True North Chili).

Fennel & Orange Salad with Black Olives

SALAD

2 cups (500 mL)	walnuts, coarsely chopped
1½ lb (750 g)	fennel bulb (white part only)
4	firm navel oranges, peeled, pithed, cut into eighths, seeded, sliced ¼ inch (5 mm)
1 lb (500 g)	Emmenthal, julienned
big handful	pitted black olives

DRESSING

3½ cups (850 mL)	plain yogurt
¼ cup (50 mL)	olive oil (or nut oil)
6 Tbsp (80 mL)	lemon juice
2 Tbsp (25 mL)	sugar
1 tsp (5 mL)	salt, more or less
1 tsp (5 mL)	black pepper, more or less

Preheat the oven to 350°F (180°C). Toast the walnuts for 8 to 10 minutes or until they smell nutty. Don't let them burn.

Quarter the fennel bulb, slice ¼ inch thick and put in a big bowl. Add the walnuts, oranges and cheese and set aside.

Whisk all the dressing ingredients together. Pour over the salad, toss, cover with plastic wrap and chill well. Toss again just before serving and scatter the olives on top.

serves 12 or more

WINE PAIRINGS

Antinori Peppoli Chianti Classico [IT]

Tohu "Mugwi" Sauvignon Blanc [NZ]

MUSIC TO COOK WITH

Mozart: *Music for Basset Horn* [PHILIPS]

This salad is, how we say at home, *ganz korrekt* ...

This salad is, how we say at home, *ganz korrekt*; I mean, there's abundant anchovy in it and fresh—and yes, raw—eggs. If either of those doesn't do it for you, you may want to go straight on to the croutons. Olympian Diane Clement is responsible for those, and I can't imagine life without them.

Sharon's Caesar Salad & Diane's State-of-the-Art Croutons

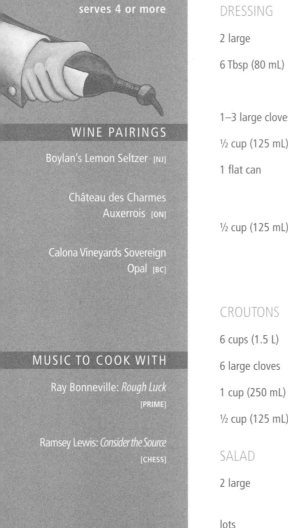

serves 4 or more

WINE PAIRINGS

Boylan's Lemon Seltzer [NJ]

Château des Charmes
Auxerrois [ON]

Calona Vineyards Sovereign
Opal [BC]

MUSIC TO COOK WITH

Ray Bonneville: *Rough Luck*
[PRIME]

Ramsey Lewis: *Consider the Source*
[CHESS]

DRESSING

2 large	very fresh eggs
6 Tbsp (80 mL)	fresh lemon juice
	black pepper to taste
1–3 large cloves	garlic, minced
½ cup (125 mL)	freshly grated Parmesan cheese
1 flat can	anchovies, with the oil (get the Italian kind that's packed in olive oil; it often comes in little cylindrical jars, and maybe put in 2, just because)
½ cup (125 mL)	olive oil (or a blend of regular, extra virgin olive oil, salad oil, grape seed oil—although it's too late to be going for the anti-cholesterol qualities of grape seed oil by this point in the game!)

CROUTONS

6 cups (1.5 L)	crusty sourdough bread, cut into small cubes
6 large cloves	garlic, crushed
1 cup (250 mL)	freshly grated Parmesan cheese
½ cup (125 mL)	olive oil (or blend of oils)

SALAD

2 large	heads really crisp romaine lettuce, torn into bite-size pieces
lots	freshly grated Parmesan cheese (the real thing, none of that wretched powdered stuff in the *tricolore* shakers)

Preheat the oven to 300°F (150°C).

In a food processor, blend together the eggs, lemon juice, pepper, garlic, Parmesan cheese and anchovies. Pour in the oil, slowly, slowly, until thickened to a creamy, smooth consistency. Set aside while you do the croutons.

In a big bowl, toss the bread cubes with the garlic and Parmesan. Drizzle enough of the oil over top to just coat the cubes. Toss well. Bake for 40–45 minutes on a big flat cookie sheet, stirring the cubes after 20 minutes, until they are golden, crisp and dry. They should be crunchy. Let cool. (They keep for weeks in the refrigerator; I like to leave some out on the counter, in a paper bag, to eat as snacks.

Now put it all together: Place the lettuce in a big salad bowl and pour enough dressing over it to coat. Toss in the croutons and sprinkle with the extra Parmesan. Toss well.

<blockquote>Artist and designer, jeweller, music lover and keen putterer-about in the kitchen, Robert Gerow ...</blockquote>

Artist and designer, jeweller, music lover and keen putterer-about in the kitchen, Robert Gerow now does his wonderful small scale creations—custom fridge magnets that look like Russian religious icons, one-of-a-kind stamps, small shadow boxes—under the *nom d'art*, Ghetto Primate. Identified as such, the following arrived not long ago, bearing quotes from Jerry Garcia and J.S. Bach. Too bad I can't show you the art card the recipe appeared on, but I've incorporated one of The Primate's earlier fridge magnets into the recipe card and it adorns my refrigerator door.

Raspberry Crab Salad

serves 2

¼ cup (50 mL)	raspberry vinegar
1 bottle	dry white wine (6 Tbsp/90 mL for the vinaigrette, a glass for the cook, the rest for the table)
4 Tbsp (60 mL)	olive oil
1 Tbsp (15 mL)	mixed fines herbes
4 Tbsp (60 mL)	liquid clover honey (anything more exotic would be lost in the vinaigrette)
2 Tbsp (25 mL)	freshly grated Parmesan cheese
1	lemon, zested, then quartered
1 large	egg
⅓ lb (170 g)	cracked crabmeat, plus 2 legs or claws
¼ cup (50 mL)	raspberries (drained if frozen)
4 Tbsp (60 mL)	sour cream
1 large head	butter lettuce

WINE PAIRINGS

Black Hills "Alibi" [BC]

Caymus "Conundrum" [CA]

Danie De Wet Chardonnay "sur lie" [SA]

Mort Subite [BL]

Absolut Raspberri Vodka shooters [SE]

MUSIC TO COOK WITH

Diana Krall: *Love Scenes* [IMPULSE]

VINAIGRETTE

Make sure all ingredients except the oil are cool. In a large bowl, combine the raspberry vinegar, 6 Tbsp (90 mL) wine, olive oil, fines herbes, honey, Parmesan cheese and half of the lemon zest. Mix well. Squeeze juice from 1 quarter of the lemon into the mixture, add the egg and whisk well. Gently fold in the crabmeat (reserving the legs or claws for garnish) and raspberries. Chill.

SOUR CREAM GARNISH

In a small bowl, mix the sour cream, the juice of a quarter lemon, a pinch of fines herbes and a pinch of lemon zest. Mix well and refrigerate.

BUTTER LETTUCE

... is rather delicate, bruising easily, so be gentle with it. Separate from the head 2 perfect, large leaves and set aside on salad plates; these will be your salad bowls.

Tear half the remaining lettuce into fork-friendly pieces in a big salad bowl. Add the vinaigrette and toss gently.

Place the salad into the butter leaf bowls. On top of each salad place a dollop of sour cream garnish and, on top of that, one crab leg or claw. Sprinkle the remaining lemon zest over both salads and serve at once.

Janet Smith is
a fan from
Roberts Creek,
British Columbia ...

Janet Smith is a fan from Roberts Creek, British Columbia, where she enjoys the proximity of the many free-spirited denizens of the Sunshine Coast, some of whom will have shared this creation with her.

Mexican-Style Chicken Salad

serves 4
needs to marinate
overnight

WINE PAIRINGS

Martin Codax Rias Biaxas
Albariño [SP]

L.A. Cetto Cabernet [MX]

MUSIC TO COOK WITH

Joe Trio: *Set 'em up Joe* [CBC]

MARINADE

¼ cup (50 mL)	lime juice
¼ cup (50 mL)	white wine vinegar
⅓ cup (75 mL)	honey
1 tsp (5 mL)	chili powder (optional)
2 Tbsp (25 mL)	corn oil
4	boneless chicken breasts

DRESSING

⅓ cup (75 mL)	corn oil
¼ cup (50 mL)	lime juice
2 Tbsp (25 mL)	chopped parsley
dash	Tabasco
1–2 Tbsp (15–25 mL)	honey
to taste	salt and pepper

SALAD

¼ cup (50 mL)	corn oil
two 8-inch (20-cm)	corn or flour tortillas cut in ¼-inch (5-mm) strips
4 cups (1 L)	lettuce, torn into bite-size pieces
2	tomatoes, cored and diced
½	onion, finely diced
2	avocados, peeled, pitted and cut in small chunks
for garnish	black olives and parsley

Combine the marinade ingredients, add the chicken and marinate in the refrigerator for up to 24 hours. Remove the chicken from the marinade and grill or sauté until the juices run clear. Slice thinly on the diagonal.

Combine all the dressing ingredients and chill until needed.

Heat the corn oil in a pan over medium heat until very hot. Fry the tortilla strips until lightly browned. Remove them with a slotted spoon and drain on paper towels.

Divide the lettuce onto 4 plates. Top with the grilled chicken, tomatoes, onion, avocado and tortilla strips. Drizzle with the dressing and garnish with sliced black olives and a sprig of parsley.

Another one to
serve as a cooling
foil for the TNC ...

Another one to serve as a cooling foil for the TNC (or any other chili or spicy stew dish you're making in the party size). I like the soft-crunchy texture of savoy, but regular green cabbage is good if you like the slaw super crunchy.

Jicama & Green Papaya Slaw with Water Chestnuts

serves 8–10

WINE PAIRINGS

Valdo Prosecco
di Valdobbiadene [IT]

Blue Mountain Brut [BC]

Hillebrand "Trius" Brut [ON]

MUSIC TO COOK WITH

Bumanis & Shaw:
Bach for 2 Harps [CBC]

DRESSING

1 cup (250 mL)	mayonnaise
1 cup (250 mL)	plain yogurt
3–5	pickled jalapeños, chopped (about ½ cup/125 mL)*
2 Tbsp (25 mL)	smooth Dijon mustard
2 Tbsp (25 mL)	sugar
¼ cup (50 mL)	fresh lemon juice
½ tsp (2 mL)	salt

SALAD

1 small	green or savoy cabbage, cored, shredded fine (about 6 cups/1.5 L)
1 large	jicama, peeled, matchsticked (just a little thinner than your average julienne)
1 large	green papaya, peeled, seeded, matchsticked
one 8-oz (227-mL) can	sliced water chestnuts, drained
½ cup (125 mL)	thinly sliced green onion
for garnish	fire-roasted red pepper (fresh or canned)

*Pickled jalapeños often come in 200-mL cans; I drain off the liquid and take out the carrots, and what's left is about the right amount.

Combine the mayonnaise, yogurt, jalapeños, mustard, sugar, lemon juice and salt in a big bowl.

Add the cabbage, jicama and green papaya. Mix everything very well. Cover with plastic wrap and refrigerate for 3–4 hours (or overnight).

Stir in the water chestnuts and green onion; taste for seasoning and garnish with the red pepper. Serve good and cold.

This brings passion to our dinner table in cold weather, says Coralee Pringle-Nelson in Saskatoon, where I understand they do get cold weather at times, certainly in July when I was last there.

This brings passion to our dinner table in cold weather ...

Italian Sausage, Eggplant & Dill Winter Soup

6–7	mild, medium or hot Italian sausages
1 medium	eggplant
4	carrots
½ head	cabbage (if desired)
two 10-oz (284-mL) cans	beef broth (equal parts water)
one 28-oz (796-mL) can	tomatoes (equal part water)
2–3 cups (500–750 mL)	water
1	bay leaf
1 bunch	fresh dill, chopped

Sauté the Italian sausages until brown and cut them into bite-size pieces. Chop the eggplant into similar-sized pieces and sauté with the sausage pieces until the eggplant is soft.

Chop the carrots and cabbage into bite-size pieces. Combine the beef broth, tomatoes, eggplant and sausage in a large soup pot. Add the water, bay leaf, dill, carrots and cabbage. Bring to a boil and simmer for 1 to 1½ hours.

Serve with fresh bread and a delectable choice of cheese (Swiss is nice) for a cozy winter meal.

serves 8–10

WINE PAIRINGS

Soloperto Primitivo [IT]

Bonny Doon "Big House Red" [CA]

MUSIC TO COOK WITH

Respighi: *Ancient Airs & Dances*
[TELARC or CBC]

John McNeish of
Ottawa, Ontario,
has rigorously
tested his bisque
over two decades
and knows its
every quirk.

John McNeish of Ottawa, Ontario, has rigorously tested his bisque over two decades and knows its every quirk. The soup best reveals its personality in placid serenity. It abhors agitated hosts who jump up and down to fuss over different courses or complicated presentations. It prefers to be made the day before, so that its flavours can repose and gather strength prior to being released through gentle reheating just before being served hot. It likes to be accompanied by

Uncle John's Nostalgic Carrot Bisque & Sweet Variation

serves 6

WINE PAIRINGS

Chapoutier "La Ciboise"
Coteaux du Tricastin
Blanc (organic) [FR]

Quinta do Noval Port [PO]

MUSIC TO COOK WITH

Robert Silverman: *The Parlor Grand* [MARQUIS]

Simon Jeffes: *Piano Music* [OBSCURE]

4 cups (1 L)	peeled, coarsely chopped carrots
2 large	coarsely chopped onions
5 cups (1.25 L)	chicken or vegetable stock
1/3 cup (75 mL)	butter
1/4 cup (50 mL)	all-purpose flour
2 cups (500 mL)	milk
1 cup (250 mL)	half-and-half cream
1/2 cup (125 mL)	Pernod or Ricard
1 Tbsp (15 mL)	fennel seeds

Place the carrots and onions in a saucepan with half of the stock. Cook until the vegetables are soft. Run through a blender until the mixture is very smooth.

Melt the butter in a large pot. Blend in the flour until a smooth roux forms. Gradually stir in the milk and cream, whisking constantly to avoid the formation of flour "dumplings." Set over a low heat, stirring constantly with the whisk until the mixture is warm. Add the vegetable purée and remaining stock and whisk for another 5 minutes. Add the Pernod/Ricard and fennel seeds. From this point, you have two choices, depending on whether you wish to serve on the same day or the next day. In either case it is very important to keep the soup from boiling, which will destroy the flavour and create little flour chips in the soup.

If you are serving the same day, leave the soup to simmer on a burner set to the lowest heat. Stir from time to time to keep the bottom from burning. The soup gets better if kept in the refrigerator overnight because the fennel seeds release their flavour. If it has been chilled overnight, put the pot on a burner on low heat an hour before serving.

Check from time to time to adjust the heat and give the soup a stir to keep the bottom from burning. Test the flavour in case you need to add more Pernod/Ricard. Five minutes before serving, raise the heat to medium and stir until the soup is hot enough to serve.

fussless finger food—Empress Hotel of Victoria sandwiches (cucumber, tomato, circles of smoked salmon rolled in white bread, pâté on buttered toast), blue and creamy cheeses, fruits, walnuts and crusty bread—which can all be prepared the day before. The wines, of course, should harmonize with the food and the occasion. Begin with crisp whites to go with the soup and sandwiches, and gradually ease into port or icewine to linger with the cheese.

This basic recipe converts into Uncle John's Summer Night Delight if you exchange the fennel and Ricard/Pernod for:

1 tsp (5 mL)	cinnamon powder
2 Tbsp (25 mL)	grated fresh ginger
1 cup (250 mL)	freshly squeezed orange juice
1 Tbsp (15 mL)	orange zest (blended with the pulp from the juiced oranges until smooth)

This version should not be served hot, but must at least be warmed up to release its flavours.

A culinary
snapshot from
Sigrid Stark: "It's a
cold winter evening
in Edmonton …

A culinary snapshot from Sigrid Stark: "It's a cold winter evening in Edmonton (−40 with the wind chill) and sauerkraut soup seems like the best remedy after the drive home. This is the closest I could come to duplicating my friend Rebi's soup that we enjoyed in her home in Zalau, Romania."

Sauerkraut Soup

**serves 6 as a main course,
8 as a starter**

WINE PAIRINGS

A hearty Rumanian red
or even better, a hearty
Moldovan red

Egri Bikaver [HU]

MUSIC TO COOK WITH

Enescu: *Octet* [NAXOS]

Alison Brown Quartet: *Replay*
[COMPASS]

2 lbs (1 kg)	stewing beef, cut in small chunks
	oil for browning
1 large	onion, diced
4–5 cups (1–1.25 L)	beef broth
28 oz (796 mL)	sauerkraut
1–2	carrots, diced
1–2 stalks	celery, diced
2–3	potatoes, diced
1	sweet red pepper, diced
3 cloves	garlic, minced
2	bay leaves
to taste	salt
for garnish	parsley and dill

In large pot, brown the meat in oil. Remove and set aside. Sauté the onion until transparent. Add the meat, broth, sauerkraut, vegetables, garlic and bay leaves and bring to a boil. Cover and simmer for a couple of hours until the meat is tender. Add salt as required.

Garnish with parsley and dill. Serve with sour cream and/or Hungarian hot sauce.

Sandra Malasky of Peterborough, Ontario, guarantees a warm and sensual afterglow from this soup. Get in touch with her if you want the terms of the guarantee.

Sandra Malasky of Peterborough, Ontario, guarantees a warm and sensual afterglow from this soup.

Spicy Sweet Potato, Roasted Corn & Chipotle Bisque

1½ cups (375 mL)	corn kernels, roasted
2 Tbsp (25 mL)	extra virgin olive oil
1 large	red onion, diced
1–2 large	diced chipotle chilies (smoked jalapeños, canned with adobo sauce)
4 large	sweet potatoes, peeled and diced
4 cups (1 L)	vegetable stock
½ cup (125 mL)	brandy (optional)
2 cups (500 mL)	light cream

serves 4

WINE PAIRINGS

Gruet Brut [NM]

Seaview Sparkling Shiraz [AU]

To roast the corn, preheat the oven to 425°F (220°C). If you're using frozen corn, allow it to thaw before roasting. Spread the kernels in a single layer on a baking sheet. Roast until the kernels begin to turn brown. Remove and set aside to cool.

Heat the oil in a large saucepan. Sauté the onion and chipotle chilies until the onion is softened. Add the sweet potatoes and sauté for 1 minute, stirring often. Add the vegetable stock and bring to a boil. Reduce the heat and simmer until the sweet potatoes are softened.

Remove the sweet potato-onion-chipotle mixture from the broth and purée in a blender until smooth. Return the purée to the broth and add the corn kernels, brandy and cream. Stir and heat through without allowing the mixture to come to a boil. Serve with hot crusty bread and mixed green salad.

MUSIC TO COOK WITH

Earl Wild: *The Romantic Master* [SONY]

Here's a Christmas
Eve or New Year's
Eve tradition from
Maureen O'Connor
in Brampton,
Ontario.

Here's a Christmas Eve or New Year's Eve tradition from Maureen O'Connor in Brampton, Ontario. This is the kind of soup that will tolerate substitutions, but this particular combination is really delicious. The recipe was originally developed by Rose Murray for *Canadian Living* magazine.

Ribollita

makes about 6 servings, but can be stretched to 8 or even 10

WINE PAIRINGS

Coltibuono Chianti Classico
[IT]

Pier Luigi Tolaini "Picconero" [IT]
(ask me about this
when we meet!)

MUSIC TO COOK WITH

Cecilia Bartoli: *Arias (Gluck)*
[LONDON]

5 cups (1.25 L)	chicken stock
1 lb (500 g)	boneless chicken breasts, skinned
2	bay leaves
3 Tbsp (45 mL)	olive oil
1	onion, chopped
2 (or more) cloves	garlic, minced
2	carrots, diced
2 stalks	celery, diced
1	green bell pepper, diced
2 cups (500 mL)	chopped savoy cabbage (about ½ regular head)
1 tsp (5 mL)	dried thyme
1 tsp (5 mL)	dried rosemary
one 19-oz (540-mL) can	tomatoes, coarsely chopped, with juice
¼ tsp (1 mL)	black pepper
one 10-oz (300-mL) package	fresh spinach, chopped
½ cup (125 mL)	chopped fresh parsley
1 small	zucchini, thinly sliced
one 19-oz (540-mL) can	white kidney (cannellini) beans, drained and rinsed
6–8 thick slices	stale French or Italian bread (depends on the size of your casserole dish)
1 cup (250 mL)	Parmesan, Romano or Asiago cheese, freshly grated
for garnish	olive oil and Parmesan cheese

In a large saucepan, bring the chicken stock, chicken breasts and bay leaves to a boil. Reduce the heat, cover and simmer for about 20 minutes or until the chicken is no longer pink inside. Remove the chicken, dice the meat and set aside. Discard the bay leaves. Keep the stock warm.

Meanwhile, in a large pan, heat 2 Tbsp (30 mL) of the olive oil over medium heat. Cook the onion, garlic, carrots and celery for 10 minutes, stirring occasionally.

Add the remaining 1 Tbsp (15 mL) of the olive oil, the green pepper, cabbage, thyme and rosemary; cook over low heat, stirring occasionally, for 10 minutes.

Add this vegetable mixture to the stock in the saucepan, along with the tomatoes with their juice, and the pepper. Bring to a boil. Reduce the heat, cover and simmer for 30 minutes.

Add the spinach, parsley, zucchini, kidney beans and the reserved diced chicken. Cook for 5 minutes. Remove 1 cup (250 mL) of the soup and set aside.

Ladle half of the remaining soup into a 24-cup (6-L) Dutch oven or casserole. Cover with the bread slices and half of the cheese. Cover with the remaining soup, then layer with remaining bread. Drizzle the reserved soup over top; sprinkle with the remaining cheese.

The recipe can be prepared to this point, cooled, covered and refrigerated for up to 24 hours. In fact, Maureen recommends it.

Bake, covered, in 350°F (180°C) oven for 20 minutes (45 minutes if the soup has been refrigerated); uncover and bake for 20 minutes longer (again, 45, if the soup has been refrigerated), or until hot.

Ladle the soup into large warmed bowls; garnish with a drizzle of olive oil and a sprinkle of Parmesan cheese.

Some days the
aromas wafting
down the hall
towards Scenic
Subterranean
Studio 20 …

Some days the aromas wafting down the hall towards Scenic Subterranean Studio 20 from the "DiscDrive" microwave are overwhelming; usually it means Mr. Wolk is heating up a big bowl of his unique Italo-Polish version of the famous soup. While he never *offers* to share, he will, if you press him on it. It's a pretty sensational soup, and he always does it up in big quantities, so I've no idea if you can halve or quarter the recipe. Try it and let us know.

Minestronska

**yields 8–10
hearty bowls**

WINE PAIRINGS

Pilsner Urquell or
Czechvar beer [CZ]

MUSIC TO COOK WITH

Django Reinhardt

for sautéing	olive oil
1	onion, diced
3–6 cloves	garlic, chopped (to taste)
4 stalks	celery, sliced
1	leek, white part only, sliced
8 cups (2 L)	chicken stock (low-salt)
one 28-oz (796-mL) can	stewed tomatoes
one 5½-oz (156-mL) can	tomato paste
one 14-oz (398-mL) can	chickpeas
to taste	salt and pepper
to taste	Italian spices mixture
½ package (about 5 oz/150 g)	dried porcini mushrooms (optional)
4	carrots, peeled, sliced or diced
1 cup (250 mL)	green beans, cut
1	parsnip, peeled, sliced or diced
2	chicken breasts (4 halves), diced
	soup-sized pasta or rice (optional)
to taste	curry powder (optional)
for garnish	Parmesan cheese and fresh dill (optional)

Heat some some olive oil in a large pot. Add the onion, garlic, celery and leek and sauté until the onion is transparent. Add the chicken stock, canned tomatoes and tomato paste.

Purée the chickpeas in a blender or food processor, then add to the mixture. Add salt, pepper and Italian spices to taste. Using a cheese grater, take the dried porcini, if using, and grate into the soup. Stir well and let the mixture cook to reduce the liquid level a little.

After 20–30 minutes on medium heat, add the carrots, green beans and parsnip. Then add chicken and cook another 20–30 minutes. During this cooking time, pasta or rice may be added. Stir often to prevent the pasta from sticking to the bottom of the pot. Optional curry can also be added at this time.

Serve in big, heated bowls. Parmesan cheese and fresh dill can be added.

Beverage suggestion:

Ede Wolk's drink with this would be "a good, true pilsner beer," and he suggests the original Urquell or Czechvar.

As for tunes, "Django Reinhardt, either performed by Mr. R. or reasonable facsimile …"

snacks & sides

Blueberry Mincemeat 36

Sautéed Grapes with Espresso & Red Wine 37

Fresh Artichokes with Sherry 38

Buttermilk Cornbread with Pine Nuts, Pumpkin & Oka 39

White Asparagus Ragout with Morels 40

Butterless Béarnaise Sauce 41

Sharpish Cheddar Thins 42

Joe Muer's De Johnge Butter Sauce 43

Piggies in the Middle 44

Dorothy's Eggs 45

Once a year a little care package arrives …

Once a year a little care package arrives from the BC Blueberries people: berries, of course, and always some interesting new recipe, usually with ingredients included, as well as instructions. I've learned over the years to try them all out; they always end up in the basic rep. Like this lovely side dish, sauce, condiment, call it anything.

Blueberry Mincemeat

serves a bunch
yields about
6 cups/1.5 L

WINE PAIRINGS

Blueberry wine
from Wellbrook Winery [BC]
or MB, ON, QC, NF

MUSIC TO COOK WITH

Terry Riley:
A Rainbow in Curved Air [SONY]

1¼ cups (300 mL)	sultana raisins
1¼ cups (300 mL)	golden raisins
½ cup (125 mL)	dried cranberries
½ cup (125 mL)	mixed peel
½ cup (125 mL)	brown sugar
¼ cup (125 mL) 1 stick	butter, cut into small pieces
1 tsp (5 mL)	grated lemon rind, yellow part only
2 Tbsp (25 mL)	brandy (oh, why be stingy?)
1 Tbsp (15 mL)	lemon juice
1 tsp (5 mL)	ground cinnamon
½ tsp (2 mL)	ground cloves
½ tsp (2 mL)	ground ginger
½ tsp (2 mL)	ground nutmeg
4 cups (1 L)	blueberries, fresh or frozen

Combine everything but the blueberries in a big mixing bowl. Mix well. Stir in the blueberries.

Pack closely in sterilized jars and cover tightly. Refrigerate for use within 2 weeks. For longer storage, freeze.

... and then, the grapes people send along some recipes, too. This one became an instant favourite from the day it arrived. Hardly a fortnight goes by without me cooking it as a warm accompaniment to some roast meat or chicken ... never found out who came up with this on-the-surface unusual combination but it sure works, so a tip of the wine glass to the anonymous creator.

I suggest that you make it at the very last minute. And don't use any kind of wimpy (or worse, powdered) espresso. Walk down the street to the coffee place and get it fresh.

... and then,
the grapes people
send along some
recipes, too.

Sautéed Grapes with Espresso & Red Wine

1 Tbsp (15 mL)	olive oil	**serves 4**
1 small	shallot, chopped	
2 cups (500 mL)	fresh grapes (I always use red, but I suppose you could do it with green; let me know if you do)	
¼ cup (50 mL)	brewed espresso	
½ cup (125 mL)	dry red wine	
½ stick	cinnamon	
1 Tbsp (15 mL)	honey	
1½ tsp (7 mL)	balsamic vinegar	
1½ tsp (7 mL)	butter	

WINE PAIRINGS

Lang Riesling [BC]

St. Innocent Pinot Noir [OR]

Le Mât Blanc Banyuls [FR]

In a medium shallow pan, heat the oil on medium heat. Add the shallot and sauté for 1 minute, or until softened. Add the grapes and sauté for 1 minute. Transfer to a bowl and set aside.

In the same pan, combine the espresso, red wine, cinnamon stick and honey. Bring to a boil. Boil for 5 minutes or until slightly syrupy.

Return the grapes to the pan and heat for 30 seconds. Remove the pan from the heat and add vinegar and butter, stirring quickly until the butter melts.

Serve with anything.

MUSIC TO COOK WITH

Dick Hyman:
The Great American Songbook
[MUSICMASTERS]

I love those little fresh artichokes that happen along during such a brief window, at least in this country. I buy 'em by the big bagful and cook them up any which way. This recipe has been rattling around with me for a couple of decades; it wound up scribbled on a serviette in a Spanish *parador* following one of those 30-course tapas dinners that usually don't start until 10:30 p.m.

Fresh Artichokes with Sherry

serves 6

24 small	fresh, tender artichokes
1 or 2	lemons
2 lb (1 kg)	fresh broad beans (or fava beans)
1 cup (250 mL) + 2 tsp (10 mL)	fino (pale dry sherry)
8 stigmas	saffron (or as much as your palate likes of this pungent spice)
for sautéing	olive oil
2 big	onions, chopped
6 big cloves	garlic, minced
1 sprig	fresh mint leaves
to taste	black pepper
2 Tbsp (25 mL)	all-purpose flour
2 cups (500 mL)	chicken stock

WINE PAIRINGS

iced fino sherry,
Casa la Luna Tempranillo [SP]

cool oloroso sherry, after

MUSIC TO COOK WITH

Rani Arbo & Daisy Mayhem:
Cocktail Swing
[SIGNATURE SOUNDS]

Peel the artichokes right down to just the hearts. Rub with lemon so they don't discolour. Blanch the artichokes in boiling salted water until tender; check after 20 minutes, depending on the size of the artichokes.

In another pot, bring lots of salted water to the boil and boil the beans till tender. Peel the beans once they are cooked.

Drain both vegetables and set aside. Pound a few of the cooked beans into the 1 cup (250 mL) of sherry, with the saffron, in a mortar and pestle. (Which is which? I always forget.)

Heat some olive oil in a big pan or wok. Sauté the onions and garlic. Add the cooked artichokes, mint and pepper. Mix the flour with the remaining 2 tsp (10 mL) sherry and mix that in too. Add the rest of the beans, cover with the stock and boil gently until the liquid is reduced by one third or so.

Serve very hot, with—what else?—crusty bread and manchego cheese.

One more for the side table of the considerable True North Chili. An easy cornbread with a couple of untraditional touches.

One more for the side-table of the considerable True North Chili.

Buttermilk Cornbread with Pine Nuts, Pumpkin & Oka

1 cup (250 mL)	all-purpose flour
1 cup (250 mL)	yellow cornmeal
¼ cup (50 mL)	sugar
1 Tbsp (15 mL)	baking powder
½ tsp (2 mL)	salt
2	eggs
1 cup (250 mL)	buttermilk
¼ cup (50 mL)	melted butter
½ cup (125 mL)	canned pumpkin
½ cup (125 mL)	pine nuts (or pecan pieces), lightly toasted in the oven
½ cup (125 mL)	grated Oka cheese, without the rind (more or less Oka to taste)

serves 6–8
(one 9-inch/23-cm round)

WINE PAIRINGS

Tinhorn Creek Cabernet Franc [BC]

Pilliterri Cabernet Franc [ON]

Sumac Ridge White Meritage [BC]

J.J. Prüm "Graacher Himmelreich" Riesling Spätlese [GY]

MUSIC TO COOK WITH

Kirk Elliott: *Moving Cloud* [KEM]

Jay Leonhardt: *Salamander Pie* [DMP]

Preheat the oven to 400°F (200°C). Grease a 9-inch (23-cm) pie plate or flan pan.

Combine the flour, cornmeal, sugar, baking powder and salt in a big mixing bowl.

In another bowl, mix the eggs, buttermilk, melted butter, pumpkin, pine nuts and cheese.

Combine the contents of both bowls into whichever one is the biggest. (Note: mix wet into dry or dry into wet ingredients as per whatever your momma done tol' you.) As they say: don't over-mix.

Pour the batter into the prepared pan. Bake for about 30 minutes, until golden around the edges, toothpick comes out clean, and all that. Let stand for 15–20 minutes before cutting into wedges to serve.

Hard to believe,
I know, but this
dish was served
to me on an
airplane once …

Hard to believe, I know, but this dish was served to me on an airplane once, and I can't remember the airline. I do remember being so taken with it I asked the purser to put me in touch with the system-chef to get the take on it. Couple of weeks later, this arrived and I've made it whenever fresh white asparagus comes around. Great midnight snack, with a glass of dry muscat.

White Asparagus Ragout with Morels

serves 4

1 oz (28 g)	dry morel mushrooms
2 lb (1 kg)	white asparagus
1 tsp (5 mL)	butter
¼ cup (50 mL)	shallots, chopped
¼ cup (50 mL)	asparagus stock or concentrated vegetable stock (see method)
¼ cup (50 mL)	crème fraîche
to taste	salt and pepper
to taste	lemon juice

Soak the dry morels for 3 hours in warm water. Rinse under running water and drain. Set aside.

Peel the asparagus and place in a pot. Barely cover with water and bring to a boil. Remove from the heat and let stand for 20 minutes (it should still be slightly crunchy). Take the asparagus out of the water, retaining the water. Drain and cut into pieces about 2½ inches (6 cm) long. Set aside.

Simmer the asparagus water to reduce it by half and set aside.

Heat the butter on low in a frying pan. Toss the shallots in the butter, add the morels and cook for 10 minutes. Add the crème fraîche and ¼ cup (50 mL) of the asparagus stock, season with salt, pepper and lemon juice, and heat through without boiling.

Serve with thinly sliced prosciutto on the side.

WINE PAIRINGS

Domaine Gres-Saint Paul
Muscat Sec [FR]

Zind-Humbrecht Sylvaner [FR]

Pfaffenheim Steinert Grand
Cru Gewürztraminer [FR]

MUSIC TO COOK WITH

Bill Frisell: *Nashville*
[NONESUCH]

Stan Getz: *Focus* [VERVE]

Sounds a bit perverse, doesn't it? Nobody's return address reads more Missouri than mine when it comes to this sort of diet-y stuff; I think the silliest is decaf espresso! But French chef Jacques Manière, on the occasion of his only visit to my home town, presided over a wonderful lunch he'd put together in advance of his *Le Grand Livre de la Cuisine à la Vapeur* text-and-recipe book. Over that lunch and a lot of good wine, we chatted about the restaurant business, his understandable dislike of Michelin restaurant inspectors and cooking with steam. This sauce has become another one of those staples that really works, and I never tell people of its butterlessness until well after; usually not until, say, we're into the St. André cheese.

Sounds a bit perverse, doesn't it?

Butterless Béarnaise Sauce

1 medium	zucchini, not peeled	serves 4
2 Tbsp (25 mL)	spreadable cream cheese	
2 Tbsp (25 mL)	sour cream	
2 branches	fresh tarragon (or 1 tsp/5 mL dry, in a pinch)	
2 Tbsp (25 mL)	white wine	
1 Tbsp (15 mL)	white wine vinegar	
1	shallot, finely chopped	
¾ tsp (4 mL)	crushed black pepper	
3	egg yolks	
½	lemon, juice of	
to taste	salt	

Cook the zucchini in a steamer or microwave until soft. In a blender or processor, purée the zucchini fine; add the cream cheese and sour cream and blend well. Transfer to a saucepan and heat.

Combine the tarragon, wine, vinegar, shallot and pepper in a saucepan. Bring to a good boil and reduce by three-quarters. Put the tarragon reduction in the top of a stainless or Pyrex double boiler, add the egg yolks and whisk continuously till the mixture is frothy and starts to thicken.

Pour the zucchini-cheese mixture into the eggs, stirring constantly. Add the lemon juice, adjust the seasonings (adding salt if desired) and keep warm.

Serve with vegetables, fish or meat.

WINE PAIRINGS

Chateau Gaudrelle Vouvray
[FR]

Chartron et Trebuchet
Meursault [FR]

Pierre André
Puligny-Montrachet [FR]

MUSIC TO COOK WITH

Eve Egoyan:
*Erik Satie: Hidden Corners
(Recoins)* [CBC]

Bill Evans & Jim Hall:
Undercurrent [BLUE NOTE]

Susan Phillips …
inspired a great
deal of Pavlovian
reaction …

Susan Phillips of Gananoque, Ontario, inspired a great deal of Pavlovian reaction with these. Just reading the ingredients does it for me.

Sharpish Cheddar Thins

**makes about
9 dozen cookies**

WINE PAIRINGS

Inniskillin Vidal Icewine [ON]

Malivoire Old Vines Foch [ON]

Inniskillin Okanagan
Zinfandel [BC]

Gehringer Brothers
"Minus 9" Icewine [BC]

MUSIC TO COOK WITH

Oscar Peterson:
Canadiana Suite [VERVE]

¾ cup (175 mL)	butter, softened
one ½-lb (250-g) package	cream cheese
1	egg
1 tsp (5 mL)	salt
½ tsp (2 mL)	chili flakes
4 cups (1 L)	grated old or very old Cheddar cheese
2 cups (500 mL)	all-purpose flour
1 cup (250 mL)	finely ground pecans

Beat the butter and cream cheese in large bowl. (I use an electric mixer.) Add the egg, salt and chili flakes; beat until well combined. Stir in the grated cheese.

Combine the flour and the ground pecans. Stir into the cream cheese mixture about a third at a time. (I use a wooden spoon, and sometimes, to mix the flour in, I knead it with my hands).

Divide the dough in half and shape each half into a log about 2 inches (5 cm) in diameter. Wrap in plastic wrap and chill overnight in the refrigerator.

Preheat the oven to 350°F (180°C).

Cut the chilled logs into ⅛-inch (3-mm) slices and place on a parchment-lined baking sheet.

Bake for 15 minutes or until the cookies are light brown around the edges. Remove them from the baking sheets and cool completely on wire racks.

These can be especially tasty with jalapeño jelly.

Joe Muer of Bloomfield, Michigan, sent in a recipe that his grandmother created in the early 1920s for the family's Detroit restaurant, Joe Muer's Sea Food. Started by Joe's grandfather, the restaurant lasted 70 years, and this was the most requested recipe.

Shrimp, scallops, lobster, fish or any seafood or chicken can be basted with the sauce in a shallow pan for broiling. Add roasted red peppers, shrimp or scallops or roasted chicken and use as a pasta sauce. Or baste sliced French bread with the sauce and toast in the broiler.

Joe Muer … sent in a recipe that his grandmother created in the early 1920s …

Joe Muer's De Johnge Butter Sauce

1 tub	Olivio* or 1 lb (500 g) butter	**serves 6**
4 cloves	garlic, minced	
1 tsp (5 mL)	salt	
¼ tsp (1 mL)	white pepper	
1	lemon	
¼ cup (50 mL)	fresh parsley	
¼ cup (50 mL)	raw almonds	
½ cup (125 mL)	regular oatmeal	

*Olivio is an olive oil product that tastes like butter but cooks better.

Melt the Olivio or butter in a 1-quart (1-L) saucepan. Add the minced garlic, salt and pepper. Quarter the lemon and remove the seeds. Squeeze the juice into the pan and throw in the rinds and parsley. Gently boil these ingredients over low heat for 10 minutes.

Chop the almonds to a medium-ground consistency and add to the pot.

Refine the oatmeal in a food processor to a flour consistency and add to thicken the mixture. Bring this to a low boil and cook, stirring, for 5 minutes.

Remove the lemon rinds, cool and refrigerate. The sauce can be frozen and will hold for a long time in the refrigerator.

WINE PAIRINGS

Roger Wong's "Focus" Riesling [BC]

Château des Charmes Viognier [ON]

Badische Winzerkellerei Red [GY]

Summerhill Blaufrankisch [BC]

MUSIC TO COOK WITH

Nuclear Whales Saxophone Orchestra: *Whalin'* [WHALECO]

Paragon Ragtime Orchestra: *That Demon Rag* [DORIAN]

Chenille Sisters: *True to Life* [RED HOUSE]

Jonathan Bingham of Regina tells us that these got their name in the Great Depression when they were a popular cheap meat course. Today, Jonathan serves them with roast pork. He remembers his mother making these using ordinary tea-cups and kitchen spoons for measures and has experimented—with an official Piggies in the Middle panel, no less—to recreate the recipe for four people.

... these got
their name in the
Great Depression ...

Piggies in the Middle

serves 4

½ lb (250 g)	pork sausage meat
2 Tbsp (25 mL)	chopped fresh herb mixture (comes in a tube at the supermarket) or 1 Tbsp (15 mL) each chopped thyme and parsley
to taste	salt and pepper
8 good-sized	green Granny Smith apples
1 Tbsp (15 mL)	butter, melted

Preheat the oven to 475°F (240°C).

In a bowl, mix the sausage meat, chopped herbs and a good seasoning of salt and pepper.

Wash and dry the apples and remove the cores using an apple corer. With a sharp knife, make the cavity larger.

Divide the sausage meat mix into 8 portions. Roll each portion into a sausage shape and fit it into the cavity of an apple. There will be some of the mix at the top that won't go into the cavity; just pat it down neatly.

Cut a line through the skin at the equator of the apple. Brush each apple with melted butter and place on a baking tray. Bake for 25 minutes.

WINE PAIRINGS

Yellow Tail Sauvignon Blanc
[AU]

De Wetshof Pinot Noir [SA]

MUSIC TO COOK WITH

Jonathan & Darlene Edwards:
Greatest Hits [CORINTHIAN]

University of Texas Winds:
Bells for Stokowski
[REFERENCE]

Dr. Emily Goetz of Vancouver has been making Dorothy's Eggs for more decades than she cares to report, usually by request. The recipe comes through a dear 45-year friend whose name isn't Dorothy. It's been handed down and adapted over three generations.

Dr. Emily Goetz … has been making Dorothy's Eggs for more decades than she cares to report …

Dorothy's Eggs

6 large	eggs, lightly beaten
2 cups (500 mL)	grated medium cheddar
to taste	Worcestershire sauce
one 4-oz (114-mL) can	diced green chilis, drained
one 14-oz (398-mL) can	creamed corn
to taste	salt and pepper

Stir everything together. Pour mixture into an oiled 9-inch (23-cm) square pan. Bake uncovered at 325°F (160°C) for 1 hour, or until the centre tests clean with a toothpick or other sensible implement.

Let sit for at least 15 minutes before cutting into squares or rectangles or … I'm aware that can sizes vary, so as you get to know the dish, alter the amounts of chilis, cheese, corn, Worcestershire, as well as the pan size, to your liking. Enjoy! It's even good at room temperature.

A note: I often serve these with an equally old fave, wonderful sautéed sausages —at some point add sliced nectarines, a bit of brown sugar, lemon juice and cardamom seeds. Let steep a bit. Consider it simply an aromatic thought.

serves 4 hungry folks

WINE PAIRINGS

mimosas

Veuve du Vernay [FR]

Gazela Vinho Verde [PO]

MUSIC TO COOK WITH

Dave Brubeck: *Time Out* [CBS]

Schubert: *Rosamunde Music* [DGG]

chapter four

pastas

Fettuccine with Rosemary & Tuna 48

Katzenthaler Fusilli 49

Egg Noodles with Gorgonzola & Pistachios 50

Far Out Noodles 51

P P P P P P P P P Pasta 52

Spaghetti with Sage & Celery 54

Ziti with Lamb, Ham & Greens 56

Penne with Fresh Vegetables 58

The Perfect Risotto, with Asparagus 59

Scallop Fettuccini with Ginger-Cream Sauce 60

Pasta with Kale & Feta Cheese 62

Linguine with Sardines, Chili & Capers 63

... get a few cans of real Italian, packed-in-olive-oil tuna ...

The delight of this dish comes from the combination of fresh rosemary and good tuna. For goodness' sake, spend the two bucks on a few sprigs of the fresh herb and go the bundle, at a good Italian deli, and get a few cans of real Italian, packed-in-olive-oil tuna, none of that spring-water-packed misery from Thailand. A quick, easy, satisfying lunch dish that's light and clean.

No cheese, please; in Italy we rarely put cheese on our fish or seafood pasta; that's reserved for tomato and meat sauces.

Fettuccine with Rosemary & Tuna

serves 4

1 lb (500 g)	fettuccine
2 Tbsp (25 mL)	olive oil
3 or 4 cloves	garlic, minced
1 small	*pepperoncino* (Italian chili pepper) or similar
two 7½-oz (213-mL) cans	Italian tuna (use the oil, too)
1 sprig	fresh rosemary, needles stripped off (or more, to taste)
to taste	black pepper

Put the pasta in plenty of boiling, salted water for 8 minutes (or whatever it says on the box), and make the sauce while it cooks.

Put the oil in a small saucepan, heat it and add the garlic. Cook nice and low till the garlic gets a golden colour to it. Add the *pepperoncino*. Mash the tuna and its oil with a fork and add it to the sauce. Add the rosemary and a couple of tablespoons of the hot pasta water. Cover the pan and cook on medium-low for 10 minutes.

Drain the cooked fettuccine and put it in a warm bowl. Pour the sauce over top, grind on some black pepper and tuck in.

WINE PAIRINGS

Fat Bastard Chardonnay [FR]

Santa Maria "La Bombarde"
Cannonau di Sardegna [IT]

MUSIC TO COOK WITH

Red Priest:
Four Seasons (Vivaldi) [DORIAN]

My favourite place for food in the whole world is Alsace. If I win the lottery you can just forward my mail to General Delivery, Alsace. Katzenthal, if you're looking, is a tiny vineyard village not far from Münster, so my take on one of the traditional ways they do pasta there—double cooking it—is to add some of that famous, if odoriferous, cheese. If you consider the second meaning of odoriferous as well, you may wish to leave it out and substitute grated Gruyère. Just as good and one of the simplest pasta recipes I know.

My favourite place for food in the whole world is Alsace.

Katzenthaler Fusilli

2 Tbsp (25 mL)	butter
½ lb (250 g)	fusilli, or other pasta that's not too stringy, cooked and drained
¼ cup (50 mL)	grated Münster cheese (or Gruyère)
to taste	salt and pepper
2 Tbsp (25 mL)	olive oil

Melt the butter in a pan and stir in half of the pasta. Add cheese, salt and pepper and simmer, stirring, for 4 minutes. Pour the pasta mixture into a heated serving dish.

Sauté the rest of the pasta in the oil in a frying pan, till it starts to brown; don't let it get too crisp.

Spoon this pasta over that in the serving dish and serve.

serves 4

WINE PAIRINGS

Laugel Rosé de Marlenheim [FR]

Willm "Edelzwicker" [FR]

eau-de-vie quetsch or celeri [FR]

MUSIC TO COOK WITH

Claude Bolling: *Suite for Flute & Jazz Piano* [CBS]

This is the sort of
dish you might not
want to tell your
doctor about.

Sometimes you want the wine to match the food and sometimes it works the other way around. After discovering a particularly tasty French country wine, called Domaine Grès-Saint Paul Muscat Sec, I decided it needed a special pasta to go along, so I rustled up a batch of very rich noodles to keep it company. It's equally at home with a country red. In various ways those who had it set before them agreed with my initial impression that this was a winner: wolfing it without words, snarfling it with purrs, and back-of-the-throat barklets of canine gustatory delight. This is the sort of dish you might not want to tell your doctor about.

Egg Noodles with Gorgonzola & Pistachios

serves 4

1 cup (250 mL)	butter
1 cup (250 mL)	Gorgonzola, crumbled
1 cup (250 mL)	whipping cream
½ cup (125 mL)	pistachios, shelled and skinned, chopped or ground (or more)
4–5 Tbsp (60–75 mL)	brandy
2–3 Tbsp (25–45 mL)	dry muscat wine (or something Alsatian)
to taste	salt (optional)
to taste	freshly ground black pepper
1 pkg. (1 lb / 500 g)	egg noodles, cooked to your liking
1 sprig	parsley, for appearances

Domaine Grès-Saint Paul
Muscat Sec [FR]

MUSIC TO COOK WITH

Lara St. John: *re: Bach* [SONY]

Melt the butter in a saucepan, on low. Blend in the Gorgonzola—it takes some stirring. Add the whipping cream—more stirring. Add the pistachios, plus the brandy and the wine; salt if you think it wants it (I don't, because the cheese seems plenty salty to me) and lots of black pepper.

Heat the lot till it simmers gently, then pour it over a batch of the cooked noodles. Garnish with a sprig of parsley.

Drink the muscat (or Alsatian Pinot Blanc or Tokay) with it and think nothing more substantial than what's in the freezer for dessert …

The name of the recipe was a giveaway as to the decade of its origin and, likely, the last time it was prepared. Handwritten on a card, reposing in a bulging file box for more decades than I'd be prepared to admit, it fell out and right back into our life again. We grinned at each other—"Let's do it." At once, waves of nostalgia came calling, complete with soundtrack: Dylan's Highway 61 Revisited, Joan Baez, Richie Havens, the music scratched out from a Seabreeze record player in a carrying case, with a nickel taped to the tone arm to cut through the gunk—mostly candle wax—on the LP's surface. Everybody was working on a collage in the basement, and herbal essence sure wasn't any sort of shampoo!

The name of the recipe was a giveaway as to the decade of its origin …

Far Out Noodles

½ lb (250 g)	noodles, cooked in lots of water with a little salt, drained
2 cups (500 mL)	cottage cheese
2 cups (500 mL)	sour cream
¼ cup (50 mL)	melted butter
½ cup (125 mL)	chopped green onions
a few cloves	garlic, minced
1 tsp (5 mL)	Worcestershire sauce, more or less
dash	Tabasco sauce
to taste	salt and pepper
½ cup (125 mL)	grated Parmesan
½ cup (125 mL)	slivered almonds, toasted

Preheat the oven to 350°F (180°C). Use a little of the butter to grease a casserole/baking dish.

Everything except the noodles, Parmesan and almonds goes into a mixing bowl: cottage cheese, sour cream, the rest of the butter, onions, garlic, sauces, salt and pepper. Blend well.

Warm noodles get dumped in the cheesy-creamy mix. Pour the glop into the casserole/baking dish and sprinkle the Parmesan on top.

Into the oven, bake for 30 minutes.

Out of the oven, and the almonds sprinkled on top. Back in for another 10 minutes or until it's all browned to your liking.

Eat with some spinach salad and bread. Brownies after (see herbal essence, above). Or Oreos. Far out.

serves 4

WINE PAIRINGS

Gamza [BU]

Labatt's Blue [CA]

MUSIC TO COOK WITH

Original London Cast: *Return to the Forbidden Planet* [VIRGIN UK]

Duane Eddy: *Twang Thang* [RHINO]

Van Morrison: *Astral Weeks* [WARNER BROS.]

Big Daddy: *Sgt. Pepper* [RHINO]

Bob Dylan: *Highway 61 Revisited* [COLUMBIA]

Aldo Ciccolini: *Erik Satie* [ANGEL]

… the nine Ps derive from the serendipitous fact that all the principal ingredients began with the letter P.

One day, after a working wine tasting, I was in the kitchen throwing stuff together to come up with one of those Unified Field Theory dishes to work with everything we'd sipped before. What ensued was this Number Niner; the nine Ps derive from the serendipitous fact that all the principal ingredients began with the letter P. (All right, I stretched it a little after seven.) Quantities are approximate. I'm still fine-tuning, so let me know how yours turns out. For the nine Ps, simply use quantities to suit.

P P P P P P P P Pasta

serves 4 or more

WINE PAIRINGS

Terruzzi & Puthod Vernaccia di San Gimignano [IT]

Saxonburg "Private Collection" Sauvignon Blanc [SA]

Frescobaldi Pomino Bianco [IT]

MUSIC TO COOK WITH

Thomas Wilbrandt: *The Electric V* [LONDON]

	potatoes
	pancetta
	oil, to sauté
3–4 cloves	garlic, minced
	porcini mushrooms, dried
	peppers (red, sun-dried)
	pine nuts
½ glass	wine (red, white or vermouth) or vodka
	peppercorns, black, crushed
½ small tin	tomato paste (about ⅓ cup/75 mL)
	peas
	water or broth (chicken or vegetable), hot, on standby
some	heavy cream, if you're being entirely excessive
dash	cheap bandy
	Italian parsley, chopped
1 tsp (5 mL)	Mexican oregano, rubbed in the palm before going in the pot
lots	Parmesan
1 lb (500 g)	pasta (penne is good, and easier to serve with all these chunky things than spaghetti)
to taste	salt and pepper

Dice and parboil the potatoes. (Drop into cold water, bring to the boil, cook 5 minutes, drain and cool.)

Sauté the pancetta in a little oil for 5 minutes, add the garlic and continue cooking on medium till garlic turns light golden. Take off the heat while you deal with the following:

Pour hot water over the porcini mushrooms and let stand for 30 minutes. Drain through a coffee filter to get the grit out; keep the liquid in case you want more later. Chop the porcini.

Soften the sun-dried red peppers with boiling water to cover, 5 minutes, then chop them.

Toast the pine nuts in the oven till light brown (10 minutes at 350°F/180°C).

Put the pancetta and garlic back on medium heat, add wine or vodka, then red peppers and peppercorns, then tomato paste. Cook through for 10 minutes.

Add the soaked mushrooms, pine nuts, potatoes and peas (fresh peas are nice but a pain to shell, so frozen peas, well-thawed are just fine. Don't use canned peas, though—they mush into green pulp.)

Heat everything through for 10 minutes more. Don't let the sauce boil. If it looks too dry or is in danger of caramelizing, add some hot broth, on standby, or mushroom liquid or more wine.

If you've chosen the cream route, add it now and heat it through. Take the sauce off the heat, add a dash of brandy if you like, then chopped Italian parsley and oregano. Mix everything thoroughly and grate vast quantities of real Parmesan over the top.

Leave out the pancetta and it's vegetarian; veganize it by dropping the cream and cheese.

Cook the pasta to desired doneness and ladle lots of sauce on, adding salt and pepper as necessary. Drink all or any of the above wines with it.

This combination
relies on celery
leaves as well
as the stalks …

This combination relies on celery leaves as well as the stalks, along with lots of fresh sage. If you delete the bacon it's a nice, surprisingly hearty vegetarian pasta.

Spaghetti with Sage & Celery

serves 4

WINE PAIRINGS

Hogue Cellars Fumé Blanc
[WA]

Carmen Pinot Noir [CH]

2 Tbsp (25 mL)	olive oil
1 medium	onion, chopped
2 stalks	celery, chopped fine (chop leaves and reserve)
2 cloves	garlic, minced
1 Tbsp (15 mL)	all-purpose flour
2 dozen	fresh sage leaves, more if you really like the flavour
3 or 4	ripe Roma tomatoes, cut into pieces (peeled if you want)
½ cup (125 mL)	hot chicken or vegetable stock
to taste	salt and pepper
6 slices	lean bacon, diced
1 Tbsp (15 mL)	oil
1 lb (500 g)	spaghetti
1 cup (250 mL)	grated Asiago and mozzarella cheeses, blended

MUSIC TO COOK WITH

Anne Sofie von Otter: *Music for a While/ Melodies Baroque* [DGG]

Diana Krall: *All for You* [IMPULSE]

Heat the olive oil in a pan and sauté the onion till it gets golden. Add the chopped celery stalks and garlic and continue cooking for 4 or 5 minutes.

Add the flour, stir and cook for 2 minutes. Add most of the sage leaves (reserve 4 or 5) and the tomatoes. Cook on moderate heat for 10 minutes.

Add the stock, salt and pepper and simmer for 20 minutes.

When the sauce is just about done, sauté the bacon in a small frying pan with 1 Tbsp (15 mL) of oil until it's golden and starting to crisp.

Take the bacon off the heat and add the rest of the sage leaves, finely chopped, and the celery leaves.

Cook the spaghetti, and while that's happening, put your sauce through one of those Italian food mills or a blender—if you like it all slurry-like, that is; I usually keep mine chunky.

Put the drained spaghetti into a big heated serving bowl. Add the bacon, sage and celery leaves and mix well. Add the sauce and half of the grated cheese and mix again. Sprinkle the rest of the cheese on top.

Ziti because it's
different from
fusilli or penne ...

Ziti because it's different from fusilli or penne; or use *radiatore* or any one of the other chunky pastas; there are a million of them. A hearty, even rich (but not fatty) pasta for early summer.

Ziti with Lamb, Ham *&* Greens

serves 4

WINE PAIRINGS

a nice little Pinot Noir, from Carneros or Willamette or Niagara, or Beaune

MUSIC TO COOK WITH

Joel Quarrington: *Virtuoso Reality* [CBC]

Ukulele Orchestra of Great Britain: *A Fistful of Ukuleles* [SONY JAPAN]

3 or 4 medium	tomatoes
¼ cup (50 mL)	olive oil
1 medium	onion, chopped fine
1 lb (500 g)	ground lamb (if you're buying what's sometimes sold as "lamb burger" make sure it doesn't have all sorts of odd seasoning in it)
½ tsp (2 mL)	salt
1 tsp (5 mL)	black pepper
3 cloves	garlic, crushed
6–8 big	fresh basil leaves
big handful	Italian parsley
1 small bunch	fresh chives (or green onions, without the white)
1 lb (500 g)	ziti
2 slices	cooked ham
¼ cup (50 mL)	butter
1 cup (250 mL)	freshly grated Parmesan

Cut up the tomatoes and put them in a pan. Bring to the boil and cook for 2 minutes.

Blenderize the tomatoes.

Heat the oil in a large frying pan and sauté the onion till golden.

Add the lamb, salt and pepper and brown over moderate heat, 7 or 8 minutes.

Chop together the crushed garlic, basil, parsley and chives very finely and add to the meat. Stir thoroughly. Add the puréed tomatoes, stir and cover. Simmer 30 minutes, stirring occasionally.

Cook the ziti in salted water. Drain and put it in a serving bowl.

Cut the ham into strips or chunks and add to the sauce. A minute or two later, add the sauce to the drained pasta along with the butter and most of the cheese, reserving a little to sprinkle on top after mixing.

This is the one
for when the road-
side farm stands
start bringing out
the fresh stuff ...

This is the one for when the roadside farm stands start bringing out the fresh stuff: crunchy carrots and beans, fresh peas for the shelling, great little potatoes. These all come together in this recipe often made in Liguria.

Penne with Fresh Vegetables

serves 4

WINE PAIRINGS

Chateau Pech-Latt
(organic) Corbières [FR]

Chateau de la Gardine
Chateauneuf-du-Pape [FR]

MUSIC TO COOK WITH

Angela Hewitt:
Bach Transcriptions [HYPERION]

3 medium	potatoes
1 cup (250 mL)	green beans, thinnest possible
4 or 5	carrots
1 cup (250 mL)	freshly shelled peas
	anything else in the fresh veggie line you can get at
1 lb (500 g)	penne (or macaroni)
1 tsp (5 mL)	fresh marjoram (more or less) (or dry, to taste)
enough	extra virgin olive oil, flavoured with rosemary if you've got it
to taste	salt and pepper
lots	freshly grated off-the-slab Parmesan

Peel and dice the potatoes, clean the beans and break them in half, peel the carrots and slice into rounds, shell the peas and do whatever is required with any other fresh vegetables going in so that the pieces will all be cooked at the same time.

Bring a big pot of salted water to the boil and throw it all in—the potatoes, vegetables, pasta and marjoram.

Cook it all together for 10 minutes, less if you're using fresh penne, in which case you want to start the veggies just a few minutes ahead of the pasta. Just make sure you don't end up mush-cooking those nice fresh peas and beans and carrots.

Drain it all and scatter on to a serving plate with a few tablespoons of olive oil. Salt and pepper to taste and throw on the Parmesan.

Serve hot or cool.

There's nothing like learning to do something from an acknowledged master, and so it was for me with Italy's famous rice dish. After Gabriele Ferron toured North America, I learned from the master himself at his restaurant in Verona. It was a wonderful weekend billed as Risotto Rendezvous, organized by the Masi wine people, the highlight of it all being a 40-years-back retrospective tasting of Amarone. Both the teeth and the prose were purple that weekend.

And the secret to perfect risotto? Says Gabriele Ferron: "Seventeen minutes," that's how long you cook it, once the near-boiling broth starts going in. And don't wash the rice. And don't brown the onions. And only ever use Italian short grain. Vialone nano is my rice of choice. And don't eat it in restaurants, very few of them cook it properly. Except, of course, if you're in the countryside just out of Verona …

… I learned from the master himself …

The Perfect Risotto, with Asparagus

serves 4 with an appetite

1 lb (500 g)	fresh green asparagus, the thinnest possible
4 Tbsp (60 mL)	extra virgin olive oil
1 clove	garlic, minced
1 medium	onion, minced
⅓ cup (75 mL)	Soave white wine (might as well use Masi, you'll be drinking it)
4–5 cups (1–1.25 L)	vegetable broth, maintained at a constant simmer on the other burner
2 cups (500 mL)	Vialone nano rice (or arborio)
1 Tbsp (15 mL)	butter
to taste	salt

Cut the asparagus stalks into 1-inch (2.5-cm) pieces, discarding the tough bottoms.

Heat half the oil in a medium pot, on low. Add the garlic, onion and asparagus tops. Sauté for 3 minutes, till the onions start softening; don't let them brown. Add the wine and cook 3 minutes more. Set aside.

In another pot, simmer the broth and add the middle pieces of the asparagus.

In a pot big enough to hold everything when it comes together, heat the remaining olive oil on medium-low. Add the rice, raise the heat to medium and cook for 3 minutes, stirring often to get the rice coated with oil. Add a couple of ladlefuls of the broth, stirring gently, and lower the heat to maintain a simmer.

Keep adding broth, a ladleful at a time, and keep stirring, so the rice absorbs the liquid, before adding more. Do this for about 8 or 9 more minutes.

Add the asparagus tops and onions and simmer for 7 more minutes.

Add the butter and salt, stir gently, and serve at once or the risotto will start to lose its creaminess.

WINE PAIRINGS

Folonari Valpolicella [IT]

Masi Campofiorin Ripasso [IT]

MUSIC TO COOK WITH

Vaughan Williams: *The Lark Ascending* [CBC]

Prokofiev: *Romeo & Juliet* [PHILIPS]

Ken Friesen ...
recommends an
expensive Chablis
along with this dish.

Ken Friesen of Kingsville, Ontario, recommends an expensive Chablis along with this dish. And who can argue?

Scallop Fettuccini with Ginger-Cream Sauce

serves 4

1 cup (250 mL)	scallops
enough	fettuccine for 4
3 Tbsp (45 mL)	butter
2 Tbsp (25 mL)	all-purpose flour
2 Tbsp (25 mL)	grated fresh ginger
½ tsp (2 mL)	lemon zest
1 clove	garlic, smashed
1 cup (250 mL)	milk
2–3 cups (500–750 mL)	water
¼ tsp (1 mL)	salt
2 Tbsp (25 mL)	minced green onion
	black pepper
for garnish	lemon twist and/or parsley

WINE PAIRINGS

Moreau Chablis [FR]
of whatever level of costliness
seems appropriate

MUSIC TO COOK WITH

Handel:
The Harmonious Blacksmith [SONY]

Wanda Landowska:
Ancient Dances [RCA]

Wash and drain the scallops. Set aside in the refrigerator.

Prepare the fettuccini, drain and rinse, and keep warm.

Make a roux using 2 Tbsp (30 mL) of the butter with the flour, ginger, lemon zest and half the garlic. Add the milk a little at a time to create a sauce, stirring constantly with a whisk until thickened. Juices released from the cooking scallops will cause it to thin when you add them just before serving, so you want the sauce to be the consistency of whipping cream at this stage. Add the water as needed to thin it. The cooked fettuccini will take up the liquid quite readily; too thick a sauce will have a tacky mouth feel.

Pass the sauce through a sieve to remove the zest, garlic and coarser ginger. Add salt to taste and keep warm on low heat.

Melt the remaining 1 Tbsp (15 mL) butter in a skillet over medium heat. Add the green onion and pepper and heat through. Add the scallops and cook gently for 3 minutes, stirring often. (Scallops give off considerable liquid, do not discard!)

Pour the sauce over the scallops, stirring together to incorporate the scallop juices. Distribute the fettuccini over a serving platter and pour the sauce lovingly over the pasta. Garnish affectionately with a lemon twist and/or parsley. Serve hot.

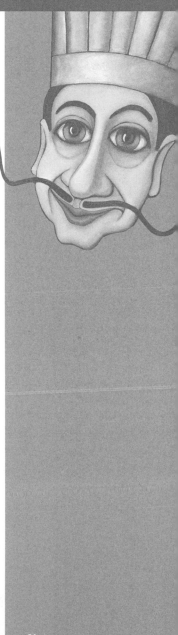

Johanna and Joe
Bergerman love to
grow kale in their
front yard …

Johanna and Joe Bergerman love to grow kale in their front yard in Saskatoon, and making this quick pasta dish keeps them connected to Johanna's Dutch roots and to the earth under their feet.

Pasta with Kale & Feta Cheese

serves 6–8

WINE PAIRINGS

iced grappa (or ouzo)

Tsantali Merlot [GR]

Manousakis Nostos [GR]

2 large bunches	kale
1–2 Tbsp (15–25 mL)	olive oil
2 cups (500 mL)	finely chopped leeks, white and green portions
1 or more large cloves	garlic, minced
4–6 cups (1–1.5 L)	of sturdy pasta such as rotini, penne, shells or fusilli
¼–½ lb (125–250 g)	feta cheese, crumbled (can be frozen)
to taste	grated Parmesan
to taste	black pepper

Strip the leafy portion off the kale spine. Discard the spines. Blanch or steam the kale until it wilts. (It can be frozen at this point to use later.)

Heat the olive oil over medium heat in a deep skillet, such as a wok, and sauté the chopped leeks and garlic. Add the blanched chopped kale and cook for 5 to 7 minutes.

Meanwhile, bring a large pot of salted water to boil and add the pasta. Cook until it is al dente. Lightly drain the pasta and add to the sautéed kale. Mix thoroughly. Stir in crumbles of feta cheese and serve with Parmesan cheese and grated black pepper.

Tip: blanch and then freeze the kale overnight or longer. Blanching and freezing is the traditional way to improve the flavour of kale. Also, kale that is partially thawed is easier to choppy finely. Finely chopped kale is also tastier in this dish.

MUSIC TO COOK WITH

Jimmy Giuffre 3: *The Train and the River* [ATLANTIC]

Andre Previn Trio: *King Size* [CONTEMPORARY]

Guitar Islancio & Don Gillis: *Connections* [ICE MUSIC]

Connie Kaldor: *Love is a Truck* [COYOTE]

Dawn Morgan of Fredericton, New Brunswick, won immediate and universal approval from the judges with this one. It's a quick workday supper that you can make in the time it takes to cook the pasta. This dish depends on flavourful tomatoes, so in winter cherry tomatoes are best. Dawn got the recipe from her brother, Theron, and he got it from Delia Smith's 1999 book, *Delia's How to Cook Book*, but he thinks he's improved it by substituting a can of grilled yellowfin tuna and half a tin of anchovies for the sardines. He drains the tuna and uses the oil from the anchovies.

Dawn Morgan ... won immediate and universal approval from the judges with this one.

Linguine with Sardines, Chili & Capers

enough	dried linguine for 1 or 2 people
1 Tbsp (15 mL)	olive oil (or more if you like) reserved from the sardines
1	red chili, deseeded and finely chopped
1 clove	garlic, peeled and chopped
4 medium	ripe tomatoes, or equivalent in cherry tomatoes, coarsely chopped
1 tin	sardines in olive oil (reserve the oil), drained and broken roughly into bite-size pieces
1 Tbsp (15 mL)	salted capers rinsed in cold water (or pickled capers—if you can't find salted capers—just drained, not rinsed)
to taste	salt and freshly ground black pepper (omit salt if using salted capers)
for garnish	fresh basil leaves, roughly torn

serves 2, or 1 with a big appetite.

Bring a big pot of salted water to boil and add the linguine.

Meanwhile, heat the olive oil from the sardines in a pot big enough to hold the cooked pasta once it is drained. Sauté the chili and garlic lightly, about 2–3 minutes.

Turn off the heat (or turn it very low) and add the tomatoes, sardines and capers. Gently heat through, stirring lightly to mix. You just want to heat the tomatoes, not cook them. Season with salt and pepper to taste.

When the pasta is ready, drain it into a colander and then quickly add it to the sauce. Toss together and serve in shallow bowls with a few torn basil leaves to garnish.

WINE PAIRINGS

Kumala Cabernet-Shiraz [SA]

Cono Sur Viognier [CH]

MUSIC TO COOK WITH

guitarists galore
Goran Söllscher: *11-String Baroque* [DGG]

Martin Taylor: *Don't Fret* [LINN]

Gordon Quinton: *North Atlantic Dance* [WOODNIGHT]

James Hill: *On the Other Hand* [JHE]

(all right, one of them plays ukulele)

chapter five

fish

Sherried, Chilied Oysters 66

Prawns & Okra over Spinach with Lemon 67

Boba Seafood Cakes with Tropical Tartar Sauce 68

Janssen's Temptation 70

Angels in E-Types (Scrumpied Oysters) 71

Mayne Island Oyster Stew (the one they call Pan Roast in some parts) 72

Tonno con Cilantro Pesto 73

Scallops with Mushrooms & Lime, in Parchment 74

Roasted Prawns with Morels & Morel Butter 76

Pappardelle with Tuna in Basil & Mint Sauce 78

Drambuie Salmon 79

... the Spanish drink sherry with fish, soup, grilled veggies, ham, chicken, garlic, ... anything.

Of course, the Spanish drink sherry with fish, soup, grilled veggies, ham, chicken, garlic, ... anything. I once cooked with a Spanish chef who insisted the best accompaniment to the leg of lamb he'd been slow-cooking all morning was a bottle of Nutty Solera. I was skeptical. He was right. It was glorious.

Somewhere in my eating, drinking travels I collected an oyster recipe that's been as much a staple in my kitchen as has Lustau Palo Cortado dry sherry in my bar.

Sherried, Chilied Oysters

serves 4

It brings together the metallic tang of fresh oysters with herbs and garlic, hot chili, cold dry sherry. You can keep on cooking fresh batches as guests arrive all afternoon, or you can do a serious supply ahead of time and leave them ready to slurp up at room temperature. Here's a double batch to pique the palates of the bridge club.

4 cups (1 L)	oysters, 2–3 dozen depending on size (mini-Malpeques are perfect)
2 Tbsp (25 mL)	olive oil
4 cloves	garlic, minced
½ cup (125 mL)	tomato paste
1½ cups (375 mL)	clam juice or oyster liquid, or chicken broth, or combination
1 Tbsp (15 mL)	hot chili sauce of choice (more or less)
1	dry chili pepper, for good luck
2 Tbsp (25 mL)	ultra-dry sherry (the aforementioned Lustau is ideal)
1 tsp (5 mL)	oregano (more if you find it fresh)
1 tsp (5 mL)	minced parsley
to taste	cracked black pepper

Shuck the oysters and reserve their liquid.

Heat the oil and sauté the garlic till golden. Stir in the tomato paste, juice/broth, chili sauce, chili pepper, sherry, oregano and parsley. Blend well and heat through.

Add the oysters. When they commence curling 'round the edges, they're done.

Sprinkle on black pepper and serve at once, with crusty bread, pouring lots more chilled sherry from the extra bottle in the door of the refrigerator, where it's been for the last hour.

WINE PAIRINGS

Lustau Palo Cortado dry [SP]

Penascal Sauvignon Blanc [SP]

MUSIC TO COOK WITH

Alfonso X, el Sabio: *Cantigas de Santa Maria* [HARMONIA MUNDI]

Frederic Hand's *Jazzantiqua* [MUSICMASTERS]

Daniel Bolshoy & Julie Nesrallah: *España* [BOLDAN MUSIC]

Why for 12? Because that's how many were sitting in the dining room waiting for dinner, of which this was only the first course—the whole dinner having to be cooked on that curious contraption called an Aga stove. Those who know and love them swear by them; those who don't swear at them. That'll be me, in my friend Erika Durlacher's kitchen, at her famous B&B, Durlacher Hof, in Whistler. I don't ski, so Erika asked if I'd cook dinner for an assembly of Pacific Coast innkeepers she'd invited. Sure, I said—I mean, how tough can a different stove be?

Prawns & Okra over Spinach with Lemon

serves 12 or more

Plenty tough: impossible if you don't know how. Couldn't have done it without Kate, traffic-controlling the whole event: "Pot #2 goes into holding oven #4 now, from which Pot #1 goes back on front burner, while Pot #3 goes into holding oven #5 …" and Benson the dog running interference around us slavering for a little taste, just a small one … Dinner went on to include soup and pasta and roast something and dessert. New appreciation was gained for working cooks everywhere. You couldn't give me one of those damn cookers!

½ cup (125 mL)	butter
2½ lb (1.2 kg)	prawns, tails on
2½ lb (1.2 kg)	fresh okra, washed, tipped and topped, halved and seeded if you want, but I like to leave them whole, providing they're small enough; if you use frozen okra, thaw, drain and wash repeatedly to de-slime
to taste	salt and pepper
2 cups (500 mL)	shredded fresh spinach
2–3	lemons, quartered

Heat the butter in a wok till it starts smoking. Sauté the prawns and okra together for 4 minutes. Add the salt and pepper and sauté for 4 minutes more.

Ladle the prawns and okra over the raw shredded spinach in a big serving bowl. Squeeze the lemon juice over top and stir through.

Serve with baguettes.

Write classified ad to sell Aga.

WINE PAIRINGS

Sazerac

Buffalo Trace Bourbon [KY]

La Frenz Muscat of Alexandria [BC]

Hillside Estate
Muscat Ottonel [BC]

MUSIC TO COOK WITH

Walt Kelly: *Songs of the Pogo* [REACTION]

Régis Gizavo: *Mikea* [SHANACHIE]

Jah Wobble & Invaders of the Heart: *English Roots Music* [30HZ]

One of my
favourite
restaurants
in Toronto
continues
to be Boba ...

One of my favourite restaurants in Toronto continues to be Boba, on Avenue Road. They come and they go, they overtrendify themselves left, right and in Oakville, but Bob Berman and Barbara Gordon's cozy place remains at the top of the list for solid satisfaction. That's because these two can cook like crazy and don't let those flavours-of-the-month get in the way. Desserts are among the best in the world, steaks are perfect and the wine list is brilliant—small, eclectic, satisfying. I asked them for a recipe for my "Chef's Table" column in *NUVO* magazine a couple of years ago and was surprised—but delighted—when they sent this one. It's become my standard for crab cakes.

Boba Seafood Cakes with Tropical Tartar Sauce

serves a group

WINE PAIRINGS

Cave Spring Cellars "CSV"
[ON]

Vignobles Germain
"Sushiwine" [FR]

Vina Antigua
Sangiovese-Bonarda [AG]

MUSIC TO COOK WITH

Noel Lee:
Gottschalk Piano Works [ERATO]

Ry Cooder: *Into the Purple Valley*
[REPRISE]

SEAFOOD CAKES

1 lb (500 g)	fresh crabmeat
½ lb (250 g)	fresh scallops, diced
¼ lb (125 g) small	shrimp, peeled, cut into small pieces
1 Tbsp (15 mL)	chives, chopped
1 Tbsp (15 mL)	parsley, chopped
1 tsp (5 mL)	fresh dill, chopped
1 Tbsp (15 mL)	Dijon mustard (more or less)
1 medium	potato, boiled, drained, mashed
to taste	salt and pepper
1 cup (250 mL)	finely ground homemade dry breadcrumbs
	vegetable oil and unsalted butter, for frying

Mix the seafood well with the herbs.

Blend the mustard into the potato gently, and carefully blend into the seafood mixture. Season with salt and pepper. Form into 3-inch (8-cm) cakes, 1 inch (2.5 cm) thick.

Put the crumbs on a plate and coat the cakes on both sides. Let rest for half an hour or longer in the fridge.

Heat ¼ inch (5 mm) of vegetable oil with 1 Tbsp (15 mL) unsalted butter in a heavy frying pan. Working in batches so as not to crowd the cakes, cook until a golden crust forms and seafood is cooked, 4–5 minutes. Drain on paper towels.

TARTAR SAUCE

1 cup (250 mL)	homemade mayonnaise
2 Tbsp (25 mL)	fresh lime juice
2 Tbsp (25 mL)	minced green onions
¼ cup (50 mL)	roasted sweet peppers (mix of red, yellow, green)
1 Tbsp (15 mL)	Caribbean hot sauce (more or less) (Bob uses Matouk's Flambeau Sauce)
to taste	salt and pepper

Blend all ingredients together, seasoning with salt and pepper. Leave at least 2 hours to marinate.

It's high on my list
of dream dinners:
four bottles of
wine ...

It's high on my list of dream dinners: four bottles of wine and the serves-six fixing of Janssen's that follows. Okay, I didn't drink all the wine; one of the cats got hold of a hefty heel of Chenin Blanc and was soon under the table. Not as bad as it sounds, he's often there, alongside the dog, particularly come dinnertime. But I did myself eat most of the dish that undid Janssen.

Janssen's Temptation

serves 6

The Temptation is a Swedish staple meant for serious indulgence. It combines potatoes, anchovies, cream, crumbs and butter; I wouldn't bother bringing it up with your doctor at the next annual.

The thing to drink with it is aquavit, iced to just above smoking stage. Easy to do: just stand the bottle in an empty two-litre milk carton, fill the carton with water and stick it in the freezer. Peel the paper away once the water's frozen and stand the bottle on the table, on a saucer to catch the melt.

WINE PAIRINGS

iced aquavit [DK]

6–8 medium	potatoes (couple of pounds), peeled and thinly sliced
lots	freshly ground black pepper
2–3 medium	onions, sliced
3 flat packs (50-g tins)	anchovy fillets in olive oil, chopped
½ cup (125 mL) medium	dry breadcrumbs
1½ cups (375 mL)	heavy cream (or make a blend using ½ half-and-half)
3–4 Tbsp (45–60 mL)	butter

MUSIC TO COOK WITH

Guitar Islancio:
Scandinavian Songs [OMI JAZZ]

Preheat the oven to 400°F (200°C).

Butter a big casserole dish. Put a layer of sliced potatoes in and sprinkle on some pepper. Cover the potatoes with a layer of onions and then some anchovies. Keep on layering till you run out of stuff, always adding a little pepper in between the layers. Sprinkle breadcrumbs over the top.

Pour in the cream—gently—so it won't come over the edge. Dot with butter. Bake till the potatoes are tender, could be an hour or so depending on how thick you sliced them.

You can also cover the dish with foil and bake and then pour a bit more cream on top after the baking is done, but I like some crunchy bits.

Serves 6. Yeah, right.

A dish that's served me well since the afternoon I invented it, upon getting stuck in a bottle of Vancouver Island Scrumpy from the Merridale Cider Works. I thought I'd bring it back here for those who (a) love oysters, (b) like real cider and (c) might have missed it in my last cookbook, over a decade ago.

A dish that's served me well since the afternoon I invented it …

Angels in E-Types (Scrumpied Oysters)

6 slices	Ayrshire bacon	
6 Tbsp (90 mL)	cold unsalted butter	
¼ cup (50 mL)	minced shallots	
1	serious chili pepper (Scotch bonnet or jalapeño), seeded and minced	
6 or 12	fresh-shucked oysters and their liquid (big West Coasters or small Easterners)	
½ cup (125 mL)	Merridale Scrumpy or other strong apple cider	
to taste	salt and pepper	
½ tub (about 90 g)	Jersey double cream or whipping cream	
1½ Tbsp (20 mL)	apple cider vinegar	
2 Tbsp (25 mL)	chopped chives	

serves 2

WINE PAIRINGS

Raven Ridge True Cider [BC]

Calvados and soda

Ketel One Citroen vodka [NL]

Start cooking the bacon in a frying pan, hot at first to sear, then medium, till semi-crisp. Drain and keep warm. Save a little bacon fat.

Meanwhile, melt half the butter in a sturdy pan. Add the shallots and hot pepper. Stir and cook for 3 minutes on medium heat. Add a little oyster liquid and cook another 2 minutes.

Add the oysters and cook briefly: no more than 2 minutes, till the edges start to curl. Remove the oysters with a slotted spoon and keep warm.

Add 1 Tbsp (15 mL) bacon fat and the scrumpy to the oyster juice. Stir and boil, reducing by half. Add salt and pepper and cream and cook 1 minute. Swirl in the remaining butter and the apple cider vinegar. Add the oysters and heat through.

Put 1 or 2 oysters on a slice of bacon, roll up à la Angels on Horseback and secure with toothpicks. Or not. Pour sauce over and sprinkle chives on top.

Make another batch if there's chilled scrumpy or wine left, and take the phone off the hook.

MUSIC TO COOK WITH

Mary Coughlan:
Tired and Emotional [WEA]

Brett Marvin: *Alias Terry Dactyl & the Dinosaurs* [MOONCREST]

Les Barker & Mrs Ackroyd Band: *Yelp!*
[MRS ACKROYD RECORDS]

Don McDougall
used to serve this
at his long-gone,
still-missed …
restaurant,
Mocha Café.

My friend and Mayne Island neighbour Don McDougall used to serve this at his long-gone, still-missed, now-legendary Vancouver restaurant, Mocha Café. I asked him for the important bits for my earlier cookbook, and have fiddled with it—not too much, just added the odd dash or splash—till it comes out like this and seems to delight every oyster fan who falls face forward into it.

If you think 16 oysters is too much—what with all that cream and butter—for two, you may not be one of the aforementioned oyster fans.

Mayne Island Oyster Stew (the one they call Pan Roast in some parts)

serves 2–4, depending on voracity

And if someone knows why some people call this a Pan Roast (since it hardly involves roasting) I'd like to know: drop around with a good bottle and I'll make dinner.

16 medium	fresh oysters, with their liquid
1 cup (250 mL)	dry white wine
1 cup (250 mL)	water
2–4 slices	good-quality smoked bacon (optional), cut in small pieces
for sautéing	vegetable oil (optional)
3 cups (750 mL)	diced vegetables (carrots, celery, onions, potatoes, celeriac)
1 cup (250 mL)	whole milk
1 cup (250 mL)	heavy cream
2 Tbsp (25 mL)	melted butter
to taste	salt and pepper
dashes	celery salt, Worcestershire sauce, paprika
to taste	chopped parsley

WINE PAIRINGS

Fetzer Bonterra (organic) Viognier [CA]

Signorello "Seta" [CA]

Saturna Island Semillon [BC]

MUSIC TO COOK WITH

Saul Berson Quartet: *Not Here Not Now* [MOCO LOCO]

Kim Darwin: *Accordion Nights* [KDA]

Jaiya: *Firedance* [JAIYA]

Poach the oysters with the wine, water and oyster liquid for 4 minutes. Remove the oysters and set aside. Strain and save the stock.

Sauté the bacon, if using, till well cooked. Otherwise, heat enough vegetable oil to cover the bottom of the pan. Add the vegetables and sauté until tender.

Add the milk and the poaching liquid to the vegetables and bring to an almost-boil. Skim off any froth and simmer for 10 minutes.

Add the oysters, heavy cream and melted butter. Simmer for 3 minutes more.

Season with salt, pepper and various dashes. Toss in the parsley and serve in warm bowls, with a dry baguette or crusty toast.

Joseph Wasielewski of Thunder Bay recommends, as a *primo piatto*, a fresh radicchio salad mixed with basil, sprinkled with pine nuts, drizzled with balsamic vinegar and olive oil and finished with a squeeze of fresh lemon juice.

Joseph Wasielewski ... recommends, as a *primo piatto*, a fresh radicchio salad ...

Tonno con Cilantro Pesto

PESTO

1 cup (250 mL)	loosely packed cilantro
¼ cup (50 mL)	olive oil
1 clove	garlic
2 Tbsp (25 mL)	pine nuts
pinch	salt
½	lime, juice of

EVERYTHING ELSE

enough	pasta for 2
for sautéing	olive oil
½ cup (125 mL)	chopped unsalted almonds
2 cloves	garlic, minced
1 Tbsp (15 mL)	fresh or dried thyme
to taste	salt and black pepper
10–12-oz (325–375-g)	Ahi tuna steak

Prepare the pesto by blending the cilantro, olive oil, garlic, pine nuts and salt in a blender and adding fresh-squeezed lime juice. Cook your choice of pasta al dente.

Heat oil in a large skillet and sauté the almonds and minced garlic with thyme and a dusting of salt and pepper until lightly browned. Remove from the pan.

Add more oil to the same skillet and sauté the tuna steak on medium heat, covered, until lightly browned on the outside and just cooked through to the centre. Add the chopped almond mixture to the pan after the ahi is turned and just about ready. Serve on a large plate with a base of the warm pasta overlaid with the pesto, which supports the sautéed ahi garnished with the seasoned chopped almonds.

Per due

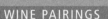

WINE PAIRINGS

Lamborghini Trescone La Fiorita [IT]

(That's the closest I'll ever get to a Lamborghini!)

MUSIC TO COOK WITH

Beppe Gambetta: *Good News from Home* [GREEN LINNET]

Giuliano Carmignola & Venice Baroque Orchestra: *Vivaldi Concertos* [SONY]

Cooking with
parchment is
fun and easy.

Cooking with parchment is fun and easy. For this dish with all its liquidity, you'll want the parchment as the inside layer and then some sturdy aluminum foil for the outside one.

Scallops with Mushrooms & Lime, in Parchment

serves 4 as a main dish

WINE PAIRINGS

De Rham Chiaretto [IT]

Bruno Sorg Pfersigberg
Muscat d'Alsace [FR]

pitcher of margaritas

MUSIC TO COOK WITH

Philip Glass: *Violin Concerto* [DGG]

3 small	carrots, julienned
2 lb (1 kg) small	bay scallops, the ones that look like an inflated dime (if you use bigger ones, halve or quarter them)
½ lb (250 g) small	white mushrooms, thinly sliced
4	green onions, julienned
3–4	fresh limes, juiced (10 seconds in the microwave before juicing does the same trick as rolling them on the counter)
½ cup (125 mL)	dry white wine
8 slices	fresh lime (see-through thin)
4 sprigs	Italian parsley
¼ cup (50 mL)	butter, from a stick, thinly sliced
4 tsp (20 mL)	extra virgin olive oil
to taste	salt and pepper

Do this: make four sheets each of parchment and foil, measuring 10 x 32 inches (25 x 80 cm) for the foil, 10 x 16 (25 x 40) for the parchment. Fold each aluminum sheet over to make a double-ply sheet and then put the sheet of parchment on that. You'll end up putting the cooked scallops and vegetables inside and folding it up to seal, so keep that in mind as you're measuring quantities. Dimensions are approximate, you'll want to experiment.

Preheat the oven to 450°F (230°C).

Drop the carrots into a pot of boiling water and when it boils again, time 2 minutes to cook. Drain.

In a mixing bowl combine the carrots, scallops, mushrooms, green onions, lime juice and white wine.

In the middle of each sheet of parchment and foil put equal measures of the vegetable-scallops mix, with liquid. Add lime slices and parsley sprigs to each. Add butter and olive oil in equal measure to each. Sprinkle with salt and pepper.

Position the mixture into an oblong in the middle of each of the sheets. Bring the long sides of the sheets to meet in the middle and fold over. Fold over again to create a double seam. Roll the ends inward till they hit the filling and fold tightly to close.

Put the packets on a baking sheet and bake for 20 minutes.

Serve hot, unopened, on individual plates, with a sharp knife for each guest to open their own and inhale the aromas.

... morel mush-
rooms, with their
honeycomb design,
require thorough
soaking in water.

Catherine Miller from Richmond, British Columbia, sent this one in with a reminder that morel mushrooms, with their honeycomb design, require thorough soaking in water. Submerge morels in a large bowl of water and agitate gently to release dirt, then lift out, leaving grit behind. Pat dry and use immediately.

Roasted Prawns with Morels & Morel Butter

serves 4

WINE PAIRINGS

Covey Run Sauvignon Blanc
[WA]

Chateau de Chamilly Aligoté
[FR]

Mission Hill Pinot Grigio [BC]

MUSIC TO COOK WITH

Lori Cullin: *So Much*
[ROSEMARY / CULLINOR]

or

Uneven Hill [LC]

Fazil Say: *Black Earth* [NAÏVE]

½ lb (250 g)	fresh morel mushrooms or 2 oz (60 g) dried*
½ cup (125 mL) (1 stick)	unsalted butter, room temperature, divided
¾ cup (175 mL)	chopped shallots, divided
1 clove	garlic, minced
1½ tsp (7 mL)	chopped fresh thyme
to taste	salt and pepper
six 4½–5-oz (130–150-g)	uncooked giant prawns (or substitute 24 large prawns)

*If using dried morels: Bring 3 cups (750 mL) water to boil in a medium saucepan. Add the dried morels. Remove from heat. Cover and let steep for 1 hour. Using a slotted spoon, transfer the morels to a bowl. Reserve soaking liquid.

Finely chop enough fresh or reconstituted morels to measure ½ cup/125 mL (packed); reserve remaining morels.

Melt 1 Tbsp (15 mL) of the butter in a medium non-stick skillet over medium heat. Add ¼ cup (50 mL) of the shallots and the garlic; sauté for 1 minute. Add the chopped morels and thyme; sauté for 2 minutes. If using dried morels, add the reserved soaking liquid to the skillet, leaving any sediment behind. Increase the heat and boil until almost all the liquid evaporates, about 8 minutes.

Transfer the morel mixture to a small bowl and cool. Mix the remaining butter into the morel mixture. Season lightly with salt and pepper. (Morel butter can be prepared 1 day ahead. Cover and chill.)

Using scissors, cut along the back shell of each prawn all the way up to the tail, exposing the vein; pull out the vein. Turn the prawns over. Using a small sharp knife and starting just below the tail end, butterfly each prawn by cutting a ¼-inch-deep slit to the opposite end. Place the prawns, shell side down, on a rimmed baking sheet. (Can be made 6 hours ahead. Cover and chill.)

Preheat the oven to 500°F (260°C). Melt 2 Tbsp (25 mL) of the morel butter in a heavy large skillet over medium-high heat. Add the remaining ½ cup (125 mL) shallots and sauté until golden, about 3 minutes. Add the remaining whole fresh or reconstituted morels and sauté until tender, about 4 minutes.

Meanwhile, spread 1 tsp (5 mL) morel butter over each giant prawn (or ¼ tsp/1 mL over each of 24 large prawns). Roast just until prawns are opaque in the centre, about 7 minutes for giant prawns or 4 minutes for large prawns. Top prawns with the remaining morel butter, dividing equally. Return to the oven just long enough to melt the butter slightly, about 10 seconds.

Transfer the prawns to plates. Serve sautéed morels alongside.

I ate something
similar somewhere
in Sicily once …

I ate something similar somewhere in Sicily once and tried to reconstruct it. No idea if this is how they did it at the name-long-forgotten seaside eatery, but it's become a tasty staple with several decades of tweaking. Fresh tuna and fresh herbs are essential here; fresh tomatoes if you've got 'em. Flash-frozen tuna steaks, good 'n' thick, are workable too.

Pappardelle with Tuna in Basil & Mint Sauce

serves 4

2 lb (1 kg)	fresh tuna steaks, as above
2 Tbsp (25 mL)	all-purpose flour
6 Tbsp (90 mL)	olive oil
2 medium	onions, cut up into eighths or so
6 cloves	garlic, quartered
to taste	salt and pepper
1½ cups (375 mL)	white wine
4 medium	tomatoes, seeds squeezed out, coarsely chopped; or one 14-oz (398-mL) can diced tomatoes + 2 Tbsp (25 mL) tomato paste
8–10	fresh basil leaves, coarsely chopped
10–12	fresh mint leaves, coarsely chopped
1 lb (500 g)	pappardelle pasta

WINE PAIRINGS

Settesoli Porta Palo Resso
di Sicilia [IT]

St Hallett "Faith" Shiraz [AU]

MUSIC TO COOK WITH

Fiamma Fumana: *1.0* [OMNIUM]

Nino Rota: *Fellini Film Music*
[CHANDOS]

Nino Rota: *Bassoon Concerto*
[CBC]

Wash the tuna and dry it with paper towels. Sprinkle flour on both sides. Heat the oil in a pan big enough to hold the rest of the ingredients. Brown the fish in the hot oil.

Throw the onions and garlic all around the fish and continue cooking, making sure to keep turning the fish for even browning. Add salt and pepper and white wine and, stirring frequently, continue cooking till some of the wine has evaporated. Add the tomatoes, basil and mint, stir gently and cover. Simmer for 30 minutes on low heat. Meanwhile, cook the pasta according to package directions and drain.

Mix the sauce with the pasta, reserving some to spoon over the tuna. Put the fish on top of the pasta in big pasta bowls and spoon the remaining sauce on top.

Jackie Wheatland of Regina adapted this from a recipe for trout and Drambuie. I think just about anything can do with a splash of Drambuie. Maybe not the oyster …

I think just about anything can do with a splash of Drambuie.

Drambuie Salmon

1	whole salmon, cleaned, without head
¼ cup (50 mL)	soft butter
1 level tsp (5 mL)	dried oregano
⅔ cup (150 mL)	natural yogurt
⅔ cup (150 mL)	thick cream (whipping cream or similar)
2 Tbsp (25 mL)	Drambuie
to taste	salt and pepper
for garnish	lemon twists

Preheat the oven to 350°F (180°C).

Wash and thoroughly dry the fish. Grease an ovenproof dish with half the butter. Put the fish in the dish, spread with the rest of the butter and sprinkle the oregano on top.

Mix the yogurt, cream and Drambuie together, season the mixture, then pour it over the salmon. Bake the fish, uncovered, for 20 minutes. Garnish with lemon twists before serving.

serves 6 to 10, depending on the size of the salmon

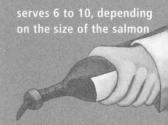

WINE PAIRINGS

Shot of iced Drambuie [SC]

Clynelish 14-year old malt [SC]

MUSIC TO COOK WITH

Ken Hyder & Talisker: *Land of Stone* [ECM]

Puirt a Baroque: *Bach Meets Cape Breton* [MARQUIS]

chapter six

chicken et cetera

Marietta's Anatra all'Arancio (the Other Duck à l'Orange) 82

Coq au Gewürztraminer 83

Gingered Goose with Apples & Calvados, Pink Peppercorns & Coriander 84

Margaritaville Chicken 87

Cornish Game Hens with Sauerkraut 88

A Chicken Full of Lemon, Garlic & Rosemary (with Truffles for Lily-Gilding) 90

Passion Poulet à la DiscDrive 92

Spicy Thai & Luscious Basil Chicken 94

Crêpes Singhiozzando (Crêpe of Smoked Duck Breast with Goat Cheese) 96

Chicken Provençal 98

The Marietta in the
title is my friend
Marietta Menghi
Malacarne of
Villa Delia
in Ripoli di Lari …

That Catherine de Medici, always putting her foot in it. Figuratively, anyway. When she went to marry one of the Louises she figured the French didn't know from cooking, so she brought her own culinary troupe along. Certainly kept her in decent pasta, but a couple of other dishes showed up frequently, including some variant or other of this one. The Marietta in the title is my friend Marietta Menghi Malacarne of Villa Delia in Ripoli di Lari, prime Tuscan grape-and-olive country, a place where I spent seven successive springs helping her cook for the guests. This is one of the dishes we'd do, usually about the fourth or fifth day. Simple, hearty, plentiful; grazie, Marietta. You too, Ms. Medici.

Marietta's Anatra all'Arancio (the Other Duck à l'Orange)

serves 6

This can be cooked on stovetop or baked in the oven. If you're using only two ducks don't alter the rest of the ingredients; get more orange and herb flavours that way.

3	ducks
2 cups (500 mL)	best-quality white wine vinegar
10 big cloves	garlic (or more), chopped
1 big bunch	fresh rosemary, chopped
1 big bunch	fresh sage, chopped
to taste	salt and pepper
3 big	oranges, zest only
	broth (basic chicken or veal) only if needed during cooking

WINE PAIRINGS

Villa Delia Bambolo [IT]

Prunetto Dolcetto d'Alba [IT]

Machiavelli Prosecco [IT]

Biondi-Santi anything [IT]

MUSIC TO COOK WITH

Joe Craven: *Camptown*
[ACORN MUSIC]

Get the butcher to cut the ducks into same-sized pieces. (Mine trims the wings off, then does it with the meat saw down the middle, then crosswise, so we end up with about 8 pieces per duck; save wings, leg bones, etc., for making stock.)

In a big roasting pan, brown the duck pieces, skin side down, over high heat, for about 10 minutes. Turn the duck pieces over and brown lightly on the other side. (If you want, you can pour off some of the duck fat at this point—but leave some, it adds to the flavour—or just leave it where it is and let the wine vinegar take care of it.)

Pour the wine vinegar over the duck pieces and let most of it boil off.

Add everything else—garlic, rosemary, sage, salt and pepper, orange zest—just scatter it all over the duck pieces.

Cook for 1 hour over medium heat, covered, stirring a few times. (Add broth only if it looks like it's drying out.)

Take the lid off, turn the heat up and cook another 10 minutes.

Serve with polenta or pasta or just fresh Tuscan bread, with oil and rock salt on the side.

In Alsace, my favourite food corner of the world, where the white wines outshine the reds, the classic coq au vin gets this twist. Riesling's fine too, and you can do it with some Kronenbourg or Fischer bière d'Alsace for a tasty change of pace. Reheats magnificently, if there's any left over—yes, even with all that cream. This recipe makes a lot of sauce. Reduce liquids if you like it more stewy and less soupy. Any kind of pasta is great with it, especially those big shells that hold the sauce.

In Alsace … the classic coq au vin gets this twist.

Coq au Gewürztraminer

12 pieces	chicken	
6 Tbsp (90 mL)	butter	
1 Tbsp (15 mL)	oil	
6	shallots, chopped	
1½ cups (375 mL)	Gewürztraminer (or Riesling, or beer)	
1½ cups (375 mL)	chicken stock	
1 lb (500 g)	mushrooms, cleaned, sliced not too thin	
to taste	salt and pepper	
1	lemon, juice of	
1 pint (250 mL)	heavy or whipping cream	
lots	fresh parsley, chopped	

serves 4

WINE PAIRINGS

Trimbach "Cuveé Emile" [FR]

Domaine Weinbach Riesling [FR]

Fischer Bière d'Alsace [FR]

Dry the chicken pieces with paper towels.

Melt half the butter and all of the oil in a big cooking pan and brown the chicken, about 5 minutes per side. Take out with a slotted spoon and in the same fat sauté the shallots without letting them brown.

Add the wine and chicken stock. With a spatula, scrape up the brown sticky bits from the bottom of the pan. Add the chicken pieces and simmer gently for 45 minutes (till no more pink juice appears when you prick the pieces in the middle).

In another pan, melt the remaining 3 Tbsp (45 mL) butter and slowly sauté the mushrooms with salt and pepper and lemon juice.

Remove the chicken pieces from the cooking pan and keep warm with the mushrooms. Boil down the pan juices until reduced to 1½ cups (375 mL) or so, then whisk in the cream. Bring to the boil again and check seasoning.

Put the mushrooms and chicken in a heated serving dish and pour on the liquid. Sprinkle with parsley.

Serve the same wine (or beer) you cooked with.

MUSIC TO COOK WITH

Koechlin:
Etudes for Saxophone & Piano
[CHANDOS]

Waldteufel: *Waltzes* [CHANDOS]

One day, in another life, I'm going to assemble a Book of Goosies. There are so many wonderful ways of cooking them it might be worth a Project: cook one a week for a year and see which turns out the favourite. This one will be high on the list, I think, along with *à l'alsacienne* (stuffed with pork and garnished with sauerkraut); *à la Bismarck* (on shredded cabbage with white wine, apples and chestnuts); *à la bordelais* (stuffed with sautéed mushrooms, soaked bread, anchovy butter, green olives, eggs and garlic); *aux marrons* (stuffed with ground pork mixed with chestnuts, half-cooked first in stock, then roasted); *chipolata* (braised, carved, garnished with pearl onions, carrots, chestnuts, bacon, sausage); *à la danoise* (stuffed with apples and raisins and caraway); *à l'anglaise* (stuffed with sage and onion and bread, with warm apple sauce on the side); *à la*

One day,
in another life,
I'm going
to assemble a
Book of Goosies.

Gingered Goose with Apples & Calvados, Pink Peppercorns & Coriander

serves 6		
	one 8–10-lb (3.5–4.5-kg)	goose
	10 small	Macintosh apples, smaller the better (those little ones from around Lac Brome are perfect)
	5 sticks	cinnamon
	½ cup (125 mL)	seedless raisins
	2 Tbsp (25 mL)	chopped fresh ginger
	6	whole cloves
	1 Tbsp (15 mL)	juniper berries
	1 tsp (5 mL)	coriander seeds
	2 tsp (10 mL)	whole pink peppercorns
	½ cup (125 mL)	Calvados (or make your own cooking Calvados by mixing brandy with apple juice, not as good, but it'll save you the 40 bucks for a bottle of the good stuff)
	1 cup (250 mL)	dry white wine
	1½ cups (375 mL)	cold water
	2 Tbsp (25 mL)	sugar
	2 tsp (10 mL)	salt
	½ cup (125 mL)	diced pancetta (or bacon)
	1 good-sized twig	fresh marjoram (or 1½ tsp/7 mL dried marjoram, crumbled in the palm of your hand)
	1 tsp (5 mL)	freshly ground black pepper
	1 cup (250 mL)	boiling water

WINE PAIRINGS

Calvados [FR]

St Ursula Devil's Rock Riesling [GY]

Chateau Musar [LB]

MUSIC TO COOK WITH

Anton Kuerti:
Beethoven Piano Sonatas [CBC]

Pat Metheny & Charlie Haden:
Beyond the Missouri Sky [VERVE]

hambourgeoise (stuffed with peeled apple wedges simmered in butter, pitted prunes and peppercorns); *à la petite-russienne* (stuffed with buckwheat gruel and braised with sliced onions, finished with sour cream); *aux griottes* (browned, braised with *mirepoix*, red wine and demi-glace, carved, covered with the sauce mixed with pitted sour cherries); *en daube* (de-boned, stuffed with pork and tongue, salt pork and truffles and brandy); cooked in a clay pot half filled with a stock of the bones, calf's foot and white wine, steamed in the oven and served cold in the jellied stock; and maybe even *à la nordique* (seasoned with salt and crushed caraway, stuffed with sliced apples and pears and onions seasoned with marjoram, flamed at the table with aquavit). See, there's a dozen to get you started on your first three months' worth.

GRAVY

2 cups (500 mL)	chicken stock
6 Tbsp (90 mL)	roast goose drippings
1 small	onion, chopped
2 Tbsp (25 mL)	all-purpose flour
to taste	salt and pepper

Preheat the oven to 325°F (160°C).

Get as much fat off the goose (inside, tail part) as you can. Rinse and pat dry.

Peel and core 5 of the apples but leave them whole. Put a cinnamon stick in each, and a few raisins, using up about half your supply.

To poach the apples, sprinkle ginger, cloves, juniper berries, coriander seeds and pink peppercorns over the bottom of a medium pan. Put the apples on top. Add the calvados, wine, cold water, sugar and 1 tsp (5 mL) of the salt. Cook over moderate heat till it boils. Adjust the heat so the liquid simmers, cover and cook for 8 minutes.

Cool the apples in the liquid, then remove. Pour the juice through a sieve to separate the spices from the liquid. Reserve the liquid. Sprinkle the spices and juniper on the bottom of a big shallow roasting pan that will fit a rack. Set aside.

Briefly sauté the pancetta till it starts to crisp.

Now peel, core and dice the remaining 5 apples and put the pieces in a bowl. Add the rest of the raisins, some salt, pancetta, the marjoram and half the pepper and mix well. Stuff the neck cavity with some of the mix and skewer it shut. Stuff the body with the rest of the mix and use poultry pins to close, and then twine, folding the wings flat against the back.

continues on next page ...

Prick the skin of the goose with a fork or skewer, sprinkle with the rest of the salt and pepper. Put the bird breast-side down on the rack in the roasting pan and pour boiling water over top. Roast uncovered for 1½ hours, basting with the apple-poaching liquid half a dozen times.

Now turn the goose breast-side up and pour 1 cup (250 mL) of the apple liquid over it, roasting uncovered for another 1½ hours, again basting with pan juices. You want to end up with a 175°F (80°C) reading on your meat thermometer.

Put the goose on a heated platter, tent with foil and let it stand while you make the gravy. Spoon off 6 Tbsp (90 mL) of the pan drippings for the gravy and toss out the rest.

Add 1 cup (250 mL) of the stock to the roasting pan and deglaze over moderate heat for 3 minutes, scraping up all the brown bits. Set aside.

Heat the goose drippings in a small saucepan for 1 minute. Add onion and sauté for 5 minutes. Blend in the flour and cook, stirring, for 2 minutes. Add the deglazing liquid and the rest of the stock and simmer for 10 minutes, stirring. Season with salt and pepper. Keep warm.

Remove the skewers and string from the goose and surround the bird with the stuffed apples. Serve gravy on the side. Red cabbage with a few cloves and a star anise is nice as a side dish; potato dumplings, too.

One day we'll talk about that "lost shaker of salt" and all, but not here. You won't be needing much of it anyway, but you'll need a weekend's supply of tequila, so don't use the designer stuff. Good old tequila-in-a-drum is just fine.

One day we'll talk about that "lost shaker of salt" …

Margaritaville Chicken

4 cups (1 L)	tequila
1 cup (250 mL)	soda water
¼ cup (50 mL)	fresh lemon juice
¼ cup (50 mL)	fresh lime juice
¼ cup (50 mL)	triple sec
¼ cup (50 mL)	extra virgin olive oil
1 cup (250 mL)	coarsely chopped cilantro
1 cup (250 mL)	chopped mixed peppers, hot and mild, any kind you can find
3 cloves	garlic, minced
1 Tbsp (15 mL)	ground mace
1 Tbsp (15 mL)	achiote seed (try gourmet markets or stores that specialize in Mexican foods)
1 Tbsp (15 mL)	coarse salt
6	chicken breasts, split
for garnish	lemon and lime slices

serves 4
Marinates overnight.

WINE PAIRINGS

Margaritas (of Chapter 11)

Corona [MX]

Cuervo Gold [MX]

MUSIC TO COOK WITH

Jimmy Buffett

but seriously, folks …

The Angstones:
The Hills are Alive [CANAL]

Petra Haden: *The Who Sell Out*
[BAR-NONE]

Mix all liquids in a big, deep glass dish or bowl. Add everything else, except the chicken. Stir well. Put the chicken in the liquid to cover and marinate overnight in the fridge.

Pour off the marinade and grill the chicken till just done (the old non-pink-juice test applies).

Garnish with lemon and lime slices and serve with—well, what else?

Sauerkraut goes with anything.

Sauerkraut goes with anything. Maybe even cheesecake. This is a different take on the little birds (did Victor Borge really invent them for Canadian Pacific or is that apocryphal?) and the key is a sweetish white wine, Riesling or Gewürztraminer.

Cornish Game Hens with Sauerkraut

serves 4

WINE PAIRINGS

Cider, scrumpy

Theakston Old Peculier [UK]
(so spelled)

Yarg cheese, after

2 Tbsp (25 mL)	butter
2 medium	onions, chopped
1 lb (500 g)	fresh sauerkraut, drained (a lot of recipes call for rinsing the sauerkraut, which I've never really understood—you want it to taste sour. I suppose, if it's really, really salty …)
8 or 10	juniper berries
splash	gin
½ cup (125 mL)	heavy or whipping cream
1 cup (250 mL)	white wine (see above)
2 Tbsp (25 mL)	bacon fat (or mixture of butter and oil)
2	Cornish game hens, halved
1 tsp (5 mL)	salt
1 tsp (5 mL)	black pepper
8 or 10 small sprigs	fresh thyme (or 1 tsp/5 mL dried)
1 cup (250 mL)	beef broth
8 slices	ham or prosciutto

MUSIC TO COOK WITH

Stacey Kent: *The Boy Next Door*
[CANDID]

Brian Browne: *The Letter*
[CAPITOL]

or

Blue Browne [SEAJAM]

Preheat the oven to 350°F (180°C).

Melt the butter in a big pan. Add the onions and cook for 5 minutes, stirring often. Add the sauerkraut, juniper berries, gin, cream and wine. Bring to a simmer then turn the heat to low, cover and simmer for 60 minutes, stirring frequently. Add water if it needs it.

Heat the bacon fat (or a mixture of butter and oil) in a frying pan. Put the game hens skin-side down in the fat and brown for 5 minutes, then turn over and cook 2 minutes more. Sprinkle with half the salt and pepper.

Arrange the game hens skin-side up in an ungreased baking pan and sprinkle with the rest of the salt and pepper. Put a few sprigs of thyme under each hen, pour the pan drippings over top and roast, uncovered, for 30 minutes, basting with some broth halfway through cooking.

Put 2 slices of ham over each piece, baste with the rest of the broth and roast 10 minutes more.

Turn the ham over and baste ham 'n' hens with pan juices. Roast 10 more minutes.

Put the sauerkraut on a heated platter and arrange the game hens on top. Lose the thyme. Serve with more pan drippings and some boiled or mashed potatoes, or fluffy rice.

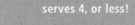

This is my favourite chicken …

This is my favourite chicken: a whole one slow-roasted with the brightness of lemon and the heartiness of garlic and the green bite of rosemary all mingling with the natural flavours. That is, natural flavours if you get yourself a natural chicken—farm-raised, free-ranged, anti-antibiotic'ed et cetera, like those my Island neighbours the McDougalls provide at the Farmers' Market, or upon a phone call.

A Chicken Full of Lemon, Garlic & Rosemary

serves 4, or less!

The truffles are optional—depending on availability and cashflow—but make a nice, over-the-top touch. Slice them very thin and, with your fingers, work loose some of the chicken skin, then slide the slices under that in half a dozen spots. Make sure none inadvertently falls to the dog.

1 whole 4–5-lb (1.4–1.8-kg)	chicken
to taste	salt and pepper
1	lemon, halved
2 heads	unblemished garlic, no green sprouts, halved crosswise
1 bunch	fresh rosemary, or more
few	truffles (optional)
1½ Tbsp (20 mL)	crushed fennel seeds
¼ cup (50 mL)	olive oil
2½ lb (1.2 kg)	baking potatoes, peeled, quartered lengthwise
	other roasting vegetables, if you like
1 cup (250 mL)	white wine

WINE PAIRINGS

your favorite roast chicken wine, or

Nichol Vineyards "Impromptu" [BC]

"Seven Deadly Zins" Zinfandel [CA]

Piramimma Petit Verdot [AU]

MUSIC TO COOK WITH

Sviatoslav Richter: *Pictures at an Exhibition (Mussorgsky)* [DGG]

Dawn Upshaw: *Theater Songs* [NONESUCH]

Preheat the oven to 375°F (190°C).

Rinse the chicken well, inside and out, with cold running water; pat fully dry with paper towels. Season the inside with lots of salt and pepper. Squeeze lemon juice over the chicken then put the halves inside the chicken with one of the halved garlic heads and the bunch of rosemary.

Do the truffle thing (see intro) if you're doing it.

Truss the chicken in your favourite way (mine usually uses about a quarter mile of twine and resembles something by Houdini by the time I'm done. There's a skill to this which I can't seem to get around to mastering).

Put the chicken, breast up, in a roasting pan (if you've got the neck, put that in the pan, too). Season the chicken exterior with more salt and pepper and the fennel seeds. Drizzle some of the olive oil all over; rub salt, pepper, fennel and oil into the skin.

Add the potatoes and other vegetables and the other halved head of garlic to the pan, season with salt and pepper and drizzle with some more oil.

Put the chicken in the hot oven on the upper rack and roast, basting every 10–15 minutes with pan drippings, until the skin and potatoes are golden brown. (Use a thermometer in the thick part of the chicken thigh, away from the bone, till it shows 175°F/80°C). This will take about an hour and a quarter, if your oven is true.

Remove the chicken to a carving board with a trough around the edge, cover with foil and let it sit 10 minutes before carving. Meanwhile, reduce the oven to about 200°F (95°C) to keep the vegetables warm in the pan.

Here's how to make pan sauce: pour the contents of the pan into a big glass measuring cup or bowl, let it stand for a few minutes and then spoon the fat off the top. The defatted juices go back into the pan on the stovetop, over high heat. Boil, adding the wine to deglaze and scraping up browned bits from the bottom with a wooden spoon; press the spoon against the garlic cloves to free them from their skins and toss away the skins. Cook the juices until reduced by half, 4 or 5 minutes, then remove from heat.

Carve the chicken and arrange on a warm platter, pour the pan sauce through a sieve and drizzle over the chicken and serve with the roasted potatoes and vegetables.

Extemporizing on the theme of passion …

Extemporizing on the theme of passion, Ferne Putnam in St. Albert, Alberta, observed, "Sometimes passion can well up at the last minute, just like this entry to the contest, which closes tonight." We felt a little tingle too when we read her recipe.

Passion Poulet à la DiscDrive

serves 6

WINE PAIRINGS

Valdizze Pinot
Frizzante Naturale [IT]

Hofstatter Gewürztraminer [IT]

Banfi Brunello di Montalcino [IT]

MUSIC TO COOK WITH

I Fiamminghi:
Music for Strings (Hovhaness)
[TELARC]

Marvin Rosen:
"Fred the Cat" & Other Piano Pieces by Alan Hovhaness [KOCH]

6	chicken thighs
6	chicken drumsticks
¾ cup (175 mL)	all-purpose flour
1½ tsp (7 mL)	salt
½ tsp (2 mL)	celery salt
½ tsp (2 mL)	poultry seasoning
½ tsp (2 mL)	dried basil leaves
¼ tsp (1 mL)	dried thyme
¼ tsp (1 mL)	marjoram
¼ tsp (1 mL)	dried savory
¼ tsp (1 mL)	dried rosemary, crumbled
¼ tsp (1 mL)	onion powder
¼ tsp (1 mL)	black pepper
¼ tsp (1 mL)	paprika
¼ tsp (1 mL)	cayenne
⅔ cup (150 mL)	buttermilk
2 Tbsp (25 mL)	vegetable oil

Preheat the oven to 350°F (180°C).

Rinse the chicken and pat dry.

In a shallow bowl combine all the dry ingredients. Put the buttermilk in another shallow bowl. Dip the chicken into the buttermilk, then coat with the flour-herb mix.

In a large skillet, heat the oil over medium-high heat. Fry 6 pieces of chicken for about 10 minutes, or until browned on both sides. Transfer with tongs to a shallow ungreased 9- x 13-inch (23- x 33-cm) pan. Repeat.

Bake uncovered in the oven for 45–50 minutes or until chicken is tender and crispy.

Serve with oven-fried potatoes and a crunchy salad. And of course, enjoy with a favourite wine, for extra passion!

Heike Cantrup of Calgary, Alberta sent us this one. It's from *Wild Women in the Kitchen: 101 Rambunctious Recipes and 99 Tasty Tales*. Where were these wild ones when I was in high school?

Spicy Thai & Luscious Basil Chicken

serves 4

WINE PAIRINGS

Bonny Doon Malvasia Bianco "Ca' del Solo" [CA]

Hoodsport Raspberry wine [OR]

Elephant Island "Little King" [BC]

MUSIC TO COOK WITH

Barbara Bonney: *Sally Chisum* [LONDON]

Andre Previn: *Ballads* [ANGEL]

COOKING SAUCE

¾ cup (175 mL)	canned coconut milk
2 Tbsp (25 mL)	soy sauce
2 Tbsp (25 mL)	rice vinegar
1½ Tbsp (20 mL)	fish sauce or soy sauce
½–1 tsp (2–5 mL)	crushed dried hot red chilies
1½ cups (375 mL)	jasmine or black Thai rice
6	dried shiitake mushrooms
2 Tbsp (25 mL)	vegetable oil
1 medium	onion, thinly sliced
3 cloves	garlic, pressed or minced
2 Tbsp (25 mL)	minced fresh ginger
2 lb (1 kg)	boneless chicken breasts, cut crosswise into ¼-inch-wide (5-mm) strips
1½ cups (375 mL)	lightly packed slivered fresh basil leaves

Combine the ingredients for the cooking sauce in a small bowl and set aside.

Prepare the rice according to the package directions. Choose black Thai rice if this is a dark, passionate night, and jasmine or any white rice (such as basmati) for those lighter, more innocent evenings.

In a bowl, soak the mushrooms in hot water to cover until soft, 10–15 minutes. Lift the mushrooms from the water, squeeze dry, and trim off and discard the rough stems. Cut the caps into ¼-inch (5-mm) slivers and set aside.

Heat 1 Tbsp (15 mL) of the oil in a 10- to 12-inch (25- to 30-cm) frying pan or wok over high heat. Add the onion, garlic and ginger; stir-fry until the onion is a light gold colour. Scoop the vegetables into a bowl and set aside.

Add the chicken strips to the pan, one-third at a time; stir occasionally until the meat is tinged with brown, about 3 minutes. Lift the strips from the pan and reserve with the cooked vegetables. Repeat to cook the remaining chicken; add oil if needed to prevent sticking.

Pour the cooking sauce into the pan and boil until reduced by one-third. Return the onion and chicken to the pan. Add the basil and mushrooms; stir to heat through—not too long! Serve over rice of your choice.

... this recipe for passion can be put on the table with candlelight and wine in less than 20 minutes.

Kern and Mary Deorksen of Ottawa claim that, with some practice and preparation, this recipe for passion can be put on the table with candlelight and wine in less than 20 minutes. Not bad for a two-pager.

Crêpes Singhiozzando (Crêpe of Smoked Duck Breast with Goat Cheese)

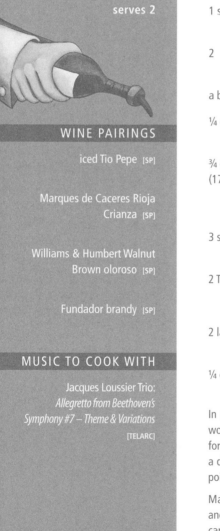

serves 2

1 small	smoked duck breast, or medium-rare roasted duck breast
2	portobello mushrooms, stems removed and caps sliced
a bit	duck fat and butter
¼ cup (50 mL)	good red wine (substitute mediocre red wine, lose 2 passion points)
¾ cup + 2 Tbsp (175 mL + 25 mL)	goose, duck or veal stock (homemade: add ½ passion point; substitute chicken or vegetable bouillon cubes, lose ½ passion point)
3 sprigs	fresh thyme (substitute dried thyme, lose ½ passion point)
2 Tbsp (25 mL)	unsalted butter in walnut-size pieces
	salt and pepper
2 large	crêpes, prepared beforehand (substitute: soft tortilla shells, lose 1 passion point)
¼ cup (50 mL)	soft unripened goat cheese, crumbled

WINE PAIRINGS

iced Tio Pepe [SP]

Marques de Caceres Rioja Crianza [SP]

Williams & Humbert Walnut Brown oloroso [SP]

Fundador brandy [SP]

MUSIC TO COOK WITH

Jacques Loussier Trio: *Allegretto from Beethoven's Symphony #7 – Theme & Variations* [TELARC]

In anticipation: Open the wine to be served with the meal (a full-bodied Rioja works wonders) allowing it to breathe during preparation (add ½ passion point for flavour). Place dining plates in a warming oven—passion, unlike revenge, is a dish best eaten warm. Light the candles, position the flowers (add ½ passion point for thoughtfulness).

Make cracklings from the duck skin and fat. Remove it from the duck breast and slice it into thin strips. Fry over low heat until very crispy (turn often and be careful not to burn). Set aside.

Slice the meat of the duck breast diagonally into thin medallions and set aside at room temperature.

For the sauce, sauté the portobello mushrooms with a small amount of duck fat and butter over medium heat until soft (cleaned stems can be included; add ½ passion point for flavour). Add the red wine, increase the heat and reduce by one-third. Add the stock and one sprig of fresh thyme; reduce by half. Lower the heat and stir the walnut-size pieces of butter one at a time into the sauce. Remove the thyme (and mushroom stems, if used) and season to taste. Pour the sauce into a warmed container.

Preheat the oven to 375°F (190°C).

Place the crêpes (1 per person) on a baking sheet or 2 small pie plates. Place in the centre of the crêpes: slices of duck breast (no need to overfill—leftovers are welcome); mushroom slices from the sauce; drizzle of sauce (enough to be moist but not sopping), holding some in reserve for the plate; crisps of fried duck skin (unless you've eaten them all already—lose 1 passion point for gluttony); goat cheese.

Fold the edges of the crêpes over the centre stuffing, then fold again, roll or bunch up the edges for a quasi-floral presentation.

Place the assembled crêpes in the oven for about 5 minutes or until the goat cheese is melted (note: when serving for 2, a toaster oven works well for this). Place on pre-warmed plates.

Finish plates with a small pool of sauce, garnish with sprigs of thyme. Serve with candlelight, flowers and a good red wine. The rest is up to you …

Susan Jaffray …
took a liking to this
recipe …

Susan Jaffray of Milford, Michigan, took a liking to this recipe when she saw it on the PBS show, "America's Test Kitchen." Rice, crusty bread or soft polenta go well.

Chicken Provençal

serves 4

8	bone-in, skin-on chicken thighs (about 3 lb/1.5 kg), trimmed of excess skin and fat
to taste	salt
1 Tbsp (15 mL)	extra virgin olive oil
1 small	onion, chopped fine (about ⅔ cup/150 mL)
6 medium cloves	garlic, minced or pressed through garlic press (about 2 Tbsp/25 mL)
1	anchovy fillet, minced (about 1 tsp/5 mL)
⅛ tsp (0.5 mL)	cayenne
1 cup (250 mL)	dry white wine
1 cup (250 mL)	low-sodium chicken broth
one 14-oz. (398-mL) can	diced tomatoes, drained
2½ Tbsp (35 mL)	tomato paste
1½ Tbsp (20 mL)	chopped fresh thyme leaves
1 tsp (5 mL) chopped	fresh oregano leaves
1	bay leaf
1 tsp (5 mL)	herbes de Provence (optional)
1½ tsp (7 mL)	grated zest from 1 lemon
½ cup (125 mL)	niçoise olives, pitted
1 Tbsp (15 mL)	chopped fresh parsley leaves

WINE PAIRINGS

Edge Napa Valley Cabernet
[CA]

Reif Meritage [ON]

Alain Faget Domaine
de Sancet red [FR]

MUSIC TO COOK WITH

Christa Grix Trio: *Cheek to Chic*
[FREEFALL]

Adjust an oven rack to the lower-middle position and preheat the oven to 300°F (150°C).

Sprinkle both sides of the chicken thighs with salt to taste. Heat 1 tsp (5 mL) of the oil in a large Dutch oven over medium-high heat until shimmering but not smoking. Add 4 chicken thighs, skin-side down, and cook without moving them until the skin is crisp and well browned, about 5 minutes. Turn the chicken pieces and brown on the second side, about 5 minutes longer. Transfer to a large plate. Repeat with the remaining 4 chicken thighs. Discard all but 1 Tbsp (15 mL) of fat from the pot.

Add the onion to the fat and sauté, stirring occasionally, over medium heat until softened and browned, about 4 minutes. Add the garlic, anchovy and cayenne; cook, stirring constantly, until fragrant, about 1 minute. Add the wine and scrape up browned bits from the pan bottom with a wooden spoon. Stir in the chicken broth, tomatoes, tomato paste, thyme, oregano, bay leaf and herbes de Provence (if using). Remove and discard the skin from the chicken thighs, then submerge the chicken pieces in the liquid and add the accumulated chicken juices to the pot. Increase the heat to high, bring to a simmer, cover, then set the pot in the oven. Cook until the chicken offers no resistance when poked with the tip of a paring knife but is still clinging to the bones, about 1¼ hours.

Using a slotted spoon, transfer the chicken to a serving platter and tent with foil. Discard the bay leaf. Set the Dutch oven over high heat, stir in 1 tsp (5 mL) of the lemon zest, bring to a boil and cook, stirring occasionally, until slightly thickened and reduced to 2 cups (500 mL), about 5 minutes. Stir in the olives and cook until heated through, about 1 minute. Meanwhile, mix the remaining ½ teaspoon zest with the parsley.

Spoon the sauce over the chicken, drizzle the chicken with the remaining 2 tsp (10 mL) olive oil, sprinkle with the parsley mixture and serve.

chapter seven

meats

Portuguese Pork, Marinated with Garlic 102

Lamb Chops with Chorizo & Garlic 103

Cuminized Garlic-Roast Round 104

Tito's Texas Tenderloin 106

Real Man Bacon-Wrapped Anchovy Pâté Roasted Pork Steak 107

Michael James's Espresso Marinated New Zealand Lamb 108

Black Cat Lamb Roast 110

Uccellini Scappati — Those Little Disappearing Birds 112

Sausage in Bondage 114

David Veljacic's Beef Ribs Method 116

David Veljacic's "How to Grill the Perfect Steak" Lesson 117

Plymouth Martini'd Leg of Lamb with Jalapeño Olives 118

Rummy Smoky Spicy Ribs 120

Lapin aux Pommes 122

Cinnamon Roasted Pork Tenderloin with Pinot Gris Applesauce 124

Tourtière 126

Pork Loin in Tuna Sauce 128

Anything really
good is worth
waiting for, right?

Anything really good is worth waiting for, right? Okay, how about you start this on December 1st and it'll be ready to start snacking on at Christmas. What starts out looking like it's going to be pork ceviche becomes sizzling golden fried cubes of mega-garlic treats. As an appetizer, sort of like rock-salted dry ribs—bet you can't eat just 15! As a dinner, you'll add some starch, leafy greens—stir-fried kale with sprouts and red peppers, tomato and red onion salad. I first had this in one of those fabulous pousadas in the north of Portugal. The vinho verde was cold and plentiful. And about a buck-seventy-five a bottle!

Portuguese Pork, Marinated with Garlic

**serves 8 as appetizer,
4 for main course**
Requires three weeks'
marinating,
so plan ahead.

WINE PAIRINGS

Gazelo Vinho Verde [PO]

Da Fonseca Periquita [PO]

3 lb	pork, cubed
1 lb (500 g) cloves	fresh garlic, the best you can find: no spots, no green sprouts, peeled and cleaned but kept whole
2 sprigs	fresh thyme, chopped
1 sprig	fresh marjoram if you can find it; ½ tsp crumbled dry if not
1 sprig	fresh rosemary, needles stripped off stem
2 or 3	hot chili peppers, chopped (or to taste)
2 tsp (10 mL)	kosher salt
½ cup (125 mL)	whole black peppercorns, more or less
2 cups (500 mL)	white vinegar (wine vinegar may be too light for this, so use regular, glass-cleaning vinegar)
for frying	oil (Portuguese extra virgin olive oil is nice and robust, but be careful—it burns at a lower temperature than regular olive oils)

MUSIC TO COOK WITH

some good gut-
wrenching fado;
got a fave?

Gustavo Santoalalla: *Ronroco*
[NONESUCH]

Place the cubed pork in a big glass jar or stoneware crock. Mix the garlic cloves, herbs, chilies, salt and peppercorns in a bowl and add to the jar. Mix it up with the pork. Pour in the vinegar and cover tightly. Let it sit in a cool place (or the back of the fridge) for 3 weeks.

When ready to serve, take out the pork pieces with a slotted spoon (or, if you're using it all, just drain), squeeze the excess moisture out and pat dry with paper towels. Heat oil in a big frying pan till it starts to think about smoking. Fry the pork in the hot oil till brown on all sides. It'll spatter like crazy. Drain on paper towels and serve in individual bowls or one big one.

Kathleen Nichol of the wonderful and very small Okanagan Valley winery that bears her name reprinted this old recipe of mine some years ago in the winery's newsletter, saying it was one of her favourites. Now I'm reprinting her reprint of it, saying hers—the wines—are some of my favourites. Especially the iconoclastic Pinot Gris, which ain't all that gris, more a robust rosé colour! You won't find them far beyond the Naramata bench of British Columbia's wine country—although savvy restaurants in Vancouver will stock them as supplies come available—but it's well worth a visit to the winery to load up the trunk. And call ahead: they're usually off working in the vineyard and don't always hear the phone ….

Kathleen Nichol
of the wonderful
and very small
Okanagan Valley
winery …

Lamb Chops with Chorizo & Garlic

Why lamb with chorizo? We unrepentant carnivores often think the only thing better than meat is meat with more meat.

serves 4

4 good-sized	lamb chops (not those little loin ones), well trimmed of fat
splash	olive oil, for cooking
6 large cloves	garlic, peeled and halved (or thirded)
1 large	chorizo sausage cut into ½-inch (1-cm) slices
to taste	cracked black pepper
a few	fresh mint leaves, chopped (or scattering of dried)
to taste	fresh rosemary (or a few needles, dried)
to taste	additional herbs, according to your fancy or availability
1 tootle	good balsamic vinegar (white's nice if you find it)
for garnish	rock salt and parsley

Heat an unoiled iron frying pan until good and hot. Sear the chops for 1 minute per side. Remove from the pan and pour off the fat, but don't wipe out the pan.

Add a splash of olive oil and turn the heat down to medium. Add the garlic and chorizo and cook a couple of minutes, till it all starts to take on a little colour—but don't let the garlic burn.

Return the lamb chops to the pan and cook for no more than 8 minutes total, turning now and then. (If you don't like your garlic all nutty-crunchy, you might want to take it out of the pan as the lamb chops cook; the chorizo can stay in.) When the smoke alarm goes off, put a lid on the pan and open all the windows. It's almost done.

A couple of minutes before the chops have finished cooking, sprinkle on the pepper, herbs and anything else you like. A few seconds before serving, splash in the balsamic and stir everything 'round in the pan. Serve up with a little mound of rock salt and some chopped fresh parsley on the side.

WINE PAIRINGS

Nichol Vineyards Pinot Noir or "Maxine's" (rosé) [BC]

Pisse-Dru Beaujolais [FR]

Clos Jordan [ON] (when it arrives)

Southbrook "Triomphe" [ON] (for the time being)

MUSIC TO COOK WITH

Lara St. John: *Bach Concertos* [INDIE]

Yo-Yo Ma: *Bach Solo Suites* [SONY]

It was just about a year ago that I discovered the pleasures of cumin in conjunction with roast beef. And capers and vinegar and parsley and garlic as a simple condiment. No matter what your mother may have told you, it's really not about size at all, but shape. Meaning, I cook a two-pound roast the same length of time as a six pounder, provided they're both shaped like footballs.

For this, get a big, Costco-size, cheap roast of beef—eye of the round is about right—say, six to seven pounds. Dinner can be on the table within an hour and a half of starting.

For this, get a big, Costco-size, cheap roast of beef ...

Cuminized Garlic-Roast Round

serves quite a few, and endless sandwichery, stir-fries, stroganoff ...

WINE PAIRINGS

Fairview "Goat-Rotie" [SA]

Bonny Doon "Cardinal Zin Beastly Old Vines" [CA]

MUSIC TO COOK WITH

Doug Cox: *Stay Lazy*
[MALAHAT MOUNTAIN]

Marc-André Hamelin:
Percy Grainger Piano Pieces
[HYPERION]

Mikhail Pletnev:
C.P.E. Bach Piano Pieces [DGG]

MEAT

6–7 lb (2.7–3.15 kg)	eye of the round beef roast
20 cloves	garlic, peeled and halved
⅓ cup (75 mL)	kosher salt
⅓ cup (75 mL)	cracked black pepper
⅓ cup (75 mL)	ground cumin
2 Tbsp (25 mL)	sweet paprika
1 Tbsp (15 mL)	red pepper flakes (optional)
enough	potatoes, quartered lengthwise, for cooking around the roast

SAUCE

½ cup (125 mL)	chopped Italian parsley
2 Tbsp (25 mL)	minced garlic
½ cup (125 mL)	dry, salted capers (or the wet ones, in a jar, well drained)
½ cup (125 mL)	extra virgin olive oil
¼ cup (50 mL)	red wine vinegar
1	lemon, juice of
to taste	pepper (salt too, if you're not using the dry-salted capers)

Preheat the oven to 475°F (240°C) to start, 325°F (160°C) thereafter.

Unsheath the roast, rinse it and pat dry well. Make a whole lot of slits in the roast, all over, and insert the 40 half cloves of garlic everywhere there's room.

Mix together the salt, pepper, cumin, paprika and red pepper flakes in a bowl. Rub the roast all over with all of the mixture and pat it on so it won't fall off when you put it in the pan. Put the roast on a rack in a big roasting pan. Put the potatoes all around it.

Put into the 475°F (240°C) oven for 15 minutes. Reduce the heat to 325°F (160°C) and roast for another 50 minutes. Start checking for rarity. It might want another 10 for medium-rare, but anything more than that and we're not on the same page, roast beef-wise.

Take the roast out and let it rest under foil for a few minutes.

Meanwhile, make the sauce. Mix all the sauce ingredients together in a bowl. If you want the sauce saucier, put it in the blender for a few seconds till it's the consistency you like.

The roast makes for great sandwiches, with red onion and tomatoes on crusty olive bread, some of the sauce on top, Caesar salad on the side.

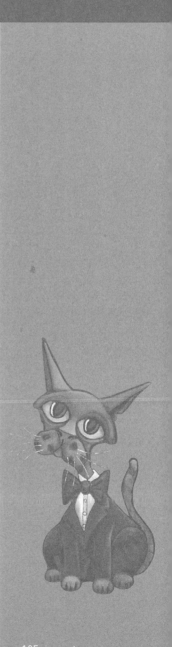

A man named
Tito Beveridge—
really!—makes the
best vodka on
the planet ...

A man named Tito Beveridge—really!—makes the best vodka on the planet: Tito's Handmade Texas Vodka. Don't think there's any difference in vodkas? Neither did I, till I tasted this one. Now, it's not at the cheap end of the price spectrum, nor right at the top, but somewhere in the middle. Sure is good, though, and a bottle has a permanent place in my freezer, alongside all those fruit eaux-de-vie, and the gin and the aquavit.

I used to make this roast with gin and junipers, but these days I'm happy doing it up with Tito's. Try it and see.

Tito's Texas Tenderloin

serves 6

WINE PAIRINGS

Tito's Handmade
Texas Vodka [TX]

Llano Estacado
Cabernet Sauvignon [TX]

Nk'Mip Cellars
"Qwam Qwmt" Merlot [BC]
(600 cases made!)

MUSIC TO COOK WITH

Brave Combo: *Polkatharsis*
[ROUNDER]

Van Cliburn: *My Favorite Chopin*
[RCA]

ZZ Top: *Antenna* [RCA]

6 cloves	garlic, peeled and halved
3 lb (1.5 kg)	beef tenderloin, sliced into 1½-inch (4-cm) rounds
2 Tbsp (25 mL)	butter
1 cup (250 mL)	Tito's Handmade Texas vodka
36	juniper berries
10	coriander seeds
2 tsp (10 mL)	fresh thyme, stripped from stems
1 Tbsp (15 mL)	whole black peppercorns
1 cup (250 mL)	mascarpone cheese or Jersey double cream
to taste	salt and pepper
for garnish	parsley, chopped

Rub garlic all over the slices of beef. Put the same halves of garlic in a heavy pan with just a smidge of the butter over medium-low heat for a couple of minutes, till the garlic gets fragrant. Lose the garlic and set the pan aside.

Put the beef slices in a single layer in a big, flat dish. Pour half the vodka over the meat. Bruise 24 of the juniper berries and the coriander seeds and sprinkle on the meat. Add the thyme and peppercorns. Cover the dish and refrigerate for 3 or 4 hours, turning a few times.

Pat the meat dry and wipe off bits of herbs. Place the heavy, pre-garlicked pan on high heat. When the pan is good and hot, add the rest of the butter and let it foam up. Arrange as many slices of meat as will fit easily in the pan in a single layer and sear about 1½–2 minutes per side, till browned. Put on a warm platter and finish with the rest of the meat.

Turn the heat down to medium-low and add the rest of the juniper and vodka. Cook for 1 minute. Stir in the mascarpone or cream and cook till blended, 2 or 3 minutes, stirring all the while. Add salt and pepper to taste. Return the meat to the pan and cover with sauce. Heat through. Serve with the sauce spooned on top of the meat and sprinkled with parsley. Keep the remaining sauce warm for seconds.

Ian McConnell of Victoria invented this recipe while he was living in the West Kootenays in 1980. He says it would do well in this cookbook "next to all the girlie desserts, pastas and all that healthy icky stuff." It can also be done with beef or venison … but not tofu.

By the way, Ian, I think you'll find some pretty virile pastas and desserts in these pages, recipes that will never earn a cardiologist's seal of approval.

Ian McConnell of Victoria invented this recipe …

Real Man Bacon-Wrapped Anchovy Pâté Roasted Pork Steak

PORK STEAKS

2 large	boneless pork steaks
½ cup (125 mL)	sherry
to taste	salt and pepper
3 slices	bacon, cut lengthwise into thirds
enough to cover	pimento-stuffed olives, sliced crosswise

ANCHOVY PÂTÉ

2	hard-cooked egg yolks
1 small	onion, finely chopped
1 clove	garlic, chopped
1 flat tin	anchovies, mashed and cut into small pieces
2 Tbsp (25 mL)	salted butter

Marinate the pork steaks in sherry for several hours, turning frequently.

While the pork is marinating, make the anchovy pâté: combine all pâté ingredients in a food processor and blend to a pasty consistency.

Preheat the oven to 350°F (180°C).

Remove the pork from the marinade and pat dry. Salt and pepper both sides, then spread a layer of pâté over one side of each steak. Take thin strings of bacon and weave in a diagonal pattern around the steaks. Place olive slices in areas of the steaks that bacon strips don't cover.

Put the wrapped steaks on a rack in a roasting pan. Roast, uncovered, for 40–50 minutes. The bacon should turn crispy.

serves 2 with manly appetite
Needs a couple of hours of marinating.

WINE PAIRINGS

Beyerskloof Stellenbosch Pinotage [SA]

Bonny Doon "Le Cigare Volante" [CA]

Guigal "La Turque" [FR]

MUSIC TO COOK WITH

Toby Keith!

Claude Bolling Big Band [FRÉMAUX]

Can: *Cannibalism* [RESTLESS / MUTE / SPOON]

... don't you like cooking something good just for yourself ...?

All right, so you double it, quadruple it, but really, don't you like cooking something good just for yourself when you're home alone, with a good bit of reading at the table, dog or cat under it, waiting for windfall? In this one, it's the recipe that's from New Zealand—Michael James spent time in the kitchens of the Auckland Regency—not necessarily the lamb, although he'd be using that for sure. And espresso with lamb? There'll be more ... I still recall the dinner event when this dish first surfaced; it was the most elegant potluck dinner ever— some seared, spiced salmon with a watermelon curry condiment, vegetables

Michael James's Espresso Marinated New Zealand Lamb

serves 1

WINE PAIRINGS

Van Loveren Semillon [SA]

Columbia Crest
Sauvignon Blanc [WA]

Villa Maria
Müller-Thurgau [NZ]

MUSIC TO COOK WITH

Kiri Te Kanawa: *Maori Songs*
[PHILIPS]

Mary Lou Fallis:
Prima Donna on a Moose
[OPENING DAY]

MARINADE

1 cup (250 mL)	espresso, brewed full-strength
1 tsp (5 mL) each	ground cumin, ground coriander, fine salt (more or less)
⅓ cup (75 mL)	lightly packed brown sugar
5 oz (150 g)	lamb loin
¼ lb (125 g)	fresh ripe tomatoes, sliced (2 or 3 Romas or those on-the-vine ones)
¼ lb (125 g) small	zucchinis, sliced very thin
for drizzling	olive oil

DRESSING

4 tsp (20 mL)	sunflower oil
3 Tbsp (45 mL)	chopped mint
4 tsp (20 mL)	pine nuts
to taste	sugar and salt

and starch kept to a minimum, and a whole lot of good antipodean drinking wine, most of it white. This dish would have made Juan Valdez run up both sides of the mountain at once. The chef did leave a recipe outline behind: not so much a method of cooking as a shopping list, so you can do as I did and adapt this to make it your own. The "instructions" are mine, based on peering over the rim of my wine glass, observing; if it doesn't work blame me, not him. I wouldn't be using any of that decaf stuff, though. And I've long wondered if he could do anything with a chicken and some Darjeeling …

Mix together all the marinade ingredients and then put the lamb loin in, letting it get good and soaked through, turning once in a while—at least a couple of hours.

Preheat the oven to 300°F (150°C).

Roast the tomato and zucchini slices on a baking sheet in the oven, with a little light olive oil drizzled on top, till the tomatoes start to dry.

Stir together all the dressing ingredients in a large bowl or jar (easier to shake that way) and mix well again just before pouring it on the lamb. Sear the lamb loin in an iron pan, both sides, till it's done to your personal comfort level of pinkitude. Keep hot. Put the tomatoes artfully on a big plate, stack the zucchini atop the tomatoes, cantilevered at a rakish angle, then position the piece of lamb on top of that and drizzle the lot with a bit of dressing.

For once, not Pinot Noir with this; the chef suggests a Müller-Thurgau from New Zealand's Villa Maria. Which works fine: fresh and full, a tiny bit flowery but robust enough to fight back when faced with a coffee-minted chunk of lamb.

While we're doing lamb with coffee, here comes a return engagement of one of my long-time favourites, another one that's been in the basic rep so long I can't recall its origin. I do know that over the years the strength and style, even make, of coffee has changed. My friend Vince Piccolo and his brother Sammy operate a mini-chain of coffee houses called Caffè Artigiano—six in Vancouver and one in Seoul, Korea. Sammy has won the world cup of caffè latte artistry several times and can now do it with one hand behind his back and his eyes closed. Literally. The Black Cat Blend is one of their house-bean mixtures that has become a strong favourite morning, noon and night. And on lamb.

While we're doing lamb with coffee …

Black Cat Lamb Roast

serves 6, with leftovers

WINE PAIRINGS

Château des Charmes
"Droit" Gamay Noir [ON]

Jadot Clos de Vougeot [FR]

MUSIC TO COOK WITH

Kirk Elliott & Norm Hacking:
*Orange Cats Make
the Very Best Friends*
[3 FLAMINGOS]

4–5-lb. (2–2.2-kg)	leg of lamb, ready for roasting
	softened butter to rub over the roast
to taste	salt and pepper
2 cups (500 mL)	chopped onions
2 cups (500 mL)	chopped carrots
2 cups (500 mL)	chopped celery (if you can get all the vegetables roughly the same size, chopped, it's classy and makes for more even cooking)
1 cup (250 mL)	broth (lamb if there is any, chicken's fine, beef works)
2 cups	Caffè Artigiano Black Cat Blend coffee, brewed double strength, or your usual coffee of choice (of course, I don't expect you to come to Vancouver or fly to Seoul just for the coffee, although if you do, give me a call and we'll have a cup, or a glass)
½ cup (125 mL)	whipping cream, more or less
2 Tbsp (25 mL)	sugar
to taste	fresh dill, parsley, chives (chopped fine)

Preheat the oven to 425°F (220°C).

Rub the lamb all over with butter and sprinkle on salt and pepper. Put the lamb fat-side down in a roasting pan that's big enough to hold all the vegetables. Toss chopped onions all around and put the pan in the oven for 30 minutes.

Turn the roast fat-side up and cook for another 15 minutes. Remove the lamb from the pan and skim off as much fat as you can. Put the lamb back in the pan and toss the carrots and celery all over and around the roast. Drop the oven temperature to 350 or 375°F (180 or 190°C), depending on how true and efficient your oven is, and roast 20 minutes more. Pour in the broth and roast for another 15 minutes.

Make the coffee strong (double or better) in your usual way. Stir in the whipping cream and the sugar till it's all blended. Add the coffee to the lamb pan and continue roasting another 30 to 40 minutes, basting often.

Check for doneness, take the lamb out and carve on a hot platter. Go ahead and let it rest under foil if you need to; I've always thought that was a bit too Calvinist; I mean, let's just get to it and tuck in.

Strain the pan juices into a pan, discarding any of the veggie bits, and stir in the fresh herbs—or sprinkle in dried ones. Pour the sauce over the sliced lamb and serve. The vegetables, by the way, while looking pretty dark and foreboding, are actually very tasty if you want to save and serve them.

One of my
favourite words
in Italian is
asciugapiatti.

One of my favourite words in Italian is *asciugapiatti*. It means dish-drainer. I just love the look and sound of it; maybe name a restaurant that one day (not in Italy). A close second is the name of this dish, which loosely translates to birds that flew the coop, got away, vamoosed. Someone said it's because when they're cooked they look like quail or ortolans or some such. Easy and quick to prepare for an impromptu dinner—provided you just happen to have prosciutto, pork loin and fresh sage in the house. You can substitute pancetta for prosciutto (although prosciutto tastes more intense), but you can't substitute dried for fresh sage this time.

Uccellini Scappati — Those Little Disappearing Birds

serves 6

1 cup (250 mL)	chicken or veal stock
2 lb (1 kg)	boneless pork tenderloin, cut into 24 slices, each about ¼ inch (5 mm) thick
½ cup (125 mL)	all-purpose flour
as needed	salt and pepper
24 thin slices	prosciutto (or pancetta); have the deli do it, or buy it already thin-sliced, in the package
30–40 large	unblemished fresh sage leaves, washed and dried
¼ cup (50 mL)	butter
2 Tbsp (25 mL)	olive oil
3 medium	shallots, minced
1 small	dried pepperoncino (hot chili pepper)
lots	Italian parsley, chopped
1½ cups (375 mL)	dry red wine (Valpolicella's good)
1 tube	Italian tomato paste (about ½ cup/125 mL)
for garnish	sage leaves and parsley sprigs

Boil the stock in a small pan on high and continue boiling till it's reduced by half, about 10 minutes. Set aside.

Take each slice of pork tenderloin and flatten it out into a rectangle. Use the palm of your most dexterous hand. Mix the flour with salt and pepper and put on a plate. Dredge the pork in the flour. Shake off the excess but make sure the slices are well floured. Put a slice of prosciutto (depending on how big the slices are, a half slice might do it) and a couple of sage leaves on each piece of pork. Roll them up from the short end, and stick a toothpick through the middle to hold stuff in.

WINE PAIRINGS

Beyerskloof Pinotage Rosé
[SA]

Rabbit Ridge "Montepiano"
[CA]

Marques de Caceres Rueda
[SP]

MUSIC TO COOK WITH

Il Giardino Armonico:
Vivaldi's Four Seasons [TELDEC]

La Banda Città Ruvo di Puglia
[ENJA]

Heat the butter and oil on high in a frying pan. Add half of the "birds" (or fewer, depending on size of pan) and sear for a minute or two on each side, till brown. Transfer to a warm plate and hold. Repeat till all are done.

Lower the heat to medium and cook the shallots, chili pepper and parsley for 2 minutes, stirring all the while. Add the reduced stock, wine and tomato paste, put the heat back up to high and bring to a boil. Scrape up the bits on the bottom of the pan. Reduce liquid by half, about 6 or 7 minutes. Put the birds into the pan with any juice on the plate. Cover the pan and cook on moderate for 5 minutes. Turn with tongs once during cooking.

Put 3 or 4 birds on to each of 6 warmed plates, take out the toothpicks, spoon sauce over top and garnish with sage leaves and parsley sprigs. Polenta is great with this, or cannellini beans or plain penne pasta, even mashed potatoes.

This sausage and cooking method are well known in Modena, the home of the real-deal balsamic vinegar. It's sometimes called *cotechino in galera* or "cotechino in jail," hence my term "sausage in bondage." The sausage is the thing; accept no substitutes. I know an old-time Italian butcher who makes up a few dozen at a time and calls me, so I can stock the freezer. More recently, I've seen it sold already cooked, in which case you just skip the first part of the prep and go straight to the beef-wrapping and tying-up.

> The sausage is the thing; accept no substitutes.

Sausage in Bondage

serves 4

3–4 quarts (3–4 L)	water
2 or 3	*cotechino* sausages (about 1½–1¾ lb/800–900 g)
1¾ lb (900 g)	top round steak, butterflied by the butcher to be like 2 or 3 sheets of beef (6–8 inches/15–20 cm wide, 10–12 inches/25–30 cm long—or the same thickness as beef rouladen)
to taste	black pepper
2 small	onions, chopped
¼ cup (50 mL)	olive oil
2 large	bay leaves
4 large cloves	garlic, peeled and crushed
1 bottle	red wine (California Zinfandel is good, if not authentic)
3½ cups (850 mL)	meat stock

WINE PAIRINGS

Sangiovese:Leonetti [WA]

Sandhill Syrah [BC]

Il Bastardo [IT]

MUSIC TO COOK WITH

Palladian Ensemble:
Vivaldi's Four Seasons [LINN]

Cecilia Bartoli: *Salieri Arias*
[LONDON]

Bring the water to boil in a pot big enough to hold the sausages. Pierce the sausages with a fork and submerge. Adjust the heat for a gentle simmer and cook 30 minutes. Drain and let cool. (None of the above is necessary if the *cotechino* is already cooked.)

Season the sheets of beef with plenty of pepper and toss on some of the onion. Cut the skin from the sausages and put one on each piece of beef. Roll them up, encasing the sausages as much as possible, with just the ends showing. Tie up with kitchen string in half a dozen places.

Heat the oil in a big pan that will hold all the meat and liquid to come. Brown the meat on medium all over. Throw in the rest of the onion and the bay leaves and brown a little longer. Take the meat out, add the garlic and wine and bring to a bubble, scraping up the bits on the bottom. Boil this liquid, uncovered, for 20–30 minutes, till half of it's evaporated.

Put the meat back in, add the stock and bring to a boil again. Lower the heat to an easy bubble, partly cover the pan and cook, barely bubbling, for 1½–2 hours.

Transfer the meat to a warm platter and concentrate the sauce flavours by boiling uncovered for 5–10 more minutes. Cut the string off and slice the "sausage rolls" into ½-inch (1-cm) rounds.

Pour sauce over the slices and use the rest with small pasta, couscous, polenta, etc. Slow-cooked lentils (canned are fine) splashed with balsamic vinegar make a nice side dish, as do oven-roasted vegetables with a little truffle oil, radicchio and crisp greens in a salad and some Bosc pears with a little *torta di* mascarpone cheese and crumbled amaretti biscuits for dessert.

David Veljacic was the Fire Chef hereabouts. A working firefighter with a deep love for cooking, he published three cookbooks in quick succession, the first of which was *The Fire Chef*, which may well still be in print (Douglas & McIntyre) and is worth the price of admission for the barbecue rub recipes alone. From him I learned how to use the barbecue; it's that simple. Prior to his simple and sensible methodology, I approached that instrument with trepidation and came away from it with less than stellar results.

> David Veljacic was the Fire Chef hereabouts.

David Veljacic's Beef Ribs Method

And then, A.D. (after David), the barbecue became my friend, and my friends came back for out-on-the-deck dinners. I know that David Veljacic is in charge of the barbecue detail Up There; they never had it so good before he arrived.

Not a recipe, but a method, then: Get some seriously meaty prime-rib beef bones, the kind that weigh about a pound apiece, the ones that look like they originated on the side of some sauropod. Rub well with a couple of handfuls of sea salt and Veljacic's salt-free barbecue rub (it's in the book). Heat the barbecue but only to about 250°F (120°C), then turn off the burners on one side and put the ribs on the unfired side. Cook for 2 to as long as 3 hours, depending on the size of the ribs and your personal understanding of beef doneness. These are not intended to be rare. Turn every 20 minutes or so.

If you like barbecue sauce or have a good recipe of your own, slather it on the ribs after you've removed them from the heat and wrap 'em in foil for 20 minutes before serving. I set some sauce alongside for those who want. Bay leaf-roasted new potatoes go nicely (see "Hasselbacks," page 139).

First time I served these ribs I sent out tumblers full of Buzbag, that onomatopoetic Turkish plonk (pronounced booze-bah, but really, you've gotta say buzz-bag if only once or twice!). It's a teeth-and-countertop stainer with a little of that elusive Pine-Sol element that informs some of the wines of the Fertile Crescent and the islands to the southwest. Gamza'd be good; Egri Bikaver, an industrial-strength Zinfandel; Merlot-in-a-Drum ...

WINE PAIRINGS

Lodez Coteaux de Languedoc [FR]

Fairview "Goats to Roam" Red [SA]

MUSIC TO COOK WITH

Pete Wernick's Live Five: *I Tell You What* [SUGAR HILL]

Rodney Crowell: *Fate's Right Hand* [EPIC]

Gary Burton: *Tennessee Firebird* [RCA]

David Veljacic's "How to Grill the Perfect Steak" Lesson

… is the other important part of the Fire Chef's legacy. You have to like his point of departure: "Buy 6-ounce filet mignons 1 inch thick … bring the steaks to room temperature."

And from there it's simple and perfect: Season steaks with sea salt and teli-cherry pepper (David's favourite, which he would send me at Christmas, from his source in Texas), or a meat-seasoning rub or a no-salt seasoning. Let that sit on the steaks while you preheat the barbecue to 350°–400°F (180°–200°C). Put the steaks on the grill directly over the heat. Close the lid. In about a minute, flip the steaks. Close the lid. Continue to turn the steaks every minute for 6 minutes. (I sometimes go less). That's it. It's never failed me yet.

serves as many as you've got steaks

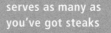

WINE PAIRINGS

Black Hills "Nota Bene" [BC]

Concha y Toro "Trio" [CH]

Henry of Pelham Merlot [ON]

Konzelmann Cabernet Sauvignon [ON]

MUSIC TO COOK WITH

Alain Trudel & Kiosque a Musique: *Kiosque 1900* [ATMA]

... here's a house-
favourite way of
doing up a fresh
leg of lamb ...

While we're on a roll with simple and easy non-recipes, here's a house-favourite way of doing up a fresh leg of lamb: marinated in a Mega-Martini.

Plymouth Martini'd Leg of Lamb with Jalapeño Olives

serves a group
Needs to marinate
8 hours or more.

WINE PAIRINGS

martinis

Bouchard Aîné "Pinossimo" [FR]

Rubens Tempranillo [SP]

MUSIC TO COOK WITH

Christopher Parkening: *Plays
Vivaldi, Warlock & Praetorius*
[ANGEL]

1 bottle	Plymouth gin
¼ cup (50 mL)	Noilly Prat Vermouth
12 dashes	Angostura Bitters
20 or 30	jalapeño-stuffed green olives (Jardine's are good, from Texas, or make your own: buy jalapeño strips in a Mexican deli, canned, buy pitted queen olives and do them yourself; fiddly but a lot cheaper, and a not-bad way to spend a rainy afternoon)
4–5-lb (2–2.2-kg)	leg of lamb, bone in or boneless, your call
for roasting	butter and oil
to taste	salt and pepper
handful	juniper berries, coriander seeds

Make a big jug of mega-martini with the gin, vermouth and Angostura. (If it's too much vermouth—or Angostura—for you, ease up there.) Put the jalapeño olives in the martini; stir or shake or whatever the movies have told you.

Put the lamb in a big bowl and pour the "martini" over. Put the bowl in the refrigerator and let marinate for at least 8 hours, preferably overnight. Turn the lamb 4 or 5 times. You can wake up if you remember what it was like when the twins were teething!

Preheat the oven to 425°F (220°C) to begin.

Take the lamb out of the marinade and pat well dry with paper towels. Rub the leg of lamb all over with butter and sprinkle with salt and pepper to taste. Put on a rack in a roasting pan. Put about an inch of marinade, including the olives, in the bottom of the pan and add a few teaspoons of oil. Sprinkle juniper berries and coriander seeds over lamb. Roast for 20 minutes at 425°F (220°C), then lower to 350°F (180°C) and continue roasting for 50–60 minutes. Baste periodically with more of the martini. When done to your satisfaction, take out and let stand under foil for 10 minutes. Skim fat from the pan and reserve ½ cup or so (125 mL) of the roasting juice.

Bring a cupful of the original marinade to the boil, add the pan juices and cook down while the lamb is resting. Add salt and pepper to season, take out the berries, seeds and cooked olives, and use as a sauce for the meat.

Slice the lamb thin and serve with English mustard, some of the uncooked olives out of the marinade, sliced red onion and tomato. You can throw out the marinade or (since it seems a waste of good gin) keep it frozen (without the olives) till the next time you decide to do this dish.

Hands up
all those who've
ever run a mill.

This may be a little more elaborate a way of prepping spare ribs, but I think you'll find the dark rum, gentle smoke and herby-spicy flavours a tasty departure from the run-of-the-mill. Hands up all those who've ever run a mill.

Rummy Smoky Spicy Ribs

serves 4
Needs to marinate overnight.

WINE PAIRINGS

Panarroz Jumilla [SP]

African Terroir
"Tribal" Pinotage [SA]

MUSIC TO COOK WITH

Kirk Elliott: *Up from the Ground*
[MARSHMELLOW]

Canadian Brass: *Magic Horn*
[OPENING DAY]

4 pods	cardamom, seeds only
6 cloves	garlic, minced
½ tsp (2 mL)	grated lime zest
¼ cup (50 mL)	fresh lime juice
2 Tbsp (25 mL)	tomato paste
2 Tbsp (25 mL)	brown sugar
1 Tbsp (15 mL)	fresh ginger, grated
6	green onions, minced
2	canned chipotle chilies in adobo (split, cored, seeded and chopped)
4 cups (1 L)	overproof dark rum
2 cups (500 mL)	water
¼ cup (50 mL)	malt vinegar (or cider vinegar)
¼ cup (50 mL)	soy sauce (I like the light kind)
3–4 Tbsp (45–60 mL)	sesame oil
2 large	onions, chopped
to taste	crushed red pepper flakes
½ cup (125 mL)	chopped parsley

2 sprigs	fresh thyme
2	whole bay leaves
½ tsp (2 mL)	celery seed
1 sprig	fresh rosemary
5	whole cloves
to taste	salt and pepper
4 lb (2 kg)	ribs, good and meaty (about a pound per person), country pork ribs are the preferred kind, but beef or even bison is tasty too

Crush the cardamom seeds in a mortar, add the garlic and pound to a paste. Stir in the lime zest and juice, tomato paste, brown sugar, ginger and green onions. Add the chipotles and mix well. Add the rum, water, vinegar, soy and sesame oil and stir well. Now add the onions, red pepper, parsley, thyme, bay leaves, celery seed, rosemary, cloves, salt and pepper and really stir well. Put the ribs in the bowl, covering them completely with the liquid. Put a tight lid or plastic wrap on the bowl and refrigerate overnight.

Now comes the option: (a) Preheat the oven to 300°F (150°C) and put the ribs in a broiling pan to roast for 3–4 hours, until the meat is good and crusty on the outside and falling off the bone. Or (b) grill on a fairly hot barbecue for about 45 minutes till the same desired effect is achieved.

Katrin Horowitz of
Victoria was
inspired by a great
meal at Millie's
Bistro in Toronto.

Katrin Horowitz of Victoria was inspired by a great meal at Millie's Bistro in Toronto. "Their wonderful chef, Gary, gave me some hints but not the whole recipe. I've been working on it over the years and, I like to think, making some improvements along the way."

Lapin aux Pommes

serves 4

1	rabbit
1 medium	onion, chopped
½ cup (125 mL)	cider vinegar
1	bay leaf
4	crushed juniper berries
2	Granny Smith apples, peeled, cored and sliced (add the apple peel to the stock)
3 cups (750 mL)	cold water
2 tsp (10 mL)	salt
to taste	pepper
1 Tbsp (15 mL)	butter
for sprinkling	cardamom
1 small	onion, finely chopped
½ cup (125 mL)	all-purpose flour
1 tsp (5 mL)	ground cardamom
1 tsp (5 mL)	ground coriander
to taste	salt and pepper
½ cup (125 mL)	dry white wine

WINE PAIRINGS

Trapiche Mendoza
Chardonnay [AG]

Cherry Point Pinot Gris [BC]

Bonny Doon Pacific Rim
Dry Riesling [CA]

Strewn Cabernet Franc [ON]

MUSIC TO COOK WITH

Garrison Keillor &
Frederica von Stade:
Songs of the Cat [RCA]

Chris Norman: *Portraits* [DORIAN]

or

Wind & Wire [BOXWOOD]

De-bone the rabbit, discarding all visible fat (it's tedious, but it's worth it). Put the bones in a stock pot, add the chopped onion, cider vinegar, bay leaf, juniper berries, apple peel, water and salt and pepper. Place on heat and simmer, uncovered, for at least 45 minutes.

While the bones are simmering, heat the butter in a non-stick frying pan and briefly sauté the apple slices over medium-high heat. Transfer to a plate and sprinkle with a little cardamom. In the same pan, sauté the finely chopped onion over medium-high heat for 1 minute, adding a little more butter if needed.

Cut the meat into bite-size pieces. Put the flour and spices into a paper bag, add salt and pepper and mix. Add the rabbit pieces, close the bag and shake so that all the meat is covered with the flour mixture.

Add the rabbit pieces to the pan and sauté them over medium-high heat until lightly browned. Add the white wine and reduce, scraping up the browned bits. Strain the stock through a sieve and add 2 cups (500 mL) to the rabbit in the pan. Simmer for 10 minutes. Add the apple slices and simmer for another 2 minutes.

Serve with garlic mashed potatoes and your best salad—and more of that white wine (Cherry Point Vineyards' Pinot Gris goes wonderfully, but so does a good Sauvignon Blanc)—to your favourite three people in the world, and have a wonderful evening.

Chef Dez …
knows the way
to DiscDrivers'
hearts …

Chef Dez, a.k.a. Gordon Desormeaux, of Abbotsford, British Columbia, knows the way to DiscDrivers' hearts with this original recipe. You can let him know what you think at www.chefdez.com.

Cinnamon Roasted Pork Tenderloin with Pinot Gris Applesauce

serves 2
Needs at least 1½ hours of marinating.

WINE PAIRINGS

Tommasini Pinot Grigio [IT]

Gaja "Promis" [IT]

MUSIC TO COOK WITH

Terem Quartet: *No, Russia Cannot be Perceived by Wit*
[INTUITION]

¼ cup (50 mL)	table salt
4 cups (1 L)	cold water
1 lb (500 g)	pork tenderloin
1 Tbsp (15 mL)	cinnamon
1 tsp (5 mL)	paprika
½ tsp (2 mL)	salt
¼ tsp (1 mL)	pepper
¼ tsp (1 mL)	cumin
1 Tbsp (15 mL)	olive oil
1 tsp (5 mL)	liquid honey
for garnish	mint leaves (optional)

APPLESAUCE

½ cup (125 mL)	Pinot Gris (or other white wine)
1 tsp (5 mL)	lemon juice
2 large	Granny Smith apples, peeled, cored and thinly sliced
1 Tbsp (15 mL)	white sugar
¼ tsp (1 mL)	allspice
pinch	salt

Dissolve the ¼ cup (50 mL) table salt in the 4 cups (1 L) of water. Add the tenderloin and brine for 1 hour in the refrigerator.

Remove the tenderloin and pat dry. Mix the seasonings, olive oil and honey in a small bowl to make a wet rub. Apply this rub to all areas of the tenderloin, and let it sit in the refrigerator for ½ hour to 12 hours.

Meanwhile, add all the applesauce ingredients to a non-reactive (stainless steel) pot. Bring to a boil over medium-high heat while breaking up the apples with a wooden spoon. Lower the heat to medium-low and simmer for 20 minutes.

Mash the apples to the desired consistency, and set aside, covered, off the heat, until needed.

Preheat the oven to 400°F (200°C). Roast the tenderloin for 20–25 minutes. Let sit for 5–10 minutes before slicing. Serve with the Pinot Gris applesauce, and a mint leaf sprig.

Cécile Daoust-Mellamphy sent this from London, Ontario. She writes, "Having the genes of a long line of good, old-fashioned *mères-de-famille* and the habit of risking new subtleties in the kitchen led to inventing a new taste from an old dish."

Tourtière

makes 2 pies, serving 4 people each

WINE PAIRINGS

V8 Juice

Unibroue "Terrible" [QC]

Fortant de France Syrah [FR]

MUSIC TO COOK WITH

La Bottine Souriante:
La Mistrine [MILLE PATTES]

Tommy Hunter:
Timeless Country Classics
[EDITH/ROCKLANDS]

2 Tbsp (25 mL)	olive oil
1 medium	onion, finely chopped
3 cloves	garlic, crushed
½ lb (250 g)	ground veal
½ lb (250 g)	ground beef
½ lb (250 g)	ground pork
1 tsp (5 mL)	salt
1 tsp (5 mL)	pepper
½ tsp (2 mL)	allspice
¼ tsp (1 mL)	ground cloves
pinch	sage
¾ cup (175 mL)	water
½ cup (125 mL)	dry breadcrumbs
enough	pastry for 4 pie crusts (2 pies)
1	egg yolk well mixed with 1 Tbsp (15 mL) water

Heat the oil in a large saucepan over medium-low heat. Add the onion and garlic and sauté for about 10 minutes, until soft. Increase the heat to high, add the meats, seasonings, spices and water, mix well and bring to a boil. Reduce the heat to low and let simmer, uncovered, for about 30 minutes, stirring occasionally, till the meat no longer shows any pink. Stir in the breadcrumbs and let cool.

Preheat the oven to 375°F (190°C).

Roll out the pastry and line one of the pie plates. Fill with half of the meat mixture. Cover with a top crust; trim and crimp the edges. Prick the top and brush with some of the egg yolk-water mixture. Repeat for the second pie. Freeze one (thaw before baking) and bake the other for about 50 minutes, until nicely golden.

Serve with a rich gravy, with cranberry sauce, or even just with ketchup!

When Louise
Merler was a new
bride arriving from
Quebec into an
Italian family ...

When Louise Merler was a new bride arriving from Quebec into an Italian family, she was totally smitten by this classic dish, prepared by her mother-in-law. As the years passed, she added it to her repertoire, and since veal is so expensive, she often prepares it with chicken breasts or this way, with pork tenderloin.

Pork Loin in Tuna Sauce

serves 6–8
Best prepared
the day before
serving.

WINE PAIRINGS

Balthasar Ress
"Hattenheimer Nussbrunnen"
Riesling Auslese [GY]

Zonin Chiaretto [IT]

Leone de Castris
Primitivo di Manduria [IT]

MUSIC TO COOK WITH

Handel: *Alexander's Feast*
[LONDON]

PORK

2 cups (500 mL)	chicken broth
1 cup (250 mL)	white wine
1	shallot
1	bay leaf
1 sprig	thyme
1 tsp (5 mL)	salt
6	peppercorns
2	pork tenderloins

TUNA SAUCE

2	egg yolks
¼ tsp (1 mL)	Dijon mustard
1 cup (250 mL)	olive oil or ½ cup (125 mL) each olive oil and salad oil (for lighter sauce)
one 7½-oz (213-mL) can	tuna in oil, drained
1	lemon, juice of
4	anchovy fillets
1 Tbsp (15 mL)	capers
	extra olive oil and lemon juice, if necessary
for garnish	thin lemon slices, black olives and capers

To poach the pork, bring the broth, wine, shallot and seasonings to boil in a saucepan. Add the tenderloins and poach them until done, 12–15 minutes or more, depending on size. Remove from the poaching liquid, cool completely and refrigerate until the sauce is ready.

For the tuna sauce, put the egg yolks and mustard in a blender. Blend a few seconds at high speed. Through the feeder cap, pour the oil very slowly in a thin stream until the sauce is very thick.

Empty the sauce into a glass bowl. Without washing the blender jar, put in the canned tuna, lemon juice, anchovy fillets and capers. Process until smooth and creamy. Add some oil if very thick. Remove from the blender jar and fold carefully into the sauce. Taste and correct the seasoning, adding lemon juice if needed for tartness.

To assemble, cut the cold pork loin in ¼-inch-thick (5-mm) slices and arrange in a shallow serving dish. Pour the tuna sauce over the meat slices to cover completely. Refrigerate, covered with plastic wrap, until serving time.

Decorate with lemon slices, black olives and capers. Serve with plenty of good bread to mop up the fabulous sauce. *Buon appetito.*

chapter eight

vegetables

Giardiniera Marietta   132

La-La Succotash (Confetti Corn)   134

Braised Celery with Mint Sauce   135

Butter Sauce with a Rumour of Tomatoes   136

West Coast Scafata   137

Baked Cholesterol (Goat Cheese 'n' Cream Potatoes)   138

Hasselbacks with Fresh Bay Leaves   139

Potato & Rosemary-Garlic Pizza   140

Shredded Brussels Sprouts with Pine Nuts & Prosciutto   141

The Brussels Sprouts Dialogues   142

Brussels Sprouts with Pine Nuts & Sage Cream   144

Escarole & Beans   145

Freedom Fries (just another word for no pounds left to lose)   146

Festive Asparagus   147

Giardiniera is one
of my favourite
condiments ...

Giardiniera is one of my favourite condiments—I eat it with everything except ice cream. You can buy it at Italian delis or make your own; it's easy enough—just takes time and space. This is the way my Tuscan mentor Marietta makes it for her own kitchen and the one in her restaurant. Lots here for keeping; it's ready to eat as soon as it cools but it keeps well in a dark cool place for up to a year. I leave the ratio and volume of vegetables up to you and your appetite.

Giardiniera Marietta

6 or 7 litres' worth

WINE PAIRINGS

Limoncello [IT] (try it, the surprise hit with pickled vegetables)

ice cold Moretti [IT]

MUSIC TO COOK WITH

Andrea Bocelli! [PHILIPS]

All right, The Pav, then! [DECCA] but without that Zucchero person! Or Beyoncé!

Better – Michael Schade [CBC]

Lots, all or any combination, of:

	celery
	onions
	cauliflower
	fennel bulbs
	red peppers
	cucumbers
	carrots
	cabbage
	yellow peppers
	zucchini
4 cups (1 L)	water
4 cups (1 L)	white wine
4 cups (1 L)	white wine vinegar
1 lb (500 g)	sugar
3½ oz (100 g)	coarse pickling salt
2 cups (500 mL)	olive oil
sufficient	bay leaves
handful per jar	black peppercorns
1 per jar	hot chili peppers (pepperoncini)

Wash and dry vegetables. Put water, wine, wine vinegar, sugar, salt and oil in a very big pot and bring to the boil.

Cook vegetables in the liquid, one batch at a time, starting with carrots. Don't forget, you want them to be crunchy—carrots will cook 5 minutes, onions 4, cabbage 3, etc. Cook each vegetable individually in boiling liquid and then take it out with a slotted spoon before putting in the next. When they're all done mix them together in a big bowl.

Have ready canning jars with new lids (sterilized by boiling). Add vegetable mix to each jar to about three-quarters full; add liquid to cover. Add 2 bay leaves to each jar, plus a handful of whole peppercorns and a *pepperoncino*. Close jars.

Put jars into a *bain-marie* or canning kettle, with a tea towel in the bottom to keep jars from banging into each other. Pour in lots of water to cover the jars and bring to a slow, rolling boil; maintain for 20 minutes. Take jars out of the hot water, set on something soft and let cool.

... you'll be
surprised how
fast it'll go ...

Sorry about the quantities; it's another accompaniment to the True North Chili. Don't worry, it reheats, but you'll be surprised how fast it'll go; it has always surprised me that such a simple dish draws such rave reactions.

La-La Succotash (Confetti Corn)

serves 10–12 as a side

¼ lb (125 g)	butter or ⅓ cup (75 mL) diced salt pork (remove salt pork before serving)
1 large	sweet red pepper, seeded and diced
3 medium cloves	garlic, minced
1–2	fresh jalapeños, seeded and minced
one 19-oz (540-mL) can	yellow hominy, drained
1 cup (250 mL)	frozen white corn, thawed and drained
1 cup (250 mL)	frozen lima beans, thawed and drained
1 cup (250 mL)	frozen edamame (green soybeans), thawed and drained (or more hominy/corn/limas)
to taste	salt and pepper
dribble	vegetable stock (optional)
2 bunches	green onions, trimmed and sliced

In a big frying pan or wok, melt the butter (or sauté the salt pork) on medium. Add the red pepper, garlic and jalapeños; cook, stirring, for about 5 minutes. Stir in hominy, corn, limas, edamame, salt and pepper. Add just a little splash of vegetable stock if it looks like it needs some liquid. Cook, covered, stirring a couple of times, for about 5 minutes, to heat through.

Add the green onions and adjust seasonings. Serve hot, warm or cool.

WINE PAIRINGS

Nekeas Navarro Rosado [SP]

Woodford Reserve Bourbon
[KY]

MUSIC TO COOK WITH

Los Angeles Philharmonic: *Stokowski Transcriptions* [DELOS]

Mose Allison: *Trilogy* [EPIC]

Celery is something I think deserves a little elevation beyond its customary crunchy-sticks-in-the-lunchbox or stuffed-with-cheese-spread status.

This makes a nice side dish for something delicate, like spring lamb loin or even a firm-fleshed white fish like halibut, olive-oiled and broiled with rhubarb. (No, the recipe isn't in here; I have to save something for the future ...)

Celery is something I think deserves a little elevation ...

Braised Celery with Mint Sauce

2 lb (1 kg)	celery stalks (without the leaves)	serves 4
2 Tbsp (25 mL)	butter	
1 Tbsp (15 mL)	olive oil	
to taste	salt	
½ cup (125 mL)	vegetable stock	
2 Tbsp (25 mL)	tarragon vinegar (or white wine vinegar with a few fresh tarragon leaves or even a handful of dry, crumbled tarragon in it)	
5 Tbsp (75 mL)	fresh mint leaves, chopped fine	
2 Tbsp (25 mL)	sugar	
to taste	mint jelly (optional)	

Preheat the oven to 375°F (190°C).

Make sure there are no brown bits on the celery and toss out any of the bruised outer stalks. Cut each stalk in half lengthwise and again in half crosswise.

Combine the butter and oil in an ovenproof pan, over medium heat. Add the celery and cook, turning once or twice, until light golden, about 10–12 minutes.

Sprinkle the celery with salt. Add the vegetable stock, vinegar, mint and sugar. Raise the heat to high, bring the liquid to a boil, then put the dish in the heated oven. Cook, uncovered, for 10 minutes.

Turn the celery over and cook another 10–12 minutes. You want the celery tender but not mushy.

Bring the pan back onto the top of the stove. Cook over medium heat to boil away any remaining liquid and get a bit of a glaze around the celery. Depending on how minty or sweet you like it, dab a little mint jelly over the celery.

WINE PAIRINGS

Cave Spring "Indian Summer" Late Harvest Riesling [ON]

St. Hubertus "Summer Symphony" [BC]

MUSIC TO COOK WITH

Miles Davis: *Sketches of Spain* [CBS]

Gabor Szabo: *Sorcerer* [IMPULSE]

Andre Previn Trio: *My Fair Lady* [CONTEMPORARY]

I like to serve
this sauce over
fresh pasta as
a *secundo* …

This time, get fresh pasta, or make your own; the flavours here are predominantly butter and tomatoes. Sad to say, I know, but canned Italian tomatoes work better here than fresh ones—unless, of course, they're homegrown and you can vouch for their taste. An old friend made the observation some years ago that tomatoes were the first true casualty of agribusiness.

I like to serve this sauce over fresh pasta as a *secundo*, that is, after the appetizer and before the main course. Sometimes we never get 'round to the main, just cook another batch of sauce …

Butter Sauce with a Rumour of Tomatoes

makes 3 cups (750 mL)

WINE PAIRINGS

Hainle "Z3" [BC]

La Vieille Ferme "Lasira" [FR]

Mommesin Beaujolais [FR]

½ cup (125 mL) (1 stick)	butter
1 medium	red onion, chopped
three 14-oz (398-mL) cans	Italian diced tomatoes
to taste	salt
to taste	black or white pepper, freshly ground
handfuls each	fresh basil and Italian parsley, chopped

Set a medium pan on low heat and warm 6 Tbsp (90 mL) of the butter. Add the onion and sauté gently till it starts to take on some colour, but don't let it get brown (10–12 minutes).

Add the tomatoes and salt and simmer another 12–15 minutes. Remove the pan from the heat and stir in the remaining butter plus freshly ground pepper. Add chopped herbs just before serving.

Be liberal to your pasta.

MUSIC TO COOK WITH

Red Priest: *Nightmare in Venice*
[DORIAN]

This is a take on a northern Italian number, basically a stew of lima or fava beans and chard in white wine and tomatoes. It's rich and hearty enough to serve as a main course for four, especially when you add pancetta. Leave the meat out and it's a fine vegetarian dish or a side to anything grilled or barbecued. The chilies, quantity-adjustable to personal Scoville tolerance, add a nice bite for the back of the mouth. And a French dry muscat is the perfect foil, with its lovely balance of fruit and acid. Just add some country bread and a few ripe pears with Gorgonzola after and move straight on to the *vin santo*.

This is a take on a northern Italian number ...

West Coast Scafata

serves 4 or more

2 or 3	dried chilies, soaked in hot water to soften, drained and chopped
½ lb (250 g)	pancetta or other cured pork, cubed small
3	carrots
2	onions
3 stalks	celery
2 or 3 sprigs	fresh rosemary needles stripped from the stems
¼ cup (50 mL)	good olive oil
1 lb (500 g)	frozen lima beans, thawed and well-drained (or fava beans if you find them)
½ bottle	dry white wine (such as French muscat)
1 cup (250 mL)	tomato sauce, thickened with 1 tsp (5 mL) tomato paste
to taste	salt
½ lb (250 g)	fresh chard, leaves stripped from the stalks and cut into thin strips
to taste	pepper

WINE PAIRINGS

Bouchard Père Meursault "Perrières" [FR]

Calona Sovereign Opal [BC]

Thomas & Vaughn Vidal [ON]

MUSIC TO COOK WITH

Michel Cardin: *The London Manuscript* (12 Volumes)— lute music of Sylvius Leopold Weiss [INDIE]

Put the chilies, pancetta, carrots, onions, celery and rosemary into the food processor and whirl around till it takes on a very fine texture. (Or, chop everything very fine with a good sharp knife.)

Put the mixture into a deep frying pan with the olive oil and sauté on medium heat for 10 minutes.

Add the beans, pour in the wine, bring to a boil and cook for 5 minutes. Add the tomato sauce and salt, cover the pan and cook gently for 1 hour, checking every 15 minutes. If the pan gets too dry add a little hot water.

Add the chard to the pan and mix well with the beans. Bring it back to the boil, cover the pan again and cook for 20 minutes more, adding hot water if needed.

Check for salt; add pepper to taste and serve hot, right out of the pan if you're all friends around the table. Wash it down with lots of wine.

Ditto the earlier reference to potatoes; these are even better because they're mashed with cream and chèvre and butter. And green onions strictly for appearances. Not something you're ever going to want to discuss with your doctor. I like to cook this when I'm home alone, and I hide the wrapping materials right after dinner.

Baked Cholesterol (Goat Cheese 'n' Cream Potatoes)

serves 4 or fewer

2 lb (1 kg)	russet potatoes
8 cloves	garlic, peeled
handful	salt
½ cup (125 mL)	whipping cream
½ cup (125 mL) 1 stick	butter
½ cup (125 mL)	creamy goat cheese
to taste	salt and pepper
¼ cup (50 mL)	green onions, chopped fine

WINE PAIRINGS

Bollinger "RD" Champagne
[FR]

De Bortoli
"Gulf Station" Shiraz [AU]

MUSIC TO COOK WITH

Renée Fleming: *Haunted Heart*
or
Bel Canto [DECCA]

Booker T. & The MGs:
Time is Tight [STAX]

Peel the potatoes and cut into pieces. Put them into a big pot with the garlic cloves, cover with cold water, add a handful of salt and put the lid on. Simmer for 20 minutes or till potatoes are tender without having turned to mush.

In a small saucepan, heat the cream, butter and goat cheese, with salt and pepper to taste. Keep stirring till the butter and cheese have melted and it's all nice and smooth. Keep warm.

Preheat the oven to Broil.

Drain the potatoes and garlic and put them through a potato ricer into a big mixing bowl. (If you don't have a potato ricer, get one; they're a fast disappearing utensil, and worth having.) Beat in the butter and cheese mixture, either by hand or with an electric mixer. Add the green onions and more salt and pepper to taste. The potatoes should be fluffy, not runny.

Put the mixture into a shallow baking dish. Broil about 4 or 5 inches (10 or 12 cm) from the heat, until the top is golden, about 5–6 minutes. Don't let it burn; you won't be able to salvage it and will have to start all over again.

Hasselbacks are a Scandinavian potato dish that makes a great side for baked fish or roasted chicken, or anything. Somewhere along the line I learned a good trick for preparing them: take two chopsticks and put them on a cutting board. You put the potato between the chopsticks, lengthwise. Hold this configuration in place and cut potatoes crosswise about one-quarter inch apart, cutting down just to the chopsticks.

Hasselbacks with Fresh Bay Leaves

If you can't get fresh bay leaves, go to a good herbs-and-garden shop and buy a bay tree in a pot. Mine cost 10 bucks and is still going after 11 years; I put it outside in the summer and bring it in for the winter and there are fresh bay leaves anytime. It's quite a different flavour from the dried.

serves 4 or 6

18 small/medium	potatoes, skin on
24	fresh bay leaves, ripped into same-sized pieces
2 Tbsp (25 mL)	butter
2 Tbsp (25 mL)	olive oil
4 or 5 large cloves	garlic, peeled and crushed
to taste	sea salt
to taste	black pepper

Preheat the oven to 375°F (190°C).

Having prepared the potatoes (sliced, but not all the way through, so they hold together at the bottom) insert a piece of bay leaf into each of the slits. Your call as to how bay-ey you're going to want the taste; put 2 or 3 into each potato, or more.

Melt the butter and oil in a roasting pan. Stir in the garlic, heat through, and add the potatoes in a single layer. Move them about for a few minutes, to take on some colour. Season with sea salt and pepper. Put the pan in the oven and roast for 30 minutes, until the potatoes are tender and golden brown.

WINE PAIRINGS

iced Kirsberry [DK]

double iced aquavit [DK]

MUSIC TO COOK WITH

Per Henrik Wallin:
Deep in a Dream
[DRAGON OF SWEDEN]

Anne Sofie von Otter:
Swedish Songs [DGG]

What? A pizza without tomato sauce? Right, and one of my favourite pizzas it is, too. In lieu of other starch, this makes a great side dish for just about anything, and a satisfying dark-night-of-the-soul snack after you've watched an old Ingmar Bergman repeat on the late show. On the matter of dough, you can always make your own, but there are so many Italian bakeries near where I live I usually buy it and keep some around in the freezer for emergencies.

Potato & Rosemary-Garlic Pizza

serves 2

1 lb (500 g)	potatoes, peeled and thinly sliced
2 Tbsp (25 mL)	extra virgin olive oil (go ahead, use the truffled stuff you got for Christmas)
6 or 8 cloves	garlic, peeled and crushed
3 or 4 sprigs	fresh rosemary, leaves stripped from the stems
1 tsp (5 mL)	*fleur de sel* or similar coarse sea salt
2 portions	fresh-rolled pizza dough (or pre-made crusts)
1 cup (250 mL)	fontina cheese, cut in small cubes (or use other favourite meltable cheese)

WINE PAIRINGS

Fraoch Heather Ale [SC]

A Notre Terre Organic
Red Wine [CA]

Monty Python's
Holy Grail [Ale] [UK]

Wild Gaucho Torrontes [AG]

MUSIC TO COOK WITH

Yo-Yo Ma: *Silk Road Project*
[SONY]

Preheat the oven to 450°F (230°C). Put two 10-inch (25-cm) baking trays in the preheated oven until they're good and hot.

Combine the potato slices, oil, garlic, rosemary and salt in a bowl and toss well to coat evenly.

Put the rolled dough (or pre-made crusts) on the hot trays. Spread the potato mixture over both pizzas and sprinkle on more oil if you like. Bake for 10 minutes.

Take the pizzas out and sprinkle on the cheese cubes. Bake another 5–10 minutes, until the cheese is well melted and starts to brown and the whole pizza is lightly golden with a crisp crust.

Serve as hot as you can stand it. Beer is good.

Here's another variation on the cured meat-nuts-Brussels sprouts combination. This is actually a Lucy Waverman recipe that Emily Lonie of Kanata, Ontario, discovered in an LCBO *Food and Drink* magazine. It's become a family favourite, and Andrew says that even people who can't stand Brussels sprouts enjoy them this way.

… Andrew says that even people who can't stand Brussels sprouts enjoy them this way.

Shredded Brussels Sprouts with Pine Nuts & Prosciutto

1½ lb (750 g)	Brussels sprouts
¼ cup (50 mL)	olive oil
6 slices	prosciutto, chopped
¾ cup (175 mL)	pine nuts
to taste	salt and freshly ground pepper

Remove the root ends and cores from the Brussels sprouts; cut them in half and thinly slice.

Heat the oil in a skillet on medium-high heat. Add the prosciutto and sauté until it begins to crisp. Add the sprouts and sauté for 3 minutes. Cover the pan and cook 2 minutes longer, or until the sprouts are crisp-tender.

Toss in the pine nuts, sauté for 1 minute and season with salt and pepper.

serves 8

WINE PAIRINGS

African Terroir Tribal
Sauvignon Blanc/Colombard
[SA]

MUSIC TO COOK WITH

Amsterdam Loeki Stardust
Quartet: *Fugue Around the Clock*
[CHANNEL CROSSING]

Here's how I do
mine, I said.
I do mine like this,
said Mr. R. Maybe
there's a cookbook
in this, I said.

It may even have been the first glimmering of this cookbook: one afternoon in Scenic Subterranean Studio 20, Mr. Rowledge and I were discussing some Weighty Issues. We often do, when there's a long piece of music playing—Mahler in the maelstrom of pre-relativistic Europe—comparative mileage (who do you know says kilometrage?) of pick-up trucks, Rick Mercer's chances in the next election or mostly, food. This afternoon it was Brussels sprouts and how we both loved ours and hated

The Brussels Sprouts Dialogues

WINE PAIRINGS

Danzante Pinot Grigio [CA/IT]

MUSIC TO COOK WITH

Winnipeg Symphony:
Klezmer Suite [CBC]

Finjan: *Crossing Selkirk Avenue*
[FAT UNCLE]

MINE

a little	olive oil (more if you use the lean prosciutto)
½ lb (250 g)	pancetta or prosciutto (Italian bacon or ham), diced
1 lb (500 g) small	Brussels sprouts, carefully hand-selected (sproutenauslese), all outer leaves trimmed off, and scored on the bottom (someone told me years ago to put a little x there and I've no idea what would happen if you don't but I've always done it and see no reason to stop now)
2 Tbsp (25 mL)	whole black peppercorns (there's no such thing as too much)
1 Tbsp (15 mL)	ground pecans (some bakery sections stock it, it's virtually powder, but crushed pecans, further pounded with mortar and pestle, work)
a hint	truffle oil

Heat the olive oil on medium, in an iron or other heavy pan. Cook the pancetta or prosciutto dice till starting to crisp. Set aside.

Depending on the amount of fat in the pan, drain some off, or not. Add the prepared whole sprouts and the peppercorns to the pan and slow cook till the outsides of the sprouts start to blacken; stir often so it happens all over. Return the pancetta/prosciutto to the pan and heat through. Sprinkle on the pecan powder and stir to coat all the sprouts. Take off the heat, drizzle a little truffle oil on top and serve with *fleur de sel* (kosher salt's fine if you can't get your hands on any of the expensive stuff) on the side, right out of the pan. With bread.

everyone else's—over-boiled, mega-mushed, barely-green, Paleozoic-tasting glop. Here's how I do mine, I said. I do mine like this, said Mr. R. Maybe there's a cookbook in this, I said. Well, we're coming up to our 20th anniversary … Wow, I thought, most marriages don't last that long anymore. Mine's first because, well, I did all the typing. It's called inputting now, isn't it?

THE ROWLEDGE VERSION

3 Tbsp (45 mL)	butter or bacon fat, for sautéing (more if the pan is larger than 9 inches (23 cm))
1 lb (500 g)	Brussels sprouts, trimmed, scored (see, he does it too!)
½ cup (125 mL)	Riesling or other naturally sweet table wine
16	whole cloves
pinches	cumin, nutmeg, allspice; one, two or all, to taste
	salt if needed

Just below medium heat in a big frying pan, heat the fat and slow cook the sprouts for 15 minutes, uncovered. The idea is not to caramelize them, but cook them through. Shake the pan to coat the sprouts every couple of minutes, otherwise they will burn.

Add the wine and spices, bring to a slow simmer for 10 more minutes, shaking the pan occasionally to coat the sprouts. It's really more like steaming than simmering. Most of the alcohol will evaporate and the wine's sweetness will seep into the sprouts. Lift sprouts out of the pan with a slotted spoon, taste for salt and serve.

WINE PAIRINGS

Gehringer Brothers
Ehrenfelser [BC]

MUSIC TO COOK WITH

Marjan Mozetich:
Affairs of the Heart [CBC]

The universal
prejudice against
Brussels sprouts …

The universal prejudice against Brussels sprouts somehow dictates that most recipes for these *petits choux* claim to appeal even to those who hate them—in this case, the offspring of David Poole of Peterborough, Ontario. He says, "The quantities are a bit rough since it's a recipe that you need to eyeball: it depends on the type of pan, the type of stove, the size of the sprouts, and probably the phases of the moon, for all I know. It's hard to ruin, but you have to be willing to add more butter or liquid if it appears necessary." Chopped, toasted hazelnuts or pecans are fine substitutes for pine nuts. Thyme, lavender or marjoram can all be used instead of sage.

Brussels Sprouts with Pine Nuts & Sage Cream

**serves 4–6
as a side dish**

2 Tbsp (30 g)	butter (or more)
¼ cup (50 mL)	pine nuts
1 large	shallot, minced
1 lb (500 g)	Brussels sprouts, trimmed and halved lengthwise
½ cup (125 mL)	chicken or vegetable stock (or more)
¼ cup (50 mL)	heavy or whipping cream
1 Tbsp (15 mL)	fresh sage, finely chopped (or 1 tsp/5 mL dried sage, crumbled)
to taste	salt and pepper

WINE PAIRINGS

Wilhelm Kraemer
Rheinhessen Liebfraumilch
[GY]

MUSIC TO COOK WITH

Bonzo Dog Band: *Best of* [RHINO]

In a large, non-stick frying pan, melt 1 Tbsp (15 mL) of the butter over medium heat and sauté the pine nuts until golden, about 3–5 minutes. Transfer to a small bowl and set aside.

In the same frying pan, melt the remaining 1 Tbsp (15 mL) butter over medium heat and cook the minced shallot until it begins to soften, about 1 minute. Add the Brussels sprouts and cook, stirring occasionally, until the sprouts are browned on all sides, about 2 to 3 minutes. (Add more butter if necessary.)

Add the stock, reduce the heat to low, cover and simmer until the sprouts are tender and the stock is reduced to about 1 Tbsp (15 mL), about 5–7 minutes. (Keep an eye on the liquid in the pan. If the stock is absorbed and/or evaporates too quickly, add a little more. If the sprouts are tender but too much liquid remains, take the lid off for a while.)

Uncover the pan and add the cream and the sage. Raise the heat until the cream simmers and toss the sprouts in the cream until the cream thickens a bit and the sprouts are completely coated, about 3 minutes.

Season with salt and pepper to taste, sprinkle with the pine nuts, and serve immediately.

Michael Wallack sent this in from St. John's, Newfoundland. His mother was born in Italy. This was one of her standard dishes. You can't beat the old standards.

Escarole & Beans

⅓ cup (75 mL)	olive oil
7 medium cloves	garlic, peeled, large ones halved
one 14-oz (398-mL) can	plum tomatoes
2 cups (500 mL)	cooked navy or cannellini beans
3 cups (750 mL)	water
1 tsp (5 mL)	salt, or to taste
2 lb (1 kg)	escarole or curly endive, washed and trimmed
to taste	freshly grated Romano cheese
to taste	freshly ground pepper

Heat the oil in a frying pan and sauté the garlic until medium brown. Add the tomatoes and cook over medium heat for 5 minutes. Add the cooked beans, water, salt and escarole. Cover the pan and wilt the escarole.

Uncover and cook about 30 minutes, or until the escarole reaches the desired degree of doneness. Midway into the cooking process, mash the browned garlic into the cooking liquid.

Top with grated Romano and black pepper to taste. Provide good-quality Italian or French bread for dipping.

Michael Wallack sent this in from St. John's, Newfoundland.

Serves 6 as a first course, 4 as a main dish

WINE PAIRINGS

Robertson Sauvignon Blanc [SA]

MUSIC TO COOK WITH

Kremerata Baltica: *Happy Birthday* [NONESUCH]

Patrick Vallely
got this potato
procedure in
Chelm in
eastern Poland.

Patrick Vallely got this potato procedure in Chelm in eastern Poland. Because Patrick believes there's no such thing as too much garlic or too much chili, you'll see the exhortation "or more" beside his conservative recommendations in the ingredient list.

Freedom Fries (just another word for no pounds left to lose)

serves as many as 6, but
4 or fewer for true
satisfaction

WINE PAIRINGS

Wyborowa
Buffalo Grass Vodka [PL]

Trapiche Sauvignon
Blanc/Semillon [AG]

MUSIC TO COOK WITH

Mike Batt: *The Aspidistra Suite*
[EMI]

Moby: *Play* [V2]

6	healthy starchy potatoes (washed, but not peeled)
about ¼ cup (50 mL)	good olive oil
1 tsp (5 mL)	cumin seeds
1 tsp (5 mL)	mustard seeds
6 (or more) cloves	garlic, crushed
½ tsp (or more)	chili powder
1 tsp (5 mL)	turmeric powder
½ Tbsp (7 mL)	salt
	fresh lemon juice, fresh dill, and fresh marjoram; are all optional

Cut the potatoes lengthwise, french-fry fashion.

Heat the oil in a heavy skillet or wok over high-medium heat. Add the cumin and mustard seeds. When they begin to pop add the crushed garlic. Keep stirring until the garlic is cooked. Add the chili, turmeric and salt. Stir well. (Patrick sometimes adds a little lemon juice at this stage).

Add the potatoes and mix well until the potatoes are all covered with the ingredients. Reduce the heat somewhat. Place a cover on the pot and cook for a few minutes. Then stir again, and continue the covered cooking until everything is done. Cooking takes about 20 minutes, sometimes a little longer, depending on the age and type of potato, but don't overcook. Remember to stir every few minutes to prevent sticking or burning.

"Depending on the mood I'm in, I toss a little freshly chopped dill or marjoram on the fries before serving," says Patrick.

Dawn Parker of Sherwood Park, Alberta, says that this attractive dish is versatile enough to go with turkey, chicken, pork or beef. Probably even with fish or seafood, although she hasn't tried it. The amount of red pepper depends on whether you're going for a mixed-vegetable look or something more distinctly asparagus.

... this attractive dish is versatile enough to go with turkey, chicken, pork or beef.

Festive Asparagus

1 large bunch	fresh asparagus
2 Tbsp (25 mL)	peanut oil
2 tsp (10 mL)	finely chopped fresh ginger
1 clove	garlic, minced
¼–½ tsp (1–2 mL)	crushed red pepper flakes
½ cup (125 mL)	coarsely chopped toasted pecans
¾ cup (175 mL)	red pepper cut into strips
2 Tbsp (25 mL)	soy sauce
2 Tbsp (25 mL)	dry sherry
½ tsp (2 mL)	sugar
1 tsp (5 mL)	cornstarch, dissolved in cold water (optional)

Wash and trim the asparagus and slice on the diagonal, making long, thin slices.

Heat the oil in a skillet or wok. Stir-fry the asparagus until tender-crisp, about 2 minutes, and remove with a slotted spoon.

Add the ginger, garlic and pepper flakes to the skillet. Stir in the pecans and red pepper. Cook for 1 minute. Add the soy sauce, sherry, sugar and cornstarch mixture, if desired. Toss in the asparagus and heat through. Serve immediately.

serves 6

WINE PAIRINGS

Tio Pepe [SP]

Pol Roger Rosé Champagne [FR]

MUSIC TO COOK WITH

Mariam Matossian:
Far From Home [MAM]

chapter nine

stews

Baeckaoffa 150

Charentais Veal Stew 152

Orange Beef Stew 153

The DiscDrive Tends-to-Get-Spicy Veggie Chili 154

TGV Paella 156

A Canadian Choucroute 158

Tagine of Beef with Prunes & Almonds 160

Old-Fashioned Chicken & Corn Stew 162

Moroccan Chicken Stew 163

This is the classic
multi-meat baked
stew of Alsace ...

This is the classic multi-meat baked stew of Alsace—a hale and hearty pot full of food that fulfils various functions: keeping the chill away, sticking to your ribs, providing good leftovers for later in the week. Like most of the world's good stews, it's pretty easy to assemble and quantities are adjustable. A lidded, earthenware pan works classically well, but a Dutch oven, stewpot or battered old Le Creuset is just fine.

Baeckaoffa

could feed 4, in a pinch
Marinates overnight.

Pfaffenheim Pinot Noir [FR]

Wolfberger Pinot Noir
"Noak Cuvée" [FR]

Pierre Sparr "Symphonie" [FR]

Orlando Consort:
Food, Wine & Song
[HARMONIA MUNDI]

1 lb (500 g)	boneless pork loin or shoulder
1 lb (500 g)	boneless lamb shoulder
1 lb (500 g)	boneless beef chuck
2	trotters (pigs' feet), optional
to taste	salt and pepper
3–4 cloves	garlic, crushed
1	bouquet garni, or quantities to taste of parsley, thyme, bay leaf, marjoram, savory
3 or 4 Tbsp (45–60 mL)	finely diced celery root, optional
1 bottle (more or less)	Tokay d'Alsace or Pinot Blanc
bit	butter or oil
2½ lb (1.2 kg)	potatoes, peeled and sliced about ¼ inch (5 mm) thick
½ lb (250 g)	onions, chopped
3 small	leeks, mostly white part, a little of the green, sliced

Cut all the meat into bite-size pieces and put in a big marinating bowl; add the pigs' feet, if using. Combine the salt, pepper, garlic, herbs and celery root (if using). Pour in half of the bottle of white wine. Cover with a lid or cling wrap and leave overnight in refrigerator or cool place.

Preheat the oven to 400°F (200°C).

Put a bit of butter or oil in a big ovenproof casserole. Pigs' feet go on the bottom, covered with a layer of potatoes, handful of onions and scattering of leeks. Lift the remaining meats out of the marinade and put on top of this layer. Add the remaining potatoes, onions and leeks. Pour on the marinade and add enough wine to just cover. Put a layer of foil over the dish and then a tight lid on top of that. Bake in the centre of the oven for 1 hour.

Lower the heat to 350°F (180°C) and bake another 1½ hours, till the meats are tender to the point of falling apart and the potatoes are cooked but still a little bit firm. Serve straight out of the pan with a green salad and crusty bread. The Alsatians say that, in order to justify the name, which just means "bakers' oven," the dish really ought to be done in the clay pot, in the village bakery's big oven.

This is a traditional dish from the heart of Cognac country …

This is a traditional dish from the heart of Cognac country, made with the region's other unique product, a *mistelle* called Pineau des Charentes. A *mistelle* is made from unfermented grape juice that goes through *mutage*, the addition of alcohol to stop the fermenting process, which leaves it fairly sweet and quite potent—15 to 20 percent alcohol. Pineau can be both aperitif and dessert companion; it combines surprisingly well with chilled oysters and other shellfish, and with melon or similar fruit.

Charentais Veal Stew

serves 4–6

It loves Roquefort and dry goat cheese after a meal and, if you add two parts Pineau to one part Cognac and serve it on the rocks, you've got a drink the locals call *Le Sauvage*. This being prime beef country, the favourite local stew goes like this:

2 lb (1 kg)	boneless veal, stew-cubed
for dredging	all-purpose flour
4 Tbsp (60 mL)	butter
4 Tbsp (60 mL)	grape seed oil (or olive oil)
2 big	onions, chopped
1 cup (250 mL)	Pineau des Charentes
2 lb (1 kg)	ripe tomatoes, chopped, or a couple cans Italian diced tomatoes, drained
2 large	carrots, sliced
1 or 2	bouquets garnis
2 or 3 cloves	garlic, minced
1	lemon, grated zest of (more or less)
1 bunch	parsley, chopped
to taste	salt and white pepper
	a mess of mashed potatoes to eat with it

Dredge the veal in flour and brown in the mix of butter and oil. Add the onions and cook until golden. Add the Pineau and scrape up the good bits from the bottom of the pan. Add everything else except the mashed potatoes and put the lid on. Simmer gently for 1 hour.

Taste for seasoning. Pour the stew out onto a deep, well-heated serving platter. Sprinkle with more parsley if you want, and circle the stew with a ring of mashed potatoes. Serve a light, fruity Beaujolais-style wine alongside. Save some Pineau for dessert.

WINE PAIRINGS

Marnier-Lapostolle
Pineau des Charentes [FR]

Georges Duboeuf Fleuri [FR]

MUSIC TO COOK WITH

Anouar Brahem:
Le pas du chat noir [ECM]

Lois Vatcher of Duncan, British Columbia, suggests green beans and garlic mashed potatoes with this. I think we need to invent a slightly more glamorous name for such a tasty dish.

Lois Vatcher … suggests green beans and garlic mashed potatoes with this.

Orange Beef Stew

2 Tbsp (25 mL)	vegetable oil (or more)
2 lb (1 kg)	beef for stew, cut in 2-inch (5-cm) cubes (a blade or cross-rib roast is a good choice for stew—trim and cube, reserving any extra to freeze and stew later)
½ tsp (2 mL)	salt
¼ tsp (1 mL)	pepper
1 medium	onion, sliced
14-oz (398-mL) can	tomatoes
1 cup (250 mL)	orange juice
1 Tbsp (15 mL)	red wine vinegar
1 clove	garlic, minced
1 tsp (5 mL)	dried rosemary
1	bay leaf
⅔ cup (150 mL)	sliced pitted black olives (optional)

Heat the oil in a large, wide saucepan over medium-high heat. Brown the beef on all sides, working in batches, adding more oil if needed. Transfer to a 2-quart (2-L) casserole dish. Sprinkle with salt and pepper.

Preheat the oven to 350°F (180°C).

Add the onion to the pan, stirring and scraping the brown bits from the bottom for about 3 minutes. Chop the tomatoes and add with their juice, orange juice and remaining ingredients, except the olives. Simmer, stirring, for 3–4 minutes. Pour over the meat.

Bake the casserole, covered, for 2 hours, or until the meat is tender. Add the olives (if using) and bake, uncovered, for 15 minutes.

Best enjoyed the day after preparation. To reheat, bake covered in a 350°F (180°C) oven for about 45 minutes, or until hot.

serves 4 to 6

WINE PAIRINGS

a big Morio Muscat from Germany

or

a sweet-edged Rosé with attitude from Spain

MUSIC TO COOK WITH

Steve Dawson:
We Belong to the Gold Coast
[BLACK HEN]

Triology:
Around the World in 77 Minutes
[EXTRAPLATTE]

This is one
of the first recipes
I muttered about
on the air …

This is one of the first recipes I muttered about on the air, semi-improvising it around a base of something I'd done a week earlier. People phoned (nobody was emailing in those days; this IS the 20th anniversary year of the show, after all) and dropped notes with additions and suggestions, and finally I got around to assembling it in this configuration. It's been satisfying ever since.

The DiscDrive Tends-to-Get-Spicy Veggie Chili

serves 6–8, easily
Requires overnight
in the fridge.

WINE PAIRINGS

Chateau Pech-Latt Domaine
de L'Olivette [FR]
(organic)
(midprice and very nice)

Casa La Luna Verdejo-Viana
[SP] (really cheap!)

MUSIC TO COOK WITH

Doug Cox: *Canadian Borderline*
[MALAHAT MOUNTAIN]

Lyle Lovett:
Step Inside this House [MCA]

Gerhard Meinl's Tuba Sextet
[ANGEL]

for sautéing	vegetable oil
3 medium	onions, chopped
4 or 5 stalks	celery, diced
¼ cup (50 mL)	garlic, minced
4 or 5	carrots, diced
2 cups (500 mL) (packed)	chopped cabbage
½ lb (250 g)	mushrooms, chopped
2 medium	red peppers, seeded and chopped
2 medium	green peppers, seeded and chopped
¼ cup (50 mL)	good-quality chili powder (more or less)
1 Tbsp (15 mL)	unsweetened cocoa powder
1 Tbsp (15 mL)	sugar
1 Tbsp (15 mL)	cumin seeds
1 Tbsp (15 mL)	oregano, plus ½ Tbsp for later
2 tsp (10 mL)	fennel seeds
1 tsp (5 mL)	thyme
½ tsp (2 mL)	cayenne, more or less
½ tsp (2 mL)	cinnamon
1 Tbsp (15 mL)	salt
1 tsp (5 mL)	ground black pepper, more or less
two 14-oz (398-mL) cans	Italian diced tomatoes

4 cups (1 L)	cold water
one 28-oz (798-mL) can	red kidney beans, drained and rinsed
4 Tbsp (60 mL)	low-salt soy sauce
4 Tbsp (60 mL)	dry sherry
1 tsp (5 mL)	hot pepper sauce, more or less, as is the call for all spices and herbs
for garnish	sour cream, chopped green onions and shredded cheddar cheese

In a big casserole, heat enough oil over medium heat to accommodate all the vegetables. Add the onions and celery and sauté till onions are translucent (6–8 minutes). Add the garlic and cook for 1 minute. Add the carrots, cabbage and mushrooms and cook till tender (10 minutes); stir while cooking. Add the red and green peppers and cook till soft (6–8 minutes).

Stir in the chili powder, cocoa, sugar, cumin, 1 Tbsp (15 mL) of the oregano, fennel seeds, thyme, cayenne, cinnamon, salt and half the black pepper. Stir in the tomatoes with their liquid. Add cold water. Bring everything to a slow boil and simmer on low, stirring now and then, till things start to get thick and rich tasting.

Start tasting after an hour or so, and cook as long as 2 hours if needed. Add the canned beans and remove from heat. Let cool to room temperature; cover and refrigerate overnight.

Reheat the chili on low. Add the remaining oregano and pepper. When heated through, remove from the heat and stir in the soy sauce, sherry and pepper sauce, tasting as you go.

Serve in big bowls topped with sour cream, green onion and cheddar. Plenty of bread alongside, and something cold and biting like true cider or beer (La Messagere). Continues to get better the next day and the day after that; freezes okay, but the beans get mushy upon reheating.

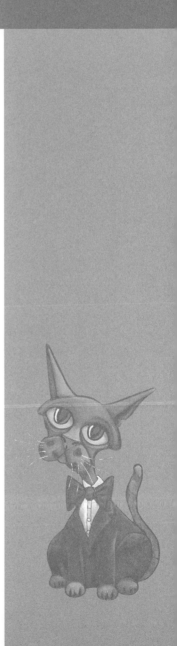

Having eaten plenty of paellas in places likely and un- (Spain, Alabama, Langley, Lebanon, Medicine Hat, Whitehorse), I was seized with the urge to make my own one day. Despite the fact that I found myself in a spot with limited options for components, there were some wine chorizos in the refrigerator and black olives in the pantry. The red peppers weren't too wrinkled, a couple of packets of Greek saffron loitered in the back of the cupboard from a long-ago excursion, and in lieu of clams there were fresh oysters and prawns with the ubiquitous "previously frozen" sticker at the little local market. What's more, there was cold dry sherry in the fridge and an interesting selection of Spanish table wines, red and white, demanding to be let out of the bottle.

> Having eaten plenty of paellas … I was seized with the urge to make my own one day.

TGV Paella

serves 4

WINE PAIRINGS

Torres Catalunya Reserve [SP]

Bodegas Nekeas Rosado [SP]

Rueda Verdejo Esperanza [SP]

MUSIC TO COOK WITH

Don Byron: *Plays the Music of Mickey Katz* [ELEKTRA/NONESUCH]

Mannheim Steamroller: *Fresh Aire I–V* [AMERICAN GRAMAPHONE]

2 Tbsp (25 mL)	olive oil
2 large	spicy sausages (I used wine chorizos)
4 medium	chicken pieces
1 medium	red pepper, cored, seeded, chunked
1 cup (250 mL)	chopped onion
3 cloves	garlic, minced
to taste	hot red chili flakes
to taste	saffron, or as available, up to 1 tsp (5 mL) of loose threads
2 medium	bay leaves
½ tsp (2 mL)	dried thyme, more or less
one 14-oz (398-mL) can	Italian diced tomatoes and their liquid
1½ cups (375 mL)	rice (I like arborio)
1 cup (250 mL)	water
to taste	salt and pepper
one 8-oz (227-g) tub	fresh shucked oysters
12	fresh prawns (or previously frozen and thawed and drained) with the tails on
lots of	fresh parsley, chopped
	shots of iced sherry for the cook

"But paella takes so long," said one of the designated eaters. I'd thought so too, but then I'd never made one before, and when I laid the puzzle pieces out on the counter it became clear that the whole exercise ought to be able to come together in less than an hour, leaving just enough time to taste through the wines before dinner. After all, what's happening here? Cook some sausage and chicken, add a few veggies and herbs, rice and tomatoes, available seafood; cover and simmer and done like dinner. It was essayed and it was excellent and, so far as I can recall, it went like this:

Heat the oil in a big pan; if you picked up one of those paella pans in Spain, now is its moment. Cut the sausages into thin slices and cook in the hot oil, turning often, for about 7 minutes. Add the chicken pieces and cook with the sausage till the chicken starts to brown, another 6 or 7 minutes, turning often. Cook everything together another 10 minutes.

While the meats are cooking, prep the veggies and garlic and throw those in the pan. Stir in the chili flakes, saffron, bay leaves and thyme. Add the tomatoes, rice, water, salt and pepper. Put a tight lid on and cook for 15 minutes.

Rinse and drain the oysters. Peel and devein the prawns, leaving the tails on for easier grabbing. When the rice is cooked but still firm, add the oysters to the rice and meat mix, cover the pot again and cook 4 minutes more. Add the prawns and cook another 2 minutes. Do the math: total time is about 50 minutes from the time you get the oil hot. That's not bad.

Sprinkle with parsley and serve with lots of bread and some chilled greens dressed with Spanish extra virgin olive oil and wine vinegar. Plenty of iced sherry, to start, and even all the way through the meal, or any one of half a dozen Spanish reds or whites.

The bland little
name they give it at
home in Alsace ...
hardly does this
magnificent
dish justice.

The bland little name they give it at home in Alsace—*choucroute garni,* garnished sauerkraut—hardly does this magnificent dish justice. It's a stew for all seasons, but especially pleasant in the fall and winter. You can't move 10 feet in Alsace without running into someone or someplace cooking and serving it. From multi-Michelin-starred world-famous restaurants to little back-street *winstuben,* everyone has a take on it. So do we—a big, time-consuming fancy one. All and any of it is adjustable, changeable, entirely to your palate, larder, time-frame.

A Canadian Choucroute

serves 6 or more

WINE PAIRINGS

Alsatian:Kronenbourg Beer [FR]

Trimbach Pinot Blanc [FR]

Ostertag Gewürztraminer [FR]

eaux-de-vie:
houx, alisier, mirabelle [FR]

MUSIC TO COOK WITH

Ben Heppner: *Songs of Strauss*
[CBC]

Isabel Bayrakdarian: *Cleopatra*
[CBC]

Taxi Chain: *James Brown Ate my
Bag-Pipes (Smarten Up)*
[NORTHERN BLUES MUSIC]

4–5 lb (2–2.2 kg)	top-grade sauerkraut
½ lb (250 g)	lean smoked bacon, julienned
3 large	onions, chopped
5–6 cloves	garlic, peeled, crushed
1 tsp (5 mL)	cumin seeds, or more to taste
10–12	juniper berries, bruised with the flat of a knife
3–4	whole cloves
2 large	bay leaves
2–3 sprigs	fresh thyme (or ½–¾ tsp/2–4 mL dry, crumbled)
1 tsp (5 mL) each	salt and black pepper, or to taste
5 or more	different sausages, cut into equal-sized pieces or left whole
½–¾-inch (1–2-cm)	smoked pork loin chops (Kassler), 1 per guest
1 lb (500 g)	good meaty bacon, in 1 piece
¾ lb (375 g)	dried pears, julienned
2 cups (500 mL)	not-too-dry white wine of the region (Riesling or Gewürztraminer)
1–2 cups (250–500 mL)	chicken or veal stock
7–8 Tbsp (105–120 mL)	Poire William or kirsch (you can use gin if you don't want to spring for a costly bottle of the famous eau-de-vie)
for garnish	smoked goose breast
for garnish	Quebec fresh foie gras (as much as you can afford)

Good sauerkraut is the principal ingredient and finding one to suit your taste can be a major quest. Lots of different mustards are required for the meats, which have to include, for my money, five or six different types of sausages, smoked pork loin, hams, bacons, the lot. Let's do the production number first:

Soak the sauerkraut for 20 minutes in cold water; drain, rinse, squeeze as dry as you can get it. Set aside.

In a big pan, cook the bacon till semi-crisp. Pour off some of the fat. Put the onions and garlic in the fat and cook, covered, over low heat, for 15 minutes.

Add the onions and garlic to the sauerkraut. Stir in the cumin, juniper berries, cloves, bay leaves, thyme, salt and pepper and mix well.

Preheat the oven to 350°F (180°C).

Spread a 1-inch (2.5-cm) layer of sauerkraut on the bottom of a lidded pot or Dutch oven big enough to eventually hold everything. Add a layer of sausages/meats and throw in some dried pears. More sauerkraut and keep layering till everything is in the pot and you can still get the lid on. Pour in the wine and stock and stir as much as possible.

Bring to a boil over medium-high heat on top of the stove. Cover the pot and put it in the oven. Cook for 30–45 minutes. Start checking for doneness after 30; don't overcook. Bring it out, add Poire William or kirsch (or gin) and maybe more wine if it looks too dry; return to the oven for another 10 minutes.

Allow to cool for a few minutes, then put the sauerkraut and meats into individual bowls. Put thinly sliced smoked goose breast and slices of foie gras on top for garnish. Or mound the whole lot on a heated serving platter, surround with boiled potatoes and tuck in.

MORE WINE PAIRINGS

Domestic: shot of Alberta Springs rye

Labatt's 50 in the quart bottle ("I said quart, yes!")

Unibroue "Trois Pistoles" [QC]

Phillips Maple Cream Ale [BC]

Konzelmann "Grand Reserve" Riesling [ON]

Sumac Ridge Gewürztraminer "Private Reserve" [BC]

Okanagan Spirits Hyslop Crab Apple eau de vie [BC]

... a Moroccan recipe that's definitely worth the effort ...

David W. Hobill of Calgary offers a Moroccan recipe that's definitely worth the effort and time it takes to make. He's tapped into the treasures assembled under the term "tagine."

Tagine of Beef with Prunes & Almonds

serves 4, more if it's served with couscous

WINE PAIRINGS

Moroccan Alicante-Bouschet, if you can find some, and real-leaf mint tea

Bouchard-Finlayson Pinot Noir [SA]

MUSIC TO COOK WITH

Jacques Loussier Trio: *Debussy* [TELARC]

2½–3 lb (1.25–1.5 kg)	beef, cut into 1½-inch (4-cm) cubes
2 large	Spanish onions, peeled and coarsely grated
2 Tbsp (25 mL)	olive oil
1 tsp (5 mL)	salt
½ tsp (2 mL)	freshly ground pepper
1 tsp (5 mL)	cinnamon
½ tsp (2 mL)	powdered saffron
¼ tsp (1 mL)	powdered ginger
½ cup (125 mL)	butter
2 cups (500 mL)	dried prunes
1 strip	lemon peel
2–3 short sticks	cinnamon
4 Tbsp (60 mL)	sugar
¾ cup (175 mL)	blanched almonds, sautéed in butter
for garnish	sprigs of fresh mint or watercress

Put the beef cubes, onions, olive oil, salt, pepper, cinnamon, saffron and ginger into a large bowl. Mix well. Rub the aromatics into each piece of meat with your fingers. If you have time, let this marinate for a couple of hours.

When ready to cook, transfer the prepared meat into a thick-bottomed flame-proof casserole (or a tagine, if in Morocco). Add the butter and enough water to just cover the meat. Cook over medium heat, covered, until the meat is tender, 45–75 minutes.

While the meat is cooking, put the prunes in a saucepan, cover with boiling water and allow to stand for 20–30 minutes. Drain the water. Add to the prunes 2 ladles of sauce from the casserole and skim off the fat. Add the lemon peel, cinnamon sticks and half the sugar. Cook the prunes in the sauce for 20 minutes (or until prunes are soft and swollen).

Add the remaining sugar to the casserole and stir well.

To serve: transfer the meat to a heated serving dish and garnish with the prunes and their sauce. Reduce the sauce remaining in the casserole to half its original volume using high heat, then pour over the meat and prunes. Sprinkle with sautéed almonds and garnish with greens. Serve immediately.

Here's a
never-fail
stew ...

Here's a never-fail stew from Jim Miller of Richmond, British Columbia. It takes about 45 minutes to prepare. That's practically what I call a zipstew.

Old-Fashioned Chicken & Corn Stew

serves 6

WINE PAIRINGS

Nk'Mip Cellars
"Qwam Qwmt" Merlot [BC]

Pelee Island
"Vinedresser" Merlot [ON]

2 lb (1 kg)	skinless boneless chicken breasts and thighs, cut into 2-inch (5-cm) pieces
to taste	salt and pepper
2 Tbsp (25 mL)	unsalted butter
1 Tbsp (15 mL)	vegetable oil
1 large	onion, halved lengthwise, then cut lengthwise into ¼-inch (5-mm) slices
1 clove	garlic, minced
2 tsp (10 mL)	chopped fresh thyme
2 Tbsp (25 mL)	all-purpose flour
1¾ cups (425 mL)	low-sodium chicken broth (one 14-oz/398-mL can)
¾ cup (175 mL)	water
1 lb (500 g)	boiling potatoes, peeled and cut into 1-inch (2.5-cm) pieces
2 ears	fresh or frozen corn, cut crosswise into 1-inch (2.5-cm) pieces (no need to thaw frozen corn)
¼ cup (50 mL)	heavy or whipping cream
to taste	salt and pepper

MUSIC TO COOK WITH

Tafelmusik: *Le Mozart Noir* [CBC]

Rolling Stones: *Aftermath* [ABKCO]

Pat the chicken dry and season with salt and pepper.

Heat the butter and oil in a wide, heavy pot over moderately high heat until foam subsides, then lightly brown the chicken in 2 batches, turning over occasionally with tongs. Transfer the browned chicken to a bowl using tongs.

Add the onion, garlic, and 1 tsp (5 mL) of the thyme to the pot and sauté, stirring occasionally, until softened, 4–5 minutes. Add the flour and cook, stirring, for 1 minute. Whisk in the broth and water and bring to a boil.

Add the potatoes and corn to the onion mixture, then cover and simmer over moderate heat, about 10 minutes. Stir in the chicken and cream, then simmer, covered, until chicken is just cooked through and potatoes are tender, 5–10 minutes. Season stew with salt and pepper and sprinkle with the remaining thyme.

By all means, take us to the casbah. Toronto's Christina Holmes homed in on the DiscDrivers' collective weakness for the flavours of North Africa.

By all means, take us to the casbah.

Moroccan Chicken Stew

2	boneless chicken breasts
1 Tbsp (15 mL)	olive oil
1	red onion, quartered lengthwise, sliced crosswise
2 cloves	garlic, finely chopped
1 tsp (5 mL)	ground cinnamon
1 tsp (5 mL)	ground ginger
¼ tsp (1 mL)	ground cumin
¼ tsp (1 mL)	cayenne pepper
one 28-oz (796-mL) can	diced tomatoes
¼ cup (50 mL)	honey
1½ tsp (7 mL)	salt
2	green peppers, cut in ½-inch (1-cm) squares
⅓ cup (75 mL)	raisins
one 14-oz (398-mL) can	chickpeas, rinsed and drained
for serving	brown rice
for garnish	almonds

serves 4

WINE PAIRINGS

ditto about the Moroccan plonk

De Wetshof Lesca Chardonnay [SA]

De Wetshof Pinot Noir [SA]

Danzante Sangiovese [CA/IT]

MUSIC TO COOK WITH

Monty Alexander: *Stir it up/The Music of Bob Marley* [TELARC]

Loretto Reid Band: *From the Inside Out* [RETA CEOL]

Slice the chicken into bite-size pieces. Heat the oil in a non-stick pan, add the chicken and brown. Transfer to a plate.

Sauté the onion and garlic in the same pan for about 7 minutes. Add the cinnamon, ginger, cumin and cayenne and cook for 1 minute. Stir in the tomatoes, honey and salt. Add the chicken and simmer, covered, for about 10 minutes.

Stir in the peppers, raisins and chickpeas and simmer, stirring occasionally, for about 15 minutes, until peppers are tender.

Serve over brown rice. Sprinkle with almonds.

a small handful of large extravaganzas

The True North Chili, Mark IV 166

David Lopez's Anti-Extravaganza 172

Tower of Pisa 173

The Pumpkin Number 176

The Lovers' Cioppino 179

Philippe Jeanty's Raspberry Milkshake in a Chocolate Bag 182

B'stillah 184

Jean's Cheese Fondue 186

After years of thinking about it, this finally came together—in the pages of *Western Living* magazine, summer of 2002. I wanted to make a chili with northern meats and other TN components. The two-day cooking was captured on film by the magazine's photographer, including all the sides (most of them found in this collection). The Emperor of Ice Cream, Hart Melvin of Toronto's Gelato Fresco, created a few new flavours for the event—Lindt Chocolate Kahlua, Jalapeño Grapefruit, Strawberry Margarita. We drank vast amounts of Shaftebury Rainforest Amber Ale and Mission Hill's Cordillera wines with the meal.

A word about chili powder. You probably have some in the cupboard. It's probably been there since before the turn of the century. Throw it out and buy fresh. Mine

> I wanted to make a chili with northern meats and other TN components.

The True North Chili, Mark IV

serves 10 or 12, with plenty for take-home, school lunches, TV snacks …

WINE PAIRINGS

Mission Hill Cordillera wines
[BC]

Shaftebury Ale [BC]

anything good 'n raunchy from Italy, Spain, Portugal

Two-Buck Chuck [CA]

MUSIC TO COOK WITH

Hot Club of Cowtown:
Continental Stomp [HIGHTONE]

Pierre Schryer Band:
Blue Drag [NEW CANADIAN]

Bob Hadley:
American Romantic Guitar [INDIE]

(1)

2–3 quarts (2–3 L)	rich chicken broth

or, if you'd rather make your own stock:

one 5-lb (2.2-kg)	free-range chicken
2–3 quarts (2–3 L)	water
to taste	salt

(2)

2 lb (1 kg)	wild boar bacon, in a piece
4 lb (2 kg)	boneless caribou shoulder
3 lb (1½ kg)	boneless muskox shoulder
4 lb (2 kg)	boneless wild boar picnic shoulder

(3)

2 cups (500 mL)	chopped celery
three 28-oz (798-mL) cans	diced tomatoes
4 Tbsp (60 mL)	sugar

(4)

four 4-oz (114-mL) cans	green chilies, stemmed, peeled (or 6 large fresh jalapeños, seeded, diced)
2 cups (500 mL)	onion, chopped
3 large	bell peppers: one each, red, yellow, green; seeded, chopped
10–12 cloves	good garlic, chopped
	fat or oil for sautéing

comes from David Lopez of La Tiendita ("on the high road to Taos"). It's the best chili powder I've ever tasted. He'll ship you some by FedEx if you call or write to him (no email last time I was in contact) and send a cheque. It's reasonable, and sensational. Phone (505) 689-2565; write Box 11-B, Trampas, NM, 87576, USA; or stop in, as readers and listeners have over the years, via the back road from Santa Fe up to Taos. They filmed *The Milagro Beanfield War* thereabouts.

This cookery thing takes forever and remains very much a work in progress. Feel free to improvise, delete, substitute, whatever. Let me know how you make out. Not for a soccer night, but a whole weekend's endeavour. And at the end, David Lopez's significantly simpler New Mexico chili "recipe" is provided for contrast.

(5)*

2 bottles	Shaftebury Rainforest Amber Ale
2 Tbsp (25 mL)	Mexican oregano
4 tsp (20 mL)	ground cumin
4 tsp (20 mL)	ground black pepper
1 Tbsp (15 mL)	salt
2 tsp (10 mL)	dried leaf cilantro
2 tsp (10 mL)	thyme
2 tsp (10 mL)	sweet or smoked paprika (not hot)
2 tsp (10 mL)	ground coriander
2 tsp (10 mL)	celery salt
2 tsp (10 mL)	dried celery leaf
10 Tbsp (150 mL)	David Lopez's Best Chimayo Red chili powder (or your best shot, fresh-bought substitute)

(6)

4	bay leaves

(7)

4 Tbsp (60 mL)	maple syrup

(8)

6 Tbsp (90 mL)	mole

continues on next page …

(9)

| 1 Tbsp (15 mL) | masa *harina* (or potato flour) |
| ½ cup (125 mL) | hot water |

(10)

⅓ cup (75 mL)	aquavit
⅓ cup (75 mL)	Canadian (rye) whisky
for serving	lime juice or ½ limes
to taste	grated cheese

OPTIONAL**

1 tsp (5 mL)	MSG
1 tsp (5 mL)	cayenne
1 tsp (5 mL)	hot sauce

NOTES

*These measurements are all plus-or-minus; your own taste (and heart tolerance) has to be your guide. Don't skimp on oregano or chili powder, though.

**MSG adds a certain something but hardly anybody likes it anymore; cayenne and hot sauce should be considered only after tasting the chili no less than a day after prep; it sneaks up on you. On the side is always wiser when it comes to extra heat.

ASSEMBLY (COOKING BY NUMBER):

1

If you feel like making your own broth, cut up the chicken, put it in a big pot, cover with water, add some salt, simmer 1½–2 hours. Save the chicken for something else; strain the broth and return to the pot. Heat it to just below boiling and keep it there till you use it. Someone-else's-toil broth is of course quicker and easier.

2

Prepare the meats: dice the bacon and sauté till crisp; remove from fat with a slotted spoon and reserve. Save the bacon fat (you want about 12 Tbsp/180 mL or more). Trim the caribou, muskox and wild boar shoulders into 1-inch (2.5-cm) cubes; keep someplace cool.

3

Combine the celery and tomatoes in a very big pot to eventually hold the entire chili (we're talking seriously large soup or stock pot). Add the sugar and bring to the boil. Reduce the heat and simmer for 60 minutes or more while you continue with other prep.

4

Prepare the hot chilies: if using fresh, dice into ¼-inch (5-mm) pieces. Otherwise open cans, drain, dice. Chop the onions into ½-inch (1-cm) pieces. Seed and dice multicoloured bell peppers into ½-inch (1-cm) pieces. Mince the garlic as small as you can stand it. Sauté all lightly in a little fat or oil and set aside.

5

Prepare the herbs and spices: pour the ale into a big glass jar with lid. Add all herbs and spices on the list and stir. Shake jar hard till everything is well mixed and dissolved (you may need to add a little warm water or more ale). Set aside.

To the celery-tomato mixture in the very big pot, add the chicken broth, chili-onion-pepper-garlic mixture and the spices-herbs-beer mixture. Bring to a simmer and hold on low simmer.

Brown the meat. Important note: make sure all the meat is well browned. Do small batches at a time, draining liquid if it gathers, adding more fat as necessary, using fairly high heat. Remove pieces as they are browned and continue till it's all done. Hire the kids, they can do this.

Using the reserved boar bacon fat, brown the boar shoulder: add to the chili mixture. Brown the muskox as above and add. Brown the caribou as above and add. Taste for salt and add if needed; do not (yet) adjust other seasonings.

continues on next page …

6

Add the bay leaves to the mixture. Bring to a gentle boil and simmer about 30 minutes. (Remove bay leaves after 30–60 minutes, if desired, or leave in, but remember to remove before serving.)

7

Add the maple syrup; maintain simmer on low for 1 hour. Add hot sauce and/or cayenne if you dare and maintain simmer. Add reserved bacon pieces after about 1 hour of cooking.

8

Add the mole after about 1½ hours of cooking. Remove from heat and let cool to room temperature. Refrigerate covered for 24 hours (up to 72 hours is okay). Take a well-deserved break and contemplate the universe.

9

Bring the chili to room temperature on the day of serving. Bring to a gentle boil and maintain. Dissolve the masa harina or potato flour in hot water; stir into chili and mix well.

10

Add aquavit and whisky, stir to blend; maintain simmer. Simmer another 30 minutes to 1 hour, checking for meat tenderness. Now's the time to also check for spices and optional seasonings; adjust as necessary.

Add—if using—MSG, cayenne, hot sauce—but be careful.

Just before serving add lime juice to taste, or serve half limes on the side and let people add their own. Ditto with cheese—about 1 cup (250 mL) of grated cheese per litre of chili will make it thicker/creamier. Again, it's better added individually, so I like to offer it on the side.

Serve with add-ons:
- sour cream
- grated cheddar and Monterey Jack cheese
- lime wedges
- sliced avocados or guacamole
- tortillas, for scooping
- slaw, ceviche, succotash and cornbread to complete menu

Hot sauces on the side for this occasion: Tapatio Salsa Picante (Mexico), Stanford Hot Pepper Sauce (Victoria, British Columbia—would I kid you on this?), Panola Clearly Hot Sauce (Louisiana), Provence Salsa de Hierbas Finas (Cuba).

Reheats splendidly. Gets better with aging. Don't we all.

We were talking
chili cookery in
his little store …

We were talking chili cookery in his little store—"Local Arts, Southwest Arts, Chili"—and David Lopez said, "I'll give you a good chili recipe." He wrote it on the back of one of the cards for his shop, which is on the high road to Taos, La Tiendita. This is it, in its entirety.

David Lopez's Anti-Extravaganza

serves 1, I think

WINE PAIRINGS

Santa Fe Pale Ale [NM]

MUSIC TO COOK WITH

Doug Wamble:
Country Libations [ROUNDER]

CHILI

1 tablespoon chili

1 tablespoon all-purpose flour or cornmeal on water (simmering)

add potato (diced raw)

add meat pork, beef, fish

add salt, garlic

So I did one and it was—well, it was okay, rudimentary. So I tweaked it a little—still keeping it simple—and came up with this version; enough for two.

1 cup (250 mL)	beer
1 cup (250 mL)	water
1 Tbsp (15 mL)	chili
1 Tbsp (15 mL)	cornmeal
1	potato
2 cloves	garlic, minced
5	pork loin chops, seared
to taste	black pepper, salt

Heat the beer and water, add the chili and cornmeal and potato. Simmer half an hour. Add the garlic. Pour it all over the pork and add pepper and salt.

Carmen Heller of Clarence Point, Ontario, learned this dish from her mother in Argentina, although she never saw it anywhere else there. She thinks it could have originated in Eastern Europe since this is the origin of her grandparents. In any case, she has served it many times, to the joy and delight of her guests.

Carmen Heller of Clarence Point, Ontario, learned this dish from her mother in Argentina ...

Tower of Pisa

CRÊPES

1 cup (250 mL)	1% milk
½ cup (125 mL)	soda water
1	egg
1 cup + 2 Tbsp (250 mL + 25 mL)	all-purpose flour
½ tsp (2 mL)	olive oil

FILLING

4 leaves	reddish-green lettuce
	mayonnaise (low-fat mayonnaise is fine), for spreading
2 oz (50 g)	sliced ham (about 1 cup/250 mL)
2 oz (50 g)	Swiss or Havarti cheese, sliced (about 1 cup/250 mL)
1 medium	potato, boiled, thinly sliced and seasoned with salt and pepper
2 Tbsp (25 mL)	chopped sweet pickles (mini-onions, cauliflower, gherkins, etc.)
1	Granny Smith apple, peeled, sliced and sprayed or brushed with lemon juice to prevent browning
2 stalks	celery, thinly sliced and seasoned with salt and pepper
2	carrots, boiled and thinly sliced
½ cup (125 mL)	frozen green peas, thawed and seasoned with salt and pepper
½ cup (125 mL)	frozen corn, thawed and seasoned with salt and pepper

continues on next page ...

WINE PAIRINGS

in Pisa we'd drink Chianti but a big, fat white would be good, like the Gaja "Rossj-Bass" Chardonnay [IT]

MUSIC TO COOK WITH

Yo-Yo Ma:
Vivaldi's Cello [SONY]

1	beet, boiled and sliced (optional)
1	red bell pepper or canned red pepper
1	green olive
1	green bell pepper
pieces of skin of	pickled cucumbers or gherkins
1–2	tomatoes, sliced

CRÊPES

Prepare the batter by mixing all the ingredients either with an electric blender or by hand. Spray a 9-inch (23-cm) non-stick pan with cooking spray and heat on medium. Pour ⅓ cup (75 mL) of batter onto the preheated frying pan. The batter should be fluid enough to easily cover the frying pan when you rotate it gently. Do not overcook. The crêpes should be very thin and lightly brown. This amount of batter will produce about 8 crêpes, and they should be made ahead of time. In the refrigerator, they keep well for up to 1 week. They also keep very well frozen, and for much longer.

FILLING

To assemble the tower, place the washed and dried lettuce leaves flat on a dinner plate large enough for the crêpes. Spread mayonnaise on the top and the bottom of the first crêpe and place it on top of the lettuce. Top the mayonnaised crêpe with ham. Continue building up layers in the same way: spread mayonnaise on one side of the next crêpe, and place this side onto the ham layer. Spread mayonnaise on the top side of this crêpe and top it with cheese. Repeat with the next layer, but using potato, sprinkled with some of the chopped pickles. Continue forming layers in this way, using the apple, celery, carrots, peas, corn and beet (if using). The apple and celery can be mixed, as can be the carrots and peas. The corn can be sprinkled with chopped pickles. Finish the top layer by spreading mayonnaise on one side of a crêpe, and placing that on top with the mayonnaised side down. Cover the tower with plastic wrap and leave it in the fridge for at least 24 hours.

Since this has the appearance of a cake, it should be decorated. Spread mayonnaise over the entire tower, including the sides. Slice a few thin rings and pieces from the red pepper and make a flower on top of the tower. For the centre of the flower, you can use a green olive. For the flower stem, use thin slices of green pepper. You can use pieces of the skin of pickled cucumbers or gherkins to form leaves. I cover the side of the tower by sticking tomato slices on it. Refrigerate for about 6 hours.

You can easily replace the ham with tuna or salmon in water. Press out the water, and mix the minced fish with mayonnaise and lemon juice, and add salt and pepper to taste.

This has been
printed in so
many places, so
many times …

This has been printed in so many places, so many times, yet people continue to clamour for it. No question but it's a winner. Around the middle of October is the best time for it—the secret is to find fresh peaches, fresh pumpkin and fresh corn, and that's about the only time, at least here in the West, when we can manage that. You can use preserved peaches—your own, or some of those wonderful ones in the big jars Italian delis sometimes carry. You can even use frozen cobs of corn, thawed. But you need a fresh, whole pumpkin, because that's your tureen.

The Pumpkin Number

serves 4 or more

WINE PAIRINGS

Errazuriz Merlot [CH]

Parducci Zinfandel [CA]

Lang Pinot Meunier [BC]

Inniskillin Pinot Noir [ON]

Chip Dry White Port, to start [PO]

Graham's Six Grapes, to end [PO]

MUSIC TO COOK WITH

Yo-Yo Ma: *Plays Ennio Morricone*
[SONY]

THE STEW

½ cup (125 mL)	olive oil
3 lb (1.5 kg)	lean beef in 1-inch (2.5-cm) cubes
2 large	onions, chopped
3 large	green peppers, chopped
6 cloves	garlic, minced
as needed	salt and pepper
2 large	bay leaves
4 Tbsp (60 mL)	tomato paste
2 tsp (10 mL)	fresh thyme (or 1 tsp/5 mL dried)
2 cups (500 mL)	hearty red wine (Zinfandel's good)
1 cup (250 mL)	beef broth
2 cups (500 mL)	squash, cut in 1-inch (2.5-cm) cubes
2 cups (500 mL)	fresh green beans, de-stringed
2 cups (500 mL)	carrots, cut in ½-inch (1-cm) rounds
2 cups (500 mL)	cabbage chopped in big pieces
1 lb (500 g)	fresh ripe tomatoes (or one 14-oz/398-mL can), diced
3 cobs	corn (or 2 cups/500 mL kernels)
8	fresh peaches, peeled, halved, pitted

Heat the oil and brown the meat, a few pieces at a time, reserving pieces in a big ovenproof pot with a lid as they brown. Add the onions, peppers and garlic to the oil and stir over medium heat till the onions get that soft but not brown appearance. Remove with a slotted spoon and add to the pot where the meat is.

Preheat the oven to 325°F (160°C).

Set the big pot over low heat and add salt and pepper, bay leaves, tomato paste and thyme. Add the wine, stir well, turn up the heat, cover the pot and cook for 10 or 15 minutes. Add the beef broth, stirring up all the gludge from the bottom of the pot, and bring to a simmer.

Cover again and put the pot in the oven. Take a look in 15 minutes and adjust the temperature if you need to, so it just keeps an easy, steady simmer. Cook for 1 hour. Check the meat for tenderness—you want it tender but not falling apart. You may have to cook it a little longer. Add all the vegetables except the corn, cover again and cook 15 minutes more—you want the veggies tender as well, but not mush. Add the corn and peaches and cook 10 minutes. Check for salt, pepper and thyme, adding more if it needs it. Take the pot out of the oven and keep warm or refrigerate covered until tomorrow.

continues on next page . . .

THE PUMPKIN

1	pumpkin, 10 inches (25 cm) diameter or bigger
for rinsing	milk
to taste	salt and pepper

Preheat the oven to 350°F (180°C).

Cut a good-sized lid off the top of the pumpkin, keeping the stalk on for a good handle. Scrape out all the seeds and fibres, being careful not to put a hole in the side or bottom of the pumpkin. Rinse inside of pumpkin well, a couple of times, with milk. Discard the milk and sprinkle a little salt and pepper inside.

Put the pumpkin, opening up, on a baking dish in the oven. Bake for 45 minutes, putting the lid on only for the last 15 minutes of baking so it doesn't shrink and end up falling into the pumpkin. Check for softness; you want the flesh tender enough so you can scrape some into the stew while serving but you don't want the walls of the pumpkin to collapse. Might take a few more minutes of baking. When ready to serve, ladle the stew gently into the pumpkin. DON'T pour it all in at once, it will split the tureen and get all over everything. Scrape out a little pumpkin flesh with each serving. Again, be careful. The pumpkin is a one-shot bowl but the stew reheats just fine in a pot.

Serve with lots of crusty bread and some quince jelly (or Portuguese *marmelada*) and Münster cheese—maybe some iced grapes.

Also referred to in my kitchen as a dish for consenting adults, this is a gloriously messy enterprise; fun to make with more than two hands on deck and definitely not meant as a prelude to any sort of new-romance liaison. In fact, it's a good dinner prelude to a brisk nap. You can begin this a day ahead if you stop prep just before adding the seafood. Next day, or later that same, about an hour before you want to eat, pick it up from "Meanwhile, scrub the clams and mussels ..." My calculations say three bottles of wine are required: one for the chef while cooking, another for the pot, a third for the table. Maybe four.

Also referred to in my kitchen as a dish for consenting adults ...

The Lovers' Cioppino

VEGETABLES

serves 2 to 4

¼ cup (50 mL)	olive oil
5 medium	onions, chopped chunky
lots	garlic, chopped
3 medium	red peppers, seeded, chopped
2 medium	green peppers, seeded, chopped
5 stalks	celery and leaves, chopped
1 bunch	fresh fennel, fronds and bulb, chopped
3 medium	zucchinis, chopped chunky
1 bottle	Zinfandel (get a good, hearty one)
8 cups (2 L)	fish stock (or vegetable stock, or any workable combination) (reserve a few spoonfuls for spread)
2 lb (1 kg)	ripe Roma tomatoes, quartered, seeded

SEASONINGS

10 medium	fresh basil leaves, chopped (or 2 Tbsp/25 ml dried)
1 tsp (5 mL)	fennel seeds
3	bay leaves
to taste	red pepper flakes (optional)
to taste	salt and pepper

continues on next page ...

WINE PAIRINGS

A Zinfandel Collection:
- Sparkling to start
- White Zin
- Burgundy style Zin (light)
- Bordeaux style Zin (medium)
- Old Vines Zin (heavy)
- Late Harvest Zin
- Zinfandel Port

[ALL FROM CALIFORNIA]

MUSIC TO COOK WITH

Jim Byrnes:
Fresh Horses [BLACK HEN]

Zubot & Dawson:
Tractor Parts [BLACK HEN]

Tangle Eye:
Alan Lomax's Southern Journey Remixed [ZOE]

Little Axe: *The Wolf That House Built* [OKEH/EPIC]

1 dozen each	clams and mussels
3 slices	white bread
2	jalapeño peppers, seeded, chopped
more	garlic, to taste
½ cup (125 mL)	olive oil
to taste	salt and pepper
1 dozen	prawns (or more)
1 whole	crab, disassembled
1 bunch	fresh parsley, chopped
1 lb (500 g)	halibut, in chunks
¾ cup (175 mL)	olive oil
24 slices	very thin French bread (baguette), toasted, rubbed with garlic, cooled

Heat the olive oil in a deep pan or wok. Add the onions and garlic and cook 10 minutes on medium. Add the peppers, celery, fennel and zucchinis and cook 10 minutes more.

Transfer everything to a big warm stew or soup pot. Pour in the bottle of Zinfandel ... yes, all of it. Pour in a similar amount of fish stock. Add the tomatoes, then the seasonings, including salt and pepper to taste. Stir well, up the heat and let it bubble once it's come to the boil. Simmer, partly covered, for 20 minutes. Check seasonings.

Meanwhile, scrub the clams and mussels thoroughly and put into another pot with a little water. Steam, covered, on high until they open. Set aside.

Soak the white bread slices in a little water and squeeze dry. Using a mortar and pestle, pound the bread and jalapeños and some garlic together into a paste. Add ½ cup oil, a small trickle at a time, as if making mayo, and keep pounding. Add a few spoonfuls of the reserved fish stock and some salt and pepper.

Bring the cioppino to another boil and add the prawns, plus the crab, and the clams and mussels in their shells. Add lots of chopped parsley. Adjust liquid (stock and wine) as needed. Heat it all through. Add halibut and heat another 3 minutes.

Take off the heat, collect yourself and set the pot before the dinner group. Serve the little garlicky toasts with the garlic-oil-pepper spread you pounded in the mortar. You can also put one in the bottom of a bowl and pour the stew over it. Roll up your sleeves and get down and messy. Drink lots more Zinfandel—starting with white if you like, moving through the lighter style and ending with one of those old vines numbers.

A dessert that's a lot of work but so dramatic your guests will talk about it for years.

A dessert that's a lot of work but so dramatic your guests will talk about it for years. Philippe Jeanty was for a long time the chef at the Napa Valley's lovely Domaine Chandon restaurant, before opening his own bistro down the road. Wherever his name appears on a door or a menu you know you'll eat spectacular food.

If you're a dab hand with chocolate tempering, and have a thermometer you can rely on, this comes a little easier.

Philippe Jeanty's Raspberry Milkshake in a Chocolate Bag

serves 6

6	paper coffee bags with wax lining
1 pair	pinking shears
2 lb (500 mL)	Belgian dark chocolate (bittersweet couverture)
3 baskets	fresh raspberries (or comparable quantity frozen)
to taste	sugar (optional)
½ gallon (2 L)	high-quality vanilla ice cream (Gelato Fresco)
3 oz (100 mL)	raspberry liqueur (or Bonny Doon Framboise)
1 cup (250 mL)	whole milk
1 Tbsp (15 mL)	lemon juice

GARNISH

6	straws (silver, with spoon on the end; Philippe: "If you find them let me know where.")
6	Peruvian lilies
6	fern tips
a few	raspberries
18	palmier cookies

WINE PAIRINGS

Kopke Port [PO]

Niepoort Port [PO]

Quinta do Crasto Vintage Port [PO]

MUSIC TO COOK WITH

John Fahey: *The Great San Bernardino Birthday Party* [TAKOMA]

Mireille Proulx: *Le jardin de nuit* [ARS MUSICA]

Cut the paper bags about 4 inches high (10 cm) with the pinking shears. Open the bags.

Formula to temper chocolate: Bring up to 110°F (53°C), down to 80°F (27°C), up to 89°F (31°C).

Chop the chocolate, place in a bowl and put the bowl over simmering water. Melt the chocolate, stirring constantly with a wooden spoon. When melted, take the bowl off the water and keep stirring until the chocolate cools down (about 10 minutes), then put it back over the water for 5 seconds.

Pour chocolate into each bag, about halfway up. Turn the bags over, making sure the chocolate coats the sides of the bags inside. Let set in the freezer or refrigerator until hardened. Then, starting at the bottom of the bag, peel the paper off very gently. Hold chocolate bags in the freezer.

Cook the raspberries for 15 minutes, adding sugar if they're not sweet enough. Put the berries in a blender with the ice cream, raspberry liqueur, milk and lemon juice and blend until smooth.

Put a chocolate bag on a plate and fill to three-quarters with the milkshake. Inside the bag, place a straw on one side, a flower on the other, and at the front right side, a fern tip, with a few berries on top and 3 palmiers at the front left.

This glorious dish from Morocco, which combines chicken and herbs with almonds, icing sugar and cinnamon, depends on a see-through thin pastry dough known as *ouarkah*—circular leaves of translucent delicacy. Well, go ahead. Me, I'm in the freezer section at the supermarket looking for a package of phyllo, ready-made and maybe not round but we can work that out.

It's the apotheosis of chicken pot pie.

B'stillah

serves 4

WINE PAIRINGS

Joie "A Noble Blend" [BC]

Malivoire Old Vines Foch [ON]

MUSIC TO COOK WITH

Vance Makin:
Bach's Goldberg Variations/The Neurology Edition [INDIE]

Martin Simpson:
Righteousness and Humidity
[RED HOUSE]

2 Tbsp (25 mL)	olive oil
4 medium	shallots, minced
4	skinned chicken thighs
2	whole boneless chicken breasts, skinned and halved
½ cup (125 mL)	parsley, stems off and chopped
3 Tbsp (45 mL)	fresh cilantro, stems off and chopped
affordable handful	saffron threads, crushed
½ tsp (2 mL)	turmeric
1 tsp (5 mL)	ground ginger
2 tsp (10 mL)	ground cinnamon
½ tsp (2 mL)	ground mace
1 cup (250 mL)	warm water
3	eggs, beaten
to taste	salt and pepper
1 cup (250 mL)	confectioner's sugar
½ cup (125 mL)	blanched almonds, whole or slivered
12–15 sheets	phyllo pastry, thawed
1 cup (250 mL)	butter, melted
for garnish	powdered sugar and cinnamon

Heat the oil in a good-sized pan and sauté the shallots for 8 minutes. Add the chicken, parsley, cilantro, saffron, turmeric, ginger, half of the cinnamon and mace, and the water. Cover and cook for 20 minutes. Take the chicken out with a slotted spoon and set aside to cool.

Continue simmering the sauce and add the eggs, salt and pepper and half the sugar. Stir to scramble the eggs.

Remove bones from the chicken, and shred the meat. Add it to the egg mixture. Set aside.

Preheat the oven to 425°F (220°C).

Grind the almonds in a food processor (or use a mortar and pestle) and mix with the remaining sugar, cinnamon and mace. Set aside.

Stack the phyllo on granite or a cutting board. Get a 12-inch (30-cm) pie plate or pizza pan as your guide and, with your kitchen equivalent of an X-acto knife, cut the phyllo sheets round. Moisten a clean tea towel and cover the phyllo sheets while you assemble.

Rub some melted butter in the pizza pan. Layer 3 sheets on the pan, brushing each one in turn with melted butter. Sprinkle the last one with the almond mixture. Layer and butter 3 more sheets. Spread the chicken mixture on top, but leave a 2-inch (5-cm) border of phyllo. Fold over the edges to partly cover the chicken. Layer and butter 3 more sheets and sprinkle the rest of the almond mixture on the top. Layer and butter 3 more sheets over the almond mixture. Tuck the edges under the whole thing. It's like making your bed at camp. Use remaining phyllo sheets to cover any gaps.

Bake b'stillah until golden brown on top, no more than 30 minutes. Cover the top with powdered sugar, in a sieve. Sprinkle ground cinnamon over the top. You can make patterns or just do it as a scatter. It must be served right away or the pastry will sog.

What better among friends and on frigid Ottawa days?

Jean Kroes of Ottawa has adapted the old Swiss standby to Canadian cheeses. What better among friends and on frigid Ottawa days? The proper Swiss-German toast to go with it is "*A Chuete.*"

Jean's Cheese Fondue

serves as many as you want

WINE PAIRINGS

Luxardo Kirsch [IT]

Quails Gate Chasselas [BC]

Fernet Branca [IT] to conclude—Italy's gift to an indigestive world

MUSIC TO COOK WITH

Jozsef Molnar: *Alphorn Concertos* [NAXOS]

Hilary Hahn: *Bach Violin Concertos* [DGG]

1 clove	garlic for up to 3 persons

Portions of wine and cheese per person:

⅔ cup (150 mL)	Fendant (or other dry Chasselas wine, or a wine fairly close in flavour and robustness, the Argentinian Trapiche Chardonnay)
7 oz (200 g)	medium aged Swiss Gruyère cheese
1 oz (25 g)	Brie or Camembert (to replace the Swiss favourite, Vacherin)
1 oz (25 g)	Danish blue (I found this to be able to replicate the Gruyère tanginess if the only Gruyère you can get is the mild one)

Plus:

to taste	pepper
	fresh nutmeg
1 generous shot glass per 4–6 persons	genuine Swiss, Austrian or German kirsch (omit if you can't get European kirsch)
1 tsp (5 mL)	cornstarch, in case the cheese doesn't want to blend
	fresh mushrooms (hey, no calories in that!)
plenty	half-white hard-crusted bread or baguette
	cauliflower (to your health and all who eat it …)

The Swiss-type cheese *caquelon* (earthenware fondue dish) is best for this, but a fondue pot will do.

Rub the bottom and sides of the *caquelon* with a peeled, halved garlic clove; this will not only give the fondue a good flavour, but also prevent the cheese from sticking. Finely chop the rest of the garlic and put in the *caquelon*. Add the wine and warm over low heat to about 150°F (50°C).

Either grate all the cheese or cut it into small cubes. Put the cheese into the warm wine, still over low heat, and slowly and continuously stir with a regular fork or small wooden spoon, making sure the full base of the *caquelon* is stirred regularly to prevent the cheese from burning. Once all the cheese is melted and blended with the wine, season with pepper and freshly grated nutmeg.

Add the kirsch; if the cheese has not fully blended, stir the cornstarch into the kirsch first, then add this mixture to the fondue, stirring continuously.

Voila, c'est prêt!

Keep the fondue warm while eating, but try to avoid boiling the cheese. We quarter the mushrooms and alternate with bread and cauliflower florets, dipping each into the cheese while turning the fork in and above the *caquelon* to gather lots of cheese but also to keep it on the fork.

Heat up the leftovers the next morning with some eggs for breakfast. Another tip: try to avoid cold, carbonated beverages (sodas or even water) during and immediately after the meal, to prevent hardening of the cheese in your stomach. (Can be a pain …)

chapter eleven

drinks

The Anasazi Margarita 190

Tea by Two: Erika's Austrian Jägertee 191

A Martini Named Robert le Pur 192

The Oceanwood Gimlet 193

Long Flat Wine Warmers in Both Official Colours 194

Gingered Rum Tea 196

Bloody Nonsense: A Garden Kick 197

Wassail & Other Hotties 198

A Yard of Flannel 200

Cider Possett 201

Whisky Mac 202

Half-Sweet Cocoa 203

Drinks Afire 204

Aberdeen Angus 205

Campfire Brulot 206

Christmas Passion 207

Amazing Eggnog 208

There's a restaurant
in Santa Fe,
New Mexico,
called Maria's …

There's a restaurant in Santa Fe, New Mexico, called Maria's, which is a shrine to the margarita: wrote the book on the subject—literally—serves a couple of hundred different ones. I did some serious undergraduate research here, but my favourite margarita occurred in the bar of the lovely Inn of the Anasazi, same town. It was so good I asked the bartender for the recipe, which he gladly gave, but with the proviso he only had the party-size version. Yours to judge who's to get into it, at these volumes.

The Anasazi Margarita

**serves a jolly group,
about to get jollier**

MUSIC TO COOK WITH

Jackalope:
Dances with Rabbits [CANYON]

Mark O'Connor:
Heroes [TELARC]

5.0 L	gold tequila
4.0 L	Cointreau
3.75 L	fresh lime juice
1.88 L	fresh lemon juice
1 lb (450 g)	berry sugar

Put everything into a suitable container with much ice.

Serve in salt-rimmed glasses if such is your pleasure.

Don't substitute any ingredients (stay with gold level tequila and Cointreau; don't use frozen juices; berry sugar is NOT icing sugar, but small-granule sugar.)

Can be downsized. Sample single serving:

1¼ oz (32 mL)	gold tequila
¾ oz (19 mL)	Cointreau
1 oz (25 mL)	fresh lime juice
½ oz (13 mL)	fresh lemon juice
1 tsp (5 mL)	berry sugar (more or less)

From the same Erika whose Whistler B&B is a favourite stop for even this non-skier, and whose Aga stove caused me considerable culinary grief. The secret of this drink is in the rum. Stroh's Austrian (!) rum is the ticket; sometimes we get to see it in Canada, but not often, and when we do it tends to cost the earth. Do experiment with other rums till you find the right one; the flavour of the rum should be light and fragrant and not overly caramelized.

From the same Erika whose Whistler B&B is a favourite stop for even this non-skier …

Tea by Two: Erika's Austrian Jägertee

½–1 L	water
2	rose hip tea bags
1	lemon, juice of
3	dried hibiscus flowers (optional but tasty)
1 tsp (5 mL)	dried juniper berries
½ tsp (2 mL)	dried lemon peel (use zest of the juiced lemon if you don't have any peel at hand; no point going out for it in the snow!)
¼ cup (50 mL)	clear honey (more or less, to taste)
¼ cup (50 mL)	Stroh Inländer rum (probably more)
for garnish	lemon slices and juniper berries

serves 2

MUSIC TO COOK WITH

Die Knoedel:
Verkochte Tiroler [RECREC]

Vienna Art Orchestra:
20th Anniversary [VERVE]

Alfred Brendel:
Diabelli Variations [PHILIPS]

Boil a big pot of water and steep the tea bags in it for 5 or 6 minutes. Take out tea bags and add the remaining ingredients except garnish; steep for 4 minutes more.

Strain, float a couple of juniper berries and a tiny slice of lemon in each cup for garnish.

"Suddenly, a
REAL martini!"
said one wag.

Some years ago I was invited, along with other food and drink media, to help celebrate an anniversary of Robert Le Crom, executive chef at the Fairmont Hotel Vancouver. All who attended were assigned to tables of six or eight, and eventually each table was to nominate a mixer to create an original martini in Robert's honour. My table nominated me, to which I protested by saying I was the arch-conservative when it came to martinis, believing there to be only one martini and only one way of making it. They insisted.

A Couple of Cool Classics: (1) A Martini Named Robert le Pur

serves 1

MUSIC TO COOK WITH

Gerald Wiggins:
At Maybeck [CONCORD]

At the bar I watched my colleagues creating curious drinks with cherries, onions, olives, cedar boughs, parasols, jujubes, ice wine (a famous television peasant chef made his with ice wine) and other liquids. Most ended up looking like antifreeze with particulate matter in the glass. Came the judging—one by one the judges wrinkled their noses, furrowed their brows and said no thanks. Came mine and there were smiles all around—"Suddenly, a REAL martini!" said one wag. Vindicated, honoured, tickled pink, I signed the glass and it remained on the Hotel's bar menu for a year or more.

No substitutions whatsoever.

9 parts	gin (Plymouth is a big favourite)
1 part	dry vermouth
2 drops	Angostura Bitters
1	olive

Mix the gin, vermouth and bitters in a shaker. Add 3 ice cubes and shake. Strain into a martini glass. Add 1 olive. Serve ice cold.

Some creative latitude is allowed in the choice of the olive—plain, pimento-, jalapeño- or almond-stuffed, but none with anchovies and especially not blue cheese. It clouds the drink and turns it into an awful mess.

At one of my favourite West-Coast food destinations, Mayne Island's Ocean-wood Country Inn, innkeeper Jonathan Chilvers delights in—insists on—a wine list that is solidly, exclusively Pacific Northwest. He hand picks the best wines from Washington and Oregon, but mostly British Columbia—big name greats as well as the little legends. But he also takes pleasure in good cocktails; Oceanwood's bar bill of fare posits one of those splendid statements upon which philosophies could be built—and given the state of a lot of latter-day philosophies, probably should be.

At one of my favourite West-Coast food destinations ...

A Couple of Cool Classics: (2) The Oceanwood Gimlet

There are, in the innkeeper's opinion, just seven great classic cocktails: the aforementioned martini is at the top of the list. Other favourites include the Manhattan, the Old Fashioned ... you fill in the rest. Finally, the Vodka Gimlet, which goes like this:

1 part	vodka
2 parts	Rose's Lime Cordial
½ part	Triple Sec
1 slice	lime

Stir or shake with ice, strain into a martini glass, serve with a slice of lime. Have a second on standby in the freezer.

serves 1

MUSIC TO COOK WITH

Dakota Staton & George Shearing:
In the Night [CAPITOL]

Lena Horne:
We'll be Together Again [BLUE NOTE]

Ralph Sharon Trio:
Plays the Frank Loesser Songbook [DRG]

Come inside, you
must be freezing.

Come inside, you must be freezing. Let me take that steaming overcoat. Sit down here by this warm cat, and I'll get you something to take the chill off. No, there isn't any *glühwein* ready yet; I usually wait till Christmas to make that. No hot toddies today, either, but I do have something nice and easy—cheap too, come to think of it, and who doesn't think of it, much of the time? Which can I get you? I have them in both official colours, red and white; could probably do up one in

Long Flat Wine Warmers in Both Official Colours

for wandering carolers

MUSIC TO COOK WITH

C.P.E. Bach:
Flute Concertos [CBC]

Red's up first:

6 cups (1.5 L)	Tyrrell's Long Flat Red wine (or similar)
1 cup (250 mL)	frozen, unsweetened raspberries, thawed, drained (or fresh, if you feel flush, in which case you might as well use the Chateau Latour)
6 slices	orange
3 slices	lemon
10	whole cloves
1 cup (250 mL)	sugar
1 Tbsp (15 mL)	whole black peppercorns
1	whole star anise
for garnish	julienned orange peel, fresh berries, halved kumquats, crystallized ginger, etc.

Put everything except the garnish in a pot and bring to the boil. Lower the heat and simmer gently for 20 minutes.

Strain through a cheesecloth or fine sieve, pushing down on the solid ingredients to get all the juice and flavours out.

Pour into warmed mugs and garnish. Serve while hot.

pink too, but the white Zinfandel delivery truck doesn't come till June. Instead, there's some nice Aussie drinking wine called Tyrrell's Long Flat (the Long Flat is the name of a long and flat vineyard), each of the current vintage, $10.95 apiece last time I looked, both decent dinner drinking wines and both fine warmer-uppers.

Now the white version:

1 cup (250 mL)	sugar
½ cup (125 mL)	water
4 cups (1 L)	Tyrrell's Long Flat White wine (or similar)
2 cups (500 mL)	clear apple juice
4 slices	lemon
2	vanilla beans, slit lengthwise
2 short sticks	cinnamon
5	whole cloves
for garnish	powdered cinnamon, grated nutmeg, more cinnamon sticks, etc.

Put the sugar and water in a pot and cook on low heat until the sugar dissolves and the mixture is clear (should take about 5 minutes). Swirl the pan once in a while.

Turn up the heat and boil until the sugar caramelizes and turns a deep brown colour.

Stand well back—the mixture will splatter—and pour in the wine and apple juice. Add the lemon slices, vanilla beans, cinnamon sticks and cloves and bring to the boil once more. Lower the heat and simmer gently for 20 minutes.

Strain through cheesecloth or sieve, pour into warmed mugs, garnish and serve while hot.

A bedtime treat, especially if you feel a cold coming on.

Gingered Rum Tea

serves 1

1 or 2	tea bags (good old Orange Pekoe, nothing too floral)
1½ oz (40 mL)	rum
1 piece	preserved or candied ginger, fingertip-size

Make a mug of good strong tea and pour in the rum and add the ginger. If it gets cold while you're on the phone fending off a marketing survey, you can reheat it in the microwave. If an unexpected heat wave appears, you can also serve it iced.

MUSIC TO COOK WITH

David Frishberg:
By Himself [ARBORS]

First seen and sipped in the assembly of Some Acquired Tastes, it remains one of my favourite vodka cocktails. You can also call it a Bloody Viking if you use tomato juice or Clamato. Hey! you can call it anything you want.

First seen and sipped in the assembly of Some Acquired Tastes …

Bloody Nonsense: A Garden Kick

serves 1

1 slice	lemon
½ tsp (2 mL)	chopped chives
3–5 drops	Tabasco or other hot sauce (Frank's Red Hot Chili Lime is really good, if not all that hot)
2 drops	Angostura Bitters
2 drops	Worcestershire sauce
2 oz (50 mL)	aquavit, straight from the freezer
	vegetable juice
	ice cubes

MUSIC TO COOK WITH

Slim Gaillard:
Laughing in Rhythm [PROPER]

Drop the lemon slice in the bottom of a tall glass and sprinkle in the chives. Drop hot sauce, Angostura and Worcestershire sauce on lemon slice. Pour in frozen aquavit. Fill glass up with vegetable juice. Plop in a couple of ice cubes to maintain chill. Fall about the garden later, if so inclined.

Traditionally, a wassail was drunk on Christmas Eve.

Traditionally, a wassail was drunk on Christmas Eve. It was wine plus ale or cider, spices, sugar and, almost always, baked apples. The name derives from *was hael* from the Norse *ves heill*, or "be in good health." Don't see how you could help but be, after two of these.

Wassail & Other Hotties

group method

MUSIC TO COOK WITH

Maddy Prior & the Carnival Band: *Sing Lustily and With Good Courage* [SAYDISC]

2 cups (500 mL)	water
1 tsp (5 mL)	ground nutmeg (use a fresh one and grate it yourself, don't use the dust in the jar you haven't opened since '97)
2 tsp (10 mL)	ground ginger
one 2-inch (5-cm) stick	cinnamon
6	whole cloves
6	allspice berries
3	coriander seeds
4	cardamom pods
12	eggs, separated
2 bottles	cream sherry (the South African is perfect in this)
8 cups (2 L)	good and hearty ale of your choice
4 cups (1 L)	sugar (sorry, you might like to downsize this part, but it's got to be sweet)
1 cup (250 mL)	brandy (ditto, South African, above)
12 slices	roasted apple or 12 tiny whole roasted apples*

*Roasting apples, sliced or small, is simple: leave skins on if you like, but remove a horizontal strip of peel so they don't explode. Place on a cookie sheet in a 325°F (160°C) oven till apples start to turn brown.

Put the water and spices in a pan and simmer 10 minutes.

Beat 12 egg yolks until pale and thick.

Beat 12 egg whites till stiff, and fold into the yolks. (No, you can't do 'em both together, you're not making scrambled eggs here.)

Add the sherry and ale to the pan and stir in the sugar. Heat to just about boiling.

Strain half the heated sherry-ale mix over the eggs and pour this mixture into a warmed punch bowl. Bring the rest of the sherry-ale mix to a boil and strain into the punch bowl. Add the brandy and roasted apples.

Quantities can be doubled or otherwise augmented.

Serve with spoons and a couple of rolls of paper towels.

If you have some extra eggs at hand, you may want to mix:

A Yard of Flannel

serves 2 or so

MUSIC TO COOK WITH

NRBQ: *Wild Weekend*
[ROUNDER]

4	egg yolks
4 Tbsp (60 mL)	brown sugar
plenty	grated nutmeg
2	egg whites
4 cups (1 L)	good ale

Beat the egg yolks until creamy and stir in the sugar and nutmeg. Beat the egg whites until creamy and fold into the mixture.

Heat the ale until it reaches boiling, then take it off the heat.

Gradually stir in the egg mixture. Pour it quickly back and forth between 2 pots until the drink is smooth and frothy.

Serve as hot as you can maintain it without boiling again.

Something similar is …

Something
similar is …

Cider Possett

… not rich or anything!

serves 3 or 4

4 cups (1 L)	cream
2 cups (500 mL)	real English (or Quebec, or Okanagan) cider
10	egg yolks
3	egg whites
1 cup (250 mL)	Madeira or cream sherry
for grating	nutmeg

Stir the cream and cider together in a pot and heat on low.

Beat egg yolks and whites separately until creamy, then add them slowly to the cider-cream, whisking all the while. Pour in the Madeira or sherry and simmer until it's like sauce (don't boil, though).

Grate nutmeg over top before serving. Serve in soup bowls. All right, mugs then.

Walk about the neighbourhood in sturdy boots and long scarves, singing old songs. Apologize to the neighbours on the nice side about the dogs barking last summer. Make rash promises to the kids for spring break. Be unconscionably merry.

MUSIC TO COOK WITH

Simon Thoumire Three:
March, Strathspey & Surreal
[GREEN LINNET]

Lamenting the loss of the bartending art and craft leads me to the fact that not even in good old Britain are the standards being maintained.

Not terribly long ago, at the recently-Gordon-Ramseyfied Claridge's in London, I asked the server if he thought the bartender could produce a Whisky Mac. He said he was sure of it, and came gliding back a few minutes later with whisky and ginger ale. "This isn't a whisky Mac, you know," I pointed out. He smoothly removed the erroneous drink to his little tray and waited politely, attentively, looking at me in a manner quite reminiscent of the dog when it desperately wants to understand a point I'm trying to make about quantum gravity.

Whisky Mac

serves 1

I opted for a martini instead, but I do miss the Mac, especially after two days travelling the Tube, when the raspy throat starts to set in. A source of Ginger Wine is worth locating.

1 oz (25 mL)	Stone's Green Ginger Wine
2 oz (50 mL)	good blended Scotch (don't use the Lagavulin or some other rare blend, one of Johnnie Walker's is the ticket)

Combine, shake—with ice if you wish—and then strain. Better yet at room temperature, if that raspy throat's about.

So now you've got a whole bottle of Ginger Wine, what else can you do with it? Substitute gin for the scotch and there's your Bishop's Cocktail. Ice that one.

Pour 3 oz (75 mL) vodka into a glass, add 1 oz (25 mL) Ginger Wine, fill it tall with soda and there's a Ginger Snap.

Get really ambitious and try for a Byculla: 1 oz (25 mL) each of sherry, port, Curaçao and Ginger Wine, shaken with ice. If you use blue Curaçao, it looks truly disgusting.

Carey Rutherford tells us that the bittersweet tinge is added by the fact that he learned this recipe from a woman he wished to enchant, but who resisted his charms for years.

Half-Sweet Cocoa

1½ mugs	2% milk
2 heaping Tbsp (30 mL)	pure cocoa
2 heaping Tbsp (30 mL)	brown sugar
3 Tbsp (45 mL)	full cream

serves 2

To make 2 large mugs of cocoa, put 1½ mugs (measured in one of the mugs) of milk in a pot and put on high to heat, covered. (The milk will boil over quickly: have all ingredients at hand before turning on the stove.)

In the dry mug, combine the cocoa and brown sugar, mixing together thoroughly. Add a few tablespoons of the cream and a few of milk (filling about half of the cup). Mix the ingredients into a thick chocolatey sauce. When it's smooth, pour into the nearly heated milk, stir thoroughly, turn the heat down to medium-low, and scoop some milk into the mixing mug to access the rest of the chocolate. Taste. Taste again. It may require more sugar, depending upon your tastes. The half-sweet cocoa flavour is stimulating and warming and sensuous.

Note: if you start smearing the undiluted cocoa/sugar mass around, be sure to turn off the stove.

Do not put marshmallows or whipped cream on top: it ruins the cocoa flavour, turning it into hot chocolate, which is everyday stuff.

MUSIC TO COOK WITH

Isabel Bayrakdarian: *Azulão*
[CBC]

Jennifer Gasoi: *Songs for You*
[SPARKLING]

Virtually any alcohol will ignite if you work at it. (All right, wine's a challenge at the best of times, and beer is downright obstinate; here, industrial applications of fire may be required—blow torches and the like.) But brandy and rum, whisky and even the "white" spirits—gin, vodka, et cetera—will happily burst into flame for you, creating a dazzling, fiery drink and singeing parts of body or raiment that come too near.

Drinks Afire

A few pointers: don't use a Bic or similar lighter; not even your good Zippo. Those long barbecue lighting things work reasonably well, and there's sufficient length to them to keep your hand unblackened.

Matches are best—especially those long wooden fireplace ones. Penny-matchbooks, no. If you do use a wooden match, make sure you let the head burn for a few seconds to burn off the sulfur or whatever it is they use. This can impart a nasty taste to your drink.

Having secured your method of fire application, next pre-warm the glass, or cup or goblet. Make sure the liquor is warm, too—if you can keep it near a heat vent, or the stove, so much the better. At least make sure it's at room temperature, not just out of the cellar, or worse, the refrigerator.

The easiest way to proceed now is to preheat a deep spoon of booze over an open flame. (In this instance, you could use a lighter under the spoon, but watch the heat doesn't travel up the handle). Set it afire and then pour the spoonful of flaming liquor into the remainder; it will set the rest aflame.

Less elegant is the old standby: light the match, let the sulfur burn off and stick it near the surface of the liquor. Whoosh it goes, and nicely too. Now you can pour it into individual glasses or whatever. No need to snuff it out, it will only burn for a few seconds and extinguish itself.

Whisky fans will either love or hate the auld AA.

Drinks Afire: Aberdeen Angus

2 oz (50 mL)	Scotch
1 Tbsp (15 mL)	clear honey
1 tsp (5 mL)	fresh lime juice
1 oz (25 mL)	Drambuie

Mix the scotch and honey in a mug until smooth. Add lime juice and stir.

Warm the Drambuie in a metal ladle over a flame (or in the microwave), ignite and pour into the mug while it's burning.

Whisky fans will either love or hate the auld AA.

Serves 1, at bedtime

MUSIC TO COOK WITH

Battlefield Band: *After Hours*
[TEMPLE]

… because it's
so easy to do in
a big iron pot over
a Coleman stove.

So named, I suppose, because it's so easy to do in a big iron pot over a Coleman stove.

Campfire Brulot

**Serves 6, before
the singalong**

MUSIC TO COOK WITH

Hein und Oss: *Cowboy Lieder*
[SONGBIRD]

1 bottle	brandy
lots	cloves, cinnamon sticks (broken into pieces), lemon and orange peel, almonds or other shelled nuts
dash	grated nutmeg
to taste	brown sugar
1 pot	strong, black coffee, just made, still hot

Pour the brandy into a big pot. Add all the spices, nuts and sugar. Set the whole brew on fire. Slowly pour in the hot coffee while the booze burns. When it goes out, let it cool a little more and pour into warm mugs.

James Romanow of Saskatoon named this drink Christmas Passion, having witnessed its efficacy first hand.

"Personally," says James, "I advise to make the recipe as written."

Christmas Passion

3	egg yolks	
½ cup (125 mL)	sugar	
⅔ cup (150 mL)	dark rum (as black as you can find, Gosling's is good)	
⅓ cup (75 mL)	Kahlua liqueur	
1 cup (250 mL)	whipping cream	
for garnish	freshly grated nutmeg	

serves 4

Beat the egg yolks with the sugar. Add the rum and Kahlua slowly, a tablespoon at a time. When the mixture is smooth, fold in the whipping cream, unwhipped or very slightly whipped. Pour into glasses, and grind a pinch of nutmeg (not too much!) on top.

If this seems too much for you, you can make it lighter by using half-and-half cream (10% BF) or even homogenized milk. You can also whip the egg whites and beat them in to diminish the booze ratio, if you like. "Personally," says James, "I advise to make the recipe as written."

MUSIC TO COOK WITH

John Fahey: *Christmas Guitar* [VARRICK]

Jane Siberry: *Child* [SHEEBA] (for the best "12 Days of Christmas" on record)

The name says
it all, according to
Sylvia Hegge
of Toronto.

The name says it all, according to Sylvia Hegge of Toronto. "I've used this recipe every Christmas since 1991 and everyone loves it," she says. "I think I'm invited to parties because people want some of my eggnog." The recipe was originally developed for *Canadian Living* magazine.

Amazing Eggnog

serves 12–16

6	eggs
½ cup (125 mL)	granulated sugar
2 cups (500 mL)	milk
1	orange
2 cups (500 mL)	light cream
½ cup (125 mL)	brandy
½ cup (125 mL)	dark rum
1 cup (250 mL)	whipping cream
for garnish	freshly grated nutmeg or shaved chocolate

MUSIC TO COOK WITH

Sharon Isbin:
Journey to the Amazon [TELARC]

Whisk together the eggs and sugar in a large saucepan until blended. Gradually whisk in the milk. Peel off thin strips of orange zest and add to the milk mixture. Cook over low heat, whisking constantly for 10–15 minutes, until a candy thermometer registers 160°F (70°C) or mixture coats the back of a spoon. Strain immediately into a bowl and whisk in the light cream. Cool slightly, then cover and refrigerate until chilled. Stir in the brandy and rum.

Whip the cream and fold into the eggnog mixture. Serve in a chilled punch bowl or individual glasses. Sprinkle with nutmeg or shaved chocolate.

chapter twelve

desserts

Sparkling Jell-O with Moscato d'Asti 210

Black Muscat Jelly with Cream 211

Strawberries in Pepper Foam (with Marzipan Ice Cream) 212

Banana-Orange & Quark Cheesecake 213

Gratin de Fruits d'Été Amandine 214

Les Amis' Pecan Cheese Shortbread 216

Madeira Jelly 217

Double Chocolate Mashed Potato Brioche with Almond Caramel Sauce 218

Tiramisù 220

Poire au Chocolat 221

Roy's Concord Grape Tart 222

Cherry Chocolate Elk 224

Pears with Pepper & Honey 227

Lancashire Sticky Toffee Pudding 228

Piña Colada Coffee Cake 230

Cherries in a Cloud 232

Summer's the right time for jellied wine—what? you haven't had any yet?—and here are two approaches, one white, one black. The first comes from Tyler Dawson, all around wine guy at the Liberty Wine Merchants, who claims it's really an old family recipe, dating back to the Renaissance. His suggestion: do it up in big batches and keep it handy, cold, for unexpected guests.

(1) Sparkling Jell-O with Moscato d'Asti

serves 4

½ cup (125 mL)	boiling water
1 package	white grape Jell-O powder (not always found in every supermarket, but it is out there)
one 13-oz (375-mL) bottle	Moscato d'Asti (Italian sweet wine, more *pétillant* than fully sparkling), chilled

Mix the boiling water and Jell-O powder and let stand to cool, about 20 minutes.

Gently pour in the bottle of cold Moscato and mix well. Pour into individual stem glasses and stand in the refrigerator for 1 hour.

Bring glasses out, whisk the setting jelly lightly and refrigerate for another 3 hours, until well set—and shot through with bubbles.

Put stuff on top: fruit slices, berries, grapes, ice cream, whatever. Eat while very cold. Take two, they're barely caloric.

WINE PAIRINGS

Mionetto Moscato Frizzante
[IT]

MUSIC TO COOK WITH

Dvorak: *Bagatelles*
[ANALEKTA]

The second jelly is based on offshore research at The Ivy, a venerable London restaurant that continues to be the rage with trendy Londoners, as it has been for decades. How do they do that? Food's one reason. After a nice bit of fish, I found a listing on the dessert cart for black muscat jelly with cream. At £9 they see you coming; it was the costliest dessert on the list. Ah, but it was good. Nothing for it but to ask the server, who all but rolled his eyes, then got conspiratorial: "All it is, is Quady Elysium (California black muscat), jellied with a little extra sugar, cream on top. Nothing to it." He was right; another nigh-perfect summer dessert.

The second jelly is based on offshore research …

(2) Black Muscat Jelly with Cream

one 13-oz (375-mL) bottle	Quady Elysium
1 envelope	Knox gelatin powder, unflavoured
sufficient	water
to taste	sugar
lashings	of whipping cream

Make the gelatin according to the package directions, using the Elysium as your liquid and sweetening it if you like. (It's sweet enough for me, straight out of the bottle.) Pour into the good glasses and put in the refrigerator overnight.

Pipe or spoon whipping cream on top and make sure there are extras because people will be wanting seconds.

serves 4, maybe 6

WINE PAIRINGS

Quady Elysium [CA]

MUSIC TO COOK WITH

Anonymous 4: *American Angels*
[HARMONIA MUNDI]

You absolutely
have to have fresh
strawberries ...

You absolutely have to have fresh strawberries for this, so wait until it's the season. It's worth the wait. This is a recipe that's been hanging around my files for a very long time, and I can't recall where it came from; if it's yours, let me know and I'll certainly credit you.

Strawberries in Pepper Foam (and to gild the lily, Marzipan Ice Cream)

serves 4

WINE PAIRINGS

a good, light *rosado*—
bubbly or still

STRAWBERRIES

2	egg yolks
1	whole egg
½ lb (250 g)	fresh strawberries, puréed
1 tsp (5 mL)	sugar
1 tsp (5 mL)	dry green peppercorns, cracked

ICE CREAM

3½ oz (100 g)	real marzipan
1 cup (250 mL)	milk
1 cup (250 mL)	cream
6	egg yolks
¾ cup (175 mL)	sugar
7 oz (200 mL)	almond liqueur (or half-and-half almond extract, and vodka or brandy)

MUSIC TO COOK WITH

some good strawberry tunes

In a double boiler over hot water, whisk together the egg yolks, egg, puréed strawberries and sugar till it becomes a thick mixture. Remove from heat and whisk for a few more minutes, then stir in the green peppercorns. Set aside.

Soak the marzipan in the milk for 1 hour. Remove the marzipan, add the cream to the milk and bring to a boil. Add the egg yolks, sugar and marzipan. Stir until smooth and shiny; continue to stir over low heat until the mixture becomes creamy. Stir in the almond liqueur and freeze.

Put a few spoonfuls of the strawberry mixture into small serving bowls and top with ice cream. Some biscotti are nice, on the side.

This cooked cheesecake (the only kind of cheesecake I really care for, sorry) came from a pastry chef named Kurt Ebert, who spent some time in the kitchens of the Vancouver Four Seasons Hotel, where I first ate this dessert as part of an Easter brunch. Had to have it. Still make it at Easter. And five or six other times of the year.

… the only kind of cheesecake I really care for, sorry …

Banana-Orange & Quark Cheesecake

¼ cup (50 g)	butter
¼ cup (50 g) fine	breadcrumbs
1 cup (250 mL)	milk
pinch	salt
⅓ cup (75 mL)	cream of wheat
⅓ cup (75 mL)	butter
4	egg yolks
½ cup (125 mL)	sugar
1	vanilla pod
1	lemon, rind of
1 cup (250 mL)	quark cheese
4	egg whites
2	oranges, peeled and cut into small pieces
1	banana, peeled and cut into small pieces
for garnish	icing sugar

serves 4

WINE PAIRINGS

Hardy's
Riesling-Gewürztraminer [AU]

MUSIC TO COOK WITH

12 Cellists of the Berlin
Philharmonic: 'Round Midnight
[EMI]

Herb Alpert & The Tijuana
Brass: Whipped Cream & Other
Delights [SHOUT]

Preheat the oven to 375°F (190°C).

Butter a 4- to 5-cup (2-L) casserole with the butter. Sprinkle with the breadcrumbs.

Combine the milk and salt in a pan. Bring to the boil. Add the cream of wheat, stirring constantly. Simmer until thick. Cool.

Combine the butter, egg yolks, half of the sugar, vanilla and lemon. Beat in a mixer at high speed until smooth. Gradually add the cream of wheat mixture and quark cheese, beating until smooth.

Beat the egg whites and remaining sugar till stiff. Fold the egg whites and fruit gently into the cheese mixture. Fold into the buttered pan. Bake for 40 minutes, until golden brown and set in the centre.

Sprinkle with icing sugar.

I'd be going
the whole milk
bundle here.

I know this is a translated recipe from a French chef—likely Jacques Manière—because of the comment, handwritten in my notebook, opposite the list of fruits: "Fruit can be substituted to your liking or availability. Canned fruits in light syrup are acceptable." Yeah, well maybe. But not as good. That, and the 2% milk thing. I'd be going the whole milk bundle here.

Gratin de Fruits d'Été Amandine

serves 4

WINE PAIRINGS

Alain Faget Domaine de
Sancet White [FR]
(one of the best cheap
whites anywhere)

Trimbach Riesling [FR]

MUSIC TO COOK WITH

Jacques Loussier Trio:
Satie [TELARC]

SYRUP

2 cups (500 mL)	water
2 Tbsp (25 mL)	sugar

FRUIT

5	apricots
10	prune plums
5	peaches
20	cherries
10	strawberries
15	raspberries

SAUCE ANGLAISE

2 cups (500 mL)	2% milk
3	egg yolks
¼ cup (50 g)	sugar
2 Tbsp (25 mL)	almond powder (ground almonds)
1 Tbsp (15 mL)	sliced almonds

Combine syrup ingredients in a large saucepan and bring to a simmer.

Cut the fruits, except for the berries, in big wedges or chunks and poach them in the simmering syrup for a few minutes. Drain and let cool.

Bring the milk to a boil. Whisk the egg yolks and sugar together until foamy and whitish. Pour a bit of the boiling milk into the eggs to temper, then add the remaining milk, stirring. Cook in a bain-marie or double boiler until thick and creamy. Don't overcook or it will curdle. When cooked, add the almond powder.

Preheat the oven to Broil.

Arrange all the fruit in a gratin dish or individual dishes. Pour the sauce anglaise over and sprinkle with the sliced almonds. Glaze rapidly in a very hot oven, being careful to watch so it doesn't burn on top.

Serve immediately.

Every neighbourhood should have a cheese shop like Les Amis du Fromage; elect me and I'll make it happen. Alice and Allison Spurrell's Vancouver emporium of imported and domestic cheeses is one of the must-stops for my Saturday morning shoppery. After all, where you gonna get some Cornish Yarg on short notice? This is their recipe for simple, sensational cheese biscuits. Make some as gifts for friends; they'll be bringing the empty tins back immediately.

Les Amis' Pecan Cheese Shortbread

serves 1 and anybody says
otherwise is going
to have to
answer to
me!

½ lb (250 g)	butter
½ lb (250 g)	Gruyère cheese, grated
½ tsp (2 mL)	salt
¼ tsp (1 mL)	cayenne (could do more …)
2½ cups (625 mL)	all-purpose flour
½ cup (125 mL)	ground pecans

Place all ingredients in a mixer in the order listed. When mixed, roll the dough into a log. Refrigerate until firm.

When ready to bake, preheat the oven to 350°F (180°C).

Cut log into ½-inch (1-cm) slices. Place the slices on an ungreased cookie sheet and bake for about 10 minutes.

WINE PAIRINGS

Jackson-Triggs Proprietors'
Reserve White Meritage [ON]

Dr. Loosen Late Harvest
Riesling [GY]

Lang Late Harvest Riesling
[BC]

MUSIC TO COOK WITH

Yolanda Kondonassis:
Music of Alan Hovhaness
[TELARC]

Diane Nalini:
Tales my Mama Told Me
[EARTHGLOW]

Shelagh W. Robinson of St. Andrews, New Brunswick, has another take on jellied wine. I figure you can't ever have too many of them.

Madeira Jelly

2¼ cups (550 mL)	water, cold
½	lemon, rind of
3	cloves
½	tangerine, rind of
1 small stick	cinnamon
½ cup (125 mL)	sugar
1 envelope	unflavoured gelatin
1 Tbsp (15 mL)	water
1	lemon, juice of
1 cup (250 mL)	sweet Madeira (Verdelho or Bual)
for serving	whipping cream

serves 6

WINE PAIRINGS

Broadbent "Rainwater" Madeira [PO]

Cossart & Gordon Bual 1963 [PO]
($200 where I shop!)

Justino Henriques Sercial 1940 [PO]
(I've got half a bottle left!)

MUSIC TO COOK WITH

Marc-André Hamelin:
Godowsky [CBC]

Put the cold water in a saucepan with the lemon rind, cloves, tangerine rind, cinnamon and sugar. Let simmer over low heat for 8 minutes.

In a bowl large enough to hold all the ingredients, soak the gelatin for 5 minutes in 1 Tbsp (15 mL) water and the lemon juice.

Pour the hot liquid over the soaked gelatin and stir until entirely dissolved. Add the Madeira and let stand until cool. Taste and add more sugar if necessary.

Strain into a screw-topped jar and cover tightly. Refrigerate overnight.

Turn into a well-chilled glass bowl and serve with a jug of rich cream, either whipped or not. This is not a stiff jelly. It's really delicious.

It's so good, it's here again for those who might have missed it.

If you're in Kelowna, in the heart of British Columbia's wine country, and you have just one night for dinner, you must go to Fresco, downtown. Here, Rodney Butters and Audrey Surrao have established the sort of legendary haven of fine food you expect to find in small French country towns that are "worth a special detour" according to *Le Guide Michelin*. Brilliant food, starter to dessert, excellent wines—of the area, of course—and great ambience. Years earlier, when Rodney Butters was cooking in Vancouver, even before he went to the

Double Chocolate Mashed Potato Brioche

could serve 8 but why be stingy?

WINE PAIRINGS

KEO Commandaria [CY]

Quinta do Portal
Moscatel Reserva [PO]

Ruby Port
(not necessarily from Portugal)

MUSIC TO COOK WITH

Owain Phyfe & The New
World Rennaissance Band:
Tales from the Vineyard
[NIGHTWATCH]

Matt Flinner Quartet:
Walking on the Moon
[COMPASS]

BRIOCHE

5 oz (140 g)	bittersweet chocolate
1 Tbsp (15 mL)	instant coffee
3 Tbsp (45 mL)	amaretto liqueur
½ cup (125 mL)	butter
4 large	eggs, separated
½ cup (125 mL)	granulated sugar
1 cup (250 mL)	mashed potatoes
½ cup (125 mL)	ground almonds
pinch	salt
½ cup (125 mL)	chocolate chips

SAUCE

⅔ cup (150 mL)	sugar
¼ cup (50 mL)	water
½ cup (125 mL)	whipping cream
4 Tbsp (60 mL)	slivered almonds, toasted
for garnish	dark and white chocolate shards

fabulous Wickaninnish Inn on the west coast of Vancouver Island, he introduced me to this dessert, which I must have eaten a half dozen times before requesting it for my cookbook a decade ago. He considers it his signature dessert, having had it on every restaurant menu where he's cooked, and planning on keeping it on every one to come. He'll tell you that his grandmother used to make something similar. It's so good that it's here again for those who might have missed it. And those who might just want another reminder …

with Almond Caramel Sauce

Preheat the oven to 350°F (180°C).

For the brioche, melt the chocolate, instant coffee, amaretto and butter in the top of a double boiler.

Beat the egg yolks with the sugar until thick and creamy. Add the chocolate mixture until blended. Add the mashed potatoes and ground almonds until thoroughly combined. Add a pinch of salt.

In a separate bowl beat the egg whites until stiff. Fold the egg whites and chocolate chips into the potato batter.

Pour into brioche moulds (or individual ramekins) and bake for about 30 minutes. Let cool for 15 minutes and remove from moulds.

To make the sauce, dissolve the sugar in the water in a pot. Caramelize the sugar till golden brown.

Heat the cream to just below boiling and add all at once to the caramel. Add the toasted almonds and cool.

Serve the warm brioche with the sauce, and dark and white chocolate shards as garnish.

All those spring cooking sessions at Villa Delia in Tuscany taught me a few things …

All those spring cooking sessions at Villa Delia in Tuscany taught me a few things for the basic repertoire; this tiramisù is one. All right, there's the fact that, like a real Caesar salad dressing, the eggs are raw. If it bothers you, stay away. As a southern sage once said, "You've put worse things in your mouth before!"

Tiramisù

serves 6

WINE PAIRINGS

Zenato Valpolicella Ripasso
[IT]

Royal Tokaj Tokaji Aszu [HU]

Il Poggione Sant'Antimo
Vin Santo [IT]

6	eggs, separated
6 Tbsp (90 mL)	sugar
1 tub (1 lb / 500 g)	mascarpone
¼ cup (50 mL)	Amaretto
1 cup (250 mL)	freshly brewed espresso, cooled
¼ cup (50 mL)	brandy
2 packages	*pavesini* (Italian ladyfinger biscuits)
for dusting	cocoa or chocolate shavings

Separate the eggs into 2 bowls. With an electric mixer, beat the egg yolks with sugar till creamy. Add the mascarpone and amaretto.

Clean the beaters and beat the egg whites until stiff and peaking. Gently fold the cheese mixture into the egg white mixture.

Stir the espresso and brandy together in a flat-bottomed dish. Dip the biscuits quickly into the liquid, one at a time. (You just want to let them absorb a little liquid, but not to get mushy.)

Put one-third of the dipped biscuits in a single layer in an 8- or 9-inch (20- or 23-cm) square glass baking dish. Spread one-third of the mascarpone mix on top, to the same level of thickness.

Repeat the process: 2 more layers of biscuits and filling, ending with mascarpone. Dust the top with cocoa or chocolate shavings.

Refrigerate for at least 3 hours before serving. It's actually best the next day and even freezes quite well; make sure you thaw it at room temperature for a couple of hours before serving.

MUSIC TO COOK WITH

Gryphon Trio:
Beethoven [ANALEKTA]

Porkbelly Futures:
Way Past Midnight
[OPENING NIGHT]

Christine J. Cannon of Kingston found herself sharing a train compartment with author Alice Munro and her daughter one day, and they talked food for the entire trip. Ms. Munro particularly wanted the recipe for this elegant dessert and, seeing that Christine wasn't able to supply it on the spot, jotted her temporary phone number on the back of her business card. Christine later phoned her with the recipe, and still has the card, now being used as a bookmark in an Alice Munro book.

Christine J. Cannon ... found herself sharing a train compartment with author Alice Munro ...

Poire au Chocolat

6	dessert pears	
4 squares	semi-sweet chocolate	
¼ cup (50 mL)	Tia Maria or other coffee-flavoured liqueur	
2 Tbsp (25 mL)	butter	
2 large	eggs, separated	
½ cup (125 mL)	chopped mixed glace fruit	
1 tsp (5 mL)	cognac or kirsch	
2 Tbsp (25 mL)	chopped pecans	
1 slice	green candied pineapple or angelica	
for garnish	whipped cream	
for garnish	finely chopped pistachio nuts	

serves 6

WINE PAIRINGS

Monimpex Golden
Pear Liqueur [HU]

Okanagan Spirits
Poire Williams [BC]

Growers Pear Cider [BC]

MUSIC TO COOK WITH

Bill Evans:
The Complete [VERVE]

Select medium-sized pears that still have the stem attached. Buy them several days ahead of time and place them stem side up on a sunny windowsill to ripen.

The day before serving, chop the chocolate into coarse pieces. In the top of a double boiler, over boiling water, melt the chocolate together with the Tia Maria, stirring from time to time. Remove from the heat and stir in the butter. Add the egg yolks one at a time and stir until the mixture is blended. Set aside to cool.

Combine the glace fruit with the cognac and pecans. Set aside.

Peel the pears and core them from the bottom, leaving the stem on. Stuff each cavity with the fruit-nut mixture. With a knife, level the bottom of each pear so that it sits firmly upright; blot with paper towels. Stand the pears on a wire rack placed over a platter.

Beat the egg whites until stiff but not dry and fold them into the cooled chocolate mixture, combining only until no white streaks remain. Spoon this mousse over the pears so that they are completely coated.

Lifting the pears by the stem, place them on serving plates and garnish each pear top with 2 leaves cut from the candied pineapple. Refrigerate at least 4 hours, or overnight. Just before serving, pipe a rosette of whipped cream beside each pear and sprinkle with pistachio nuts.

... although we
live in an area
surrounded by
vineyards, we
have never seen
a grape tart ...

Julie Rollason of Niagara-on-the-Lake, Ontario, tells us that "although we live in an area surrounded by vineyards, we have never seen a grape tart in the Niagara region ... On the other hand, we recently travelled through the Finger Lakes region in New York state and found that 'grape tart' or 'grape pie' is available in just about every restaurant, and even from many houses—Stop here for Linda's (Mary's, Martha's, et cetera) Famous Grape Pie." Julie doesn't, however, reveal who Roy is.

Roy's Concord Grape Tart

serves 6–8

WINE PAIRINGS

Concord Wine ?! [NY]

MUSIC TO COOK WITH

Vancouver Symphony:
Rumanian Rhapsody [CBC]

Nellie McKay:
Get Away From Me [COLUMBIA]

EGG GLAZE

1	egg
1 Tbsp (15 mL)	water
one 9-inch (23-cm)	unbaked pie crust

CONCORD GRAPE FILLING

2 lb (1 kg)	blue grapes, such as Concord or Fredonia
¼ cup (50 mL)	cornstarch
1 Tbsp (15 mL)	lemon juice
2 tsp (10 mL)	grated orange zest
½ cup (125 mL)	granulated sugar
2 Tbsp (25 mL)	Concord wine, optional

STREUSEL TOPPING

½ cup (125 mL)	brown sugar
1 cup (250 mL)	all-purpose flour
½ cup (125 mL)	butter

Preheat the oven to 400°F (200°C). Beat the egg and water together. Brush over the bottom, sides and edges of the pie crust. Refrigerate while preparing the filling.

Press the grapes with your fingers to pop out the fruit. Reserve the skins in a bowl. Place the skinned fruit in a pot and bring to a boil. Remove from heat. Sieve the grape seeds from the pulp. Mix the pulp with the skins and set aside.

In a large bowl, combine the cornstarch with ¼ cup (50 mL) of liquid from the reserved grape mixture. Then stir in the lemon juice, grated orange zest, sugar, wine (if using) and remaining grape mixture. Pour the mixture into the prepared pie crust.

In another large bowl, combine the brown sugar and flour for the streusel. Cut in the butter until the mixture has a crumbly texture. Sprinkle over top of the grape filling.

Bake for 35 minutes, or until grape juice is bubbling. The topping should be golden brown. Let cool completely before serving.

Note: The filling can be frozen in small containers to be used during the winter.

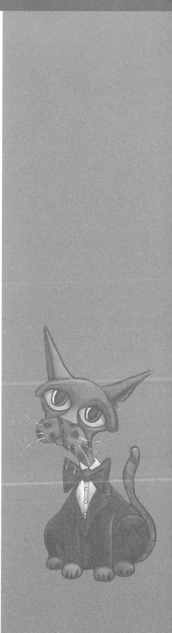

Graydon Saunders …
calls this Chocolate
Elk because it's
clearly of the
same genus as
chocolate mousse.

Graydon Saunders of Toronto calls this Chocolate Elk because it's clearly of the same genus as chocolate mousse.

What chocolate you select as an ingredient makes a big difference to the final result. You want something that's a pure dark chocolate, without the sort of addenda often made to chocolate intended to be unnaturally shiny or not melt in your hands. Since you do want it to melt, chocolate that comes in small pieces is good, too. Belgian chocolate chips are likely just the thing if you can get them, but a certain experimentation will be required to discover what works best from your local chocolate supply.

Cherry Chocolate Elk

serves 8 or more
Needs 8–10 hours to set.

WINE PAIRINGS

Godiva Chocolate Liqueur [FR]

Delamain Cognac [FR]

Marcel Trepout et
Fils Armagnac [FR]

MUSIC TO COOK WITH

Mary Lou Fallis:
Prima Donna on a Moose
[OPENING DAY]

Simon Fraser
University Pipe Band:
Down Under [SFU]

SHORTBREAD CRUST

2 cups (500 mL)	fine soft oat flour (NOT oatmeal)
¼ cup (50 mL)	whole wheat pastry flour (white pastry flour is a little too soft)
1 cup (250 mL)	butter
½ cup (125 mL)	demerara sugar
for greasing	butter

FILLING

4 cups (1 L)	whipping cream
1 lb (500 g)	semi-sweet or bittersweet chocolate, chopped
1 Tbsp (15 mL)	demerara sugar or bland liquid honey (3 Tbsp/45 mL if you're using bittersweet chocolate)

TOPPING

one 28-oz (796-mL) jar	pitted cherries in syrup (sour cherries work better than sweet)
1 Tbsp (15 mL)	frozen orange juice concentrate
½ tsp (2 mL)	ground cinnamon
3	whole cloves, crushed
pinch	dried peppermint leaves, powdered
2 Tbsp (25 mL)	cornstarch or rice flour
1 Tbsp (15 mL)	cold water

The recipes for the crust and the elk scale down or up well, between half and twice the amounts given, so long as the proportions are closely maintained.

The fruit topping is optional, but is often well received. Putting brandied whipped cream on top of that is overkill, "to the point where people fond of rich desserts asked me to please not do that anymore."

CRUST

Preheat the oven to 350°F (180°C).

For the shortbread crust, sift the oat flour. Sift the pastry flour into the oat flour, blend well, and set aside.

In a large bowl, cream together the butter and sugar, adding a quarter of each at a time; when thoroughly blended, add the flour by quarters (about ½ cup/125 mL at a time), stopping as soon as it is all blended in. You should have a sticky soft dough that you'll have to vigorously spatula off the mixer beaters and out of the bowl.

Butter an 11-inch (3.5-L) springform pan with a lavish hand. Press the short-bread dough evenly into the bottom of the pan and prick all over with a fork, being sure to pierce through to the pan. Bake for 15 minutes or until the top of the shortbread darkens evenly. Set the crust aside to cool; do not refrigerate, or the shortbread will become soggy.

FILLING

Heat the whipping cream in the top of a double boiler. When it is warm, add the chocolate in small pieces, stirring all the while. Once the chocolate is all melted, add the sugar or honey. Stir steadily for the next 45–60 minutes; you are waiting for the small dark flecks of chocolate that show on the spoon to dissolve, or at least to get very small, and the texture of the whole to thicken. (Whether or not the flecks will disappear entirely depends on the chocolate you have chosen to use. Bittersweet is sometimes regarded as producing an overly bitter result, as well as having flecks that do not entirely disappear.) Pour straight from the pot onto the cooled crust in the springform pan; refrigerate until set. This will take at least 8–12 hours; usually overnight. Once set, the elk will have a consistency like soft ice cream.

continues on next page ...

TOPPING

Pour off the syrup from the cherries into a saucepan. Put the cherries in a strainer over the saucepan and joggle it occasionally until the cherries are drained enough to not be dripping anymore. Set the strainer aside over a clean bowl to catch any remaining liquid.

Put the saucepan with the syrup over medium heat, add the frozen concentrated orange juice, and stir until it dissolves. Add the cinnamon, crushed cloves and powdered dried peppermint leaves, stirring occasionally. Pour in any additional liquid that has accumulated under the strainer.

Mix the starch and cold water together with a fork until smooth. When the mixture in the saucepan is almost boiling, add the starch mixture and stir. When the result clears and thickens, stir in the cherries, and apply to the top of the elk. There should be lots of height left to the springform pan sides to keep the topping contained while it sets. Re-refrigerate the elk until the topping sets. (A couple of hours should be plenty of time.)

Graydon says, "It is advisable to serve chocolate elk in small portions, and to promise seconds to any chocolate fiends who find that they desire same after finishing their first portion. I've served 12 people from one of these and had leftovers, but you can count on serving 8. Chocolate elk keeps well, covered in the refrigerator."

Sheer simplicity from Susan Murdoch of London, Ontario. Simple is nice sometimes, especially after the preceding elk.

Pears with Pepper & Honey

2 Tbsp (25 mL)	unsalted butter
2	firm ripe Bosc pears, halved lengthwise and cored
2 Tbsp (25 mL)	balsamic vinegar
4 oz (125 g)	mild goat cheese, cut into 4 slices
¼ cup (50 mL)	honey
to taste	freshly ground pepper

Preheat the oven to 400°F (200°C).

Melt the butter in a Pyrex baking dish. Arrange the pears cut-side down and roast for 20 minutes. Pour the vinegar over the pears and roast 5 more minutes. Transfer to serving plates cut-side down.

Top the pears with the cheese and drizzle juices from the baking dish over the cheese and pears. Drizzle with honey and give a crack of freshly ground pepper.

serves 4—easily increased or decreased

WINE PAIRINGS

Fassbind Williams [SW]

Schladerer Birnenbrand [GY]

Has anybody ever found a good pear wine?

MUSIC TO COOK WITH

Los Angeles Guitar Quartet: *Heroes* [SONY]

... from a "reliable source" at an Information Centre in Clithertoe, Lancashire, UK.

This gooey classic comes via Fabian Hugh, who says he got it from a "reliable source" at an Information Centre in Clithertoe, Lancashire, UK. Mind you, my friend Ffiona makes a fabulous one at her eponymous restaurant in the Kensington Church Street, in London. Maybe I'll get her recipe for the next cookbook. You can't ever have too many …

Lancashire Sticky Toffee Pudding

serves 8

WINE PAIRINGS

Crabbie's Green Ginger Wine
[UK]

Williams & Humbert Walnut
Brown Sherry [SP]

MUSIC TO COOK WITH

Michael Gray:
9 Blasted Notes [DUNABER]

Kathryn Tickell:
Common Ground [BLACK CROW]

PUDDING

⅔ cup (150 mL)	chopped dates
½ tsp (2 mL)	vanilla
1 tsp (5 mL)	instant coffee granules
¾ tsp (4 mL)	baking soda
¾ cup (175 mL)	boiling water
⅜ cup (40 mL)	butter
¾ cup (175 mL)	white sugar
2	eggs
1¾ cups (425 mL)	all-purpose flour

SAUCE

1¼ cups (300 mL)	brown sugar
½ cup (125 mL)	butter
6 Tbsp (90 mL)	heavy or whipping cream (or double cream, if you can get it)

PUDDING

Preheat the oven to 350°F (180°C).

Stir together the dates, vanilla, instant coffee, baking soda and water and let stand for 15 minutes.

Cream the butter and sugar until fluffy. Add the eggs and mix thoroughly. Fold in the flour, then fold in the date mixture.

Grease either 8 small ovenproof ramekins or a 7- x 11-inch (2-L) glass baking dish. Pour the pudding in and bake until a cake tester comes out clean, about 30–35 minutes. Do not overbake.

SAUCE

Preheat the oven to Broil.

Gently heat the brown sugar, butter and cream until the sugar has melted.

Arrange the pudding(s) on a heatproof plate while still hot. Pour the sauce over and put under the broiler until the sauce begins to bubble.

Judy Graschuk …
invented
this cake …

Judy Graschuk of Edmonton invented this cake and is beseiged by requests for it. Judy, get back in the kitchen at once and do some more inventing!

Piña Colada Coffee Cake

serves approximately 8

WINE PAIRINGS

Pina Coladas or amaretto

Ava Tahiti Starfruit
eau de vie [TA]

MUSIC TO COOK WITH

Valentino Orchestra:
Daybreak Express
[JUST A MEMORY]

CAKE

¾ cup (175 mL)	butter or margarine
¾ cup (175 mL)	granulated sugar
1	egg
1 cup (250 mL)	sour cream
1 tsp (5 mL)	coconut extract
2 cups (500 mL)	all-purpose flour
1 tsp (5 mL)	baking soda
1 tsp (5 mL)	baking powder
¼ tsp (1 mL)	salt
two 14- or 19-oz (398- or 540-mL) cans	crushed pineapple, well drained (reserve juice)
½ cup (125 mL)	medium-sweet shredded coconut

TOPPING

2 Tbsp (25 mL)	butter or margarine
1 Tbsp	all-purpose flour
¼ cup (50 mL)	granulated sugar
¾ cup (175 mL)	medium-sweet shredded coconut

SAUCE

	reserved pineapple juice
1 Tbsp (15 mL)	melted butter or margarine
1–1½ Tbsp	cornstarch
¼ cup (50 mL)	granulated sugar
1 tsp (5 mL)	coconut extract
for serving	whipped cream or ice cream

Preheat the oven to 350°F (180°C). Grease a 9-inch (2.5-L) springform pan.

Cream the butter with the sugar. Add the egg and beat until well blended. Stir in the sour cream and coconut extract.

In a separate bowl, combine the flour, baking soda, baking powder and salt. Add to the batter and mix well. Spread two-thirds of the batter in the prepared pan.

In another bowl, combine the pineapple and coconut. Mix well and spread evenly over the batter in the pan. Top with the remaining batter, spreading evenly.

For the topping, mix the butter, flour, sugar and coconut until crumbly; sprinkle over the top of the cake. Bake for 1 hour or until a tester comes out clean.

While the cake is baking, prepare the sauce by combining the juice, butter, cornstarch, sugar and coconut extract. Heat on the stovetop or in the microwave, stirring occasionally, until the sauce is thickened.

Serve the cake with whipped cream or ice cream and spoon warm sauce over top.

Mike Kressock not only won a trip to Montreal by submitting this recipe …

Mike Kressock not only won a trip to Montreal by submitting this recipe but he also got into the cookbook.

Cherries in a Cloud

WINE PAIRINGS

Cherry Heering [DK]

Fassbind Kirsch du Righi [SW]

Elephant Island Family Reserve Cherry Wine [BC]

MUSIC TO COOK WITH

Holst: *The Planets* for 2 Pianos [NAXOS]

6	egg whites
¾ tsp (4 mL)	cream of tartar
2 cups (500 mL)	sugar
¾ cup (175 mL)	chopped walnuts
2 cups (500 mL)	saltine crackers, crushed
2 tsp (10 mL)	vanilla extract
for serving	Cool Whip
1 can	cherry pie filling

Beat the egg whites with the cream of tartar and add in the sugar a little at a time. Beat until the mixture is shiny, white and frothy. Then fold in the walnuts, crushed crackers and vanilla.

Put the mixture into a greased baking pan and bake in a 350°F (160°C) oven for 25 minutes. Remove and cool.

When cool, spread Cool Whip over the meringue and pour the cherry pie filling on top.

index

A

Aberdeen Angus, 205
Amazing Eggnog, 208
Anasazi Margarita, The, 190
Angels in E-Types (Scrumpied Oysters), 71
Antipasto of Roasted Red Peppers, 10
Applesauce, Pinot Gris, 124
Artichokes, Fresh, with Sherry, 38
Asparagus
    Festive, 147
    Perfect Risotto, with, 59
    White, Ragout with Morels, 40

B

B'stillah, 184
Baeckaoffa, 150
Baked Cholesterol (Goat Cheese 'n' Cream
    Potatoes), 138
Banana-Orange & Quark Cheesecake, 213
Beans
    Black, Three-Alarm "Caviar," 11
    broad, Fresh Artichokes with Sherry, 38
    Escarole & Beans, 145
    lima and edamame, La-La Succotash, 134
    lima, West Coast Scafata, 137
Béarnaise Sauce, Butterless, 41
Beef
    Baeckaoffa, 150
    Cuminized Garlic-Roast Round, 104
    David Veljacic's Beef Ribs Method, 116
    David Veljacic's "How to Grill the Perfect Steak"
        Lesson, 117
    Orange Beef Stew, 153
    Pumpkin Number, The, 176
    Sauerkraut Soup, 28
    Tagine of Beef with Prunes & Almonds, 160
    Tartare with Avocado, Papaya & Lime, 6
    Tito's Texas Tenderloin, 106
    Tourtière, 126
Beef Tartare with Avocado, Papaya & Lime, 6
Black Bean "Caviar," Three-Alarm, 11
Black Cat Lamb Roast, 110
Black Muscat Jelly with Cream, 211
Bloody Nonsense: A Garden Kick, 197
Blueberry Mincemeat, 36
Boba Seafood Cakes with Tropical Tartar Sauce, 68
Braised Celery with Mint Sauce, 135
Breads and Crackers
    Buttermilk Cornbread with Pine Nuts,
        Pumpkin & Oka, 39
    Les Amis' Pecan Cheese Shortbread, 216
    Sharpish Cheddar Thins, 42
Brioche, Double Chocolate Mashed Potato
    with Almond Caramel Sauce, 218
Brussels Sprouts Dialogues, 142
Brussels Sprouts with Pine Nuts & Sage Cream, 144

Brussels Sprouts, Shredded, with Pine Nuts
    & Prosciutto, 141
Butter Sauce with a Rumour of Tomatoes, 136
Butterless Béarnaise Sauce, 41
Buttermilk Cornbread with Pine Nuts,
    Pumpkin & Oka, 39

C

Caesar Salad, Sharon's, 18
Cake, Coffee, Piña Colada, 230
Caldo Verde, 14
Campfire Brulot, 206
Canadian Choucroute, A, 158
Carrot Bisque & Sweet Variation, Uncle John's, 6
Charentais Veal Stew, 152
Cheese
    Buttermilk Cornbread with Pine Nuts,
        Pumpkin & Oka, 39
    cheddar, in Dorothy's Eggs, 45
    Crêpe of Smoked Duck Breast with Goat
        Cheese, 96
    Egg Noodles with Gorgonzola & Pistachios, 50
    Fondue, Jean's Cheese, 186
    Goat Cheese 'n' Cream Potatoes (Baked
        Cholesterol) 138
    Gruyère, in Les Amis' Pecan Cheese Shortbread, 216
    mascarpone, in Tiramisù, 220
    Münster, in Katzenthaler Fusilli, 49
    Pasta with Kale & Feta Cheese, 62
    Sharpish Cheddar Thins, 42
Cheesecake, Banana-Orange & Quark, 213
Cherries in a Cloud, 232
Cherry Chocolate Elk, 224
Chicken and Poultry, 82–99
    B'stillah, 184
    Chicken Full of Lemon, Garlic & Rosemary, 90
    Chicken Provençal, 98
    Coq au Gewürztraminer, 83
    Cornish Game Hens with Sauerkraut, 88
    Crêpe of Smoked Duck Breast with Goat
        Cheese, 96
    duck, Marietta's Anatra all'Arancio, 82
    liver, Passion Pâté, 9
    Margaritaville Chicken, 87
    Mexican-Style Chicken Salad, 22
    Minestronska, 32
    Moroccan Chicken Stew, 163
    Old-Fashioned Chicken & Corn Stew, 162
    Passion Poulet à la DiscDrive, 92
    Ribollita, 30
    Spicy Thai & Luscious Basil Chicken, 94
Chicken Full of Lemon, Garlic & Rosemary, 90
Chicken Provençal, 98
Chili
    David Lopez's Anti-Extravaganza, 172
    DiscDrive Tends-to-Get-Spicy Veggie, 154
    True North, Mark IV, 166

Chocolate
  Double Chocolate Mashed Potato Brioche with
    Almond Caramel Sauce, 218
  Half-Sweet Cocoa, 203
  Philippe Jeanty's Raspberry Milkshake in a
    Chocolate Bag, 182
  Poire au Chocolat, 221
Christmas Passion, 207
Cider Possett, 201
Cinnamon Roasted Pork Tenderloin with Pinot Gris
  Applesauce, 124
Cioppino, The Lovers', 179
Coffee
  Black Cat Lamb Roast, 110
  Campfire Brulot, 206
  Michael James's Espresso Marinated New
    Zealand Lamb, 108
  Sautéed Grapes with Espresso & Red Wine, 37
  Tiramisù, 220
Coq au Gewürztraminer, 83
Cornbread, Buttermilk, with Pine Nuts, Pumpkin
  & Oka, 39
Cornish Game Hens with Sauerkraut, 88
Crab Salad, Raspberry, 20
Crêpe of Smoked Duck Breast with Goat Cheese, 96
Crêpes Singhiozzando, 96
crêpes, in Tower of Pisa, 173
Croutons, State-of-the-Art, 18
Cuminized Garlic-Roast Round, 104

D

David Lopez's Anti-Extravaganza, 172
David Veljacic's Beef Ribs Method, 116
David Veljacic's "How to Grill the Perfect Steak"
  Lesson, 117
De Johnge Butter Sauce, Joe Muer's, 43
Desserts, 209–31
DiscDrive Tends-to-Get-Spicy Veggie Chili, 154
Dorothy's Eggs, 45
Double Chocolate Mashed Potato Brioche with
  Almond Caramel Sauce, 218
Drambuie Salmon, 79
Drinks Afire, 204
Drinks, 180–208
Duck
  Crêpe of Smoked Duck Breast with Goat
    Cheese, 96
  Marietta's Anatra all'Arancio, 82

E

Egg Noodles with Gorgonzola & Pistachios, 50
Eggplant
  Italian Sausage, Eggplant & Dill Winter Soup, 25
  Japanese Eggplant Baked with Apricots, 3
Eggs
  Amazing Eggnog, 208
  Christmas Passion, 207

Dorothy's Eggs, 45
Entrée de Tête Fromagée Maison, 8
Escarole & Beans, 145
Escarole & Tomato Soup with Lemon & Mint, 16
Extravaganzas, 165–187

F

Far Out Noodles, 51
Fennel & Orange Salad with Black Olives, 17
Festive Asparagus, 147
Fettuccine with Rosemary & Tuna, 48
Fiery Prawns in Orange Juice, 4
Fish and Shellfish, 65–79
  Angels in E-Types (Scrumpied Oysters) 71
  Boba Seafood Cakes with Tropical Tartar Sauce, 68
  Drambuie Salmon, 79
  Fettuccine with Rosemary & Tuna, 48
  Fiery Prawns in Orange Juice, 4
  Linguine with Sardines, Chili & Capers, 63
  Lovers' Cioppino, 179
  Mayne Island Oyster Stew, 72
  Pappardelle with Tuna in Basil & Mint Sauce, 78
  Prawn & Peanut Soup with Lime & Coconut, 15
  Prawns with Sugar Snap Peas & Garlic, 2
  Raspberry Crab Salad, 20
  Roasted Prawns with Morels & Morel Butter, 76
  Scallop Fettuccini with Ginger-Cream Sauce, 60
  Scallops with Mushrooms & Lime, in
    Parchment, 74
  Sherried, Chilied Oysters, 66
  Shrimp & Mango Ceviche, 5
  Tonno con Cilantro Pesto, 73
  TVG Paella, 156
flaming technique for alcohol, 204
Freedom Fries, 146
Fresh Artichokes with Sherry, 38
Fruits d'Été Amandine, Gratin, 214

G

Giardiniera Marietta, 132
Gingered Goose with Apples & Calvados, Pink
  Peppercorns & Coriander, 84
Gingered Rum Tea, 196
Goose, Gingered with Apples & Calvados, Pink
  Peppercorns & Coriander, 84
Gorgonzola with Egg Noodles & Pistachios, 50
Grape Tart, Roy's Concord, 222
Grapes, Sautéed with Espresso & Red Wine, 37
Gratin de Fruits d'Été Amandine, 214

H

Half-Sweet Cocoa, 203
Hasselbacks with Fresh Bay Leaves, 139
Head Cheese, Homemade, 8

I

Italian Sausage, Eggplant & Dill Winter Soup, 25

J

Janssen's Temptation, 70
Japanese Eggplant Baked with Apricots, 3
Jean's Cheese Fondue, 186
Jelly
  Black Muscat, with Cream, 211
  Madeira, 217
  Sparkling Jell-O with Moscato d'Asti, 210
Jicama & Green Papaya Slaw with Water
  Chestnuts, 24
Joe Muer's De Johnge Butter Sauce, 43

K

Kale
  Caldo Verde, 14
  Pasta with Kale & Feta Cheese, 62
Katzenthaler Fusilli, 49

L

La-La Succotash (Confetti Corn), 134
Lamb
  Baeckaoffa, 150
  Chops with Chorizo & Garlic, 103
  Michael James's Espresso Marinated New
    Zealand, 108
  Plymouth Martini'd Leg of, with Jalapeño Olives,
    118
  Ziti with Lamb, Ham & Greens, 56
Lamb Chops with Chorizo & Garlic, 103
Lancashire Sticky Toffee Pudding, 228
Lapin aux Pommes, 122
Les Amis' Pecan Cheese Shortbread, 216
Linguine with Sardines, Chili & Capers, 63
Long Flat Wine Warmers in Both Official Colours,
  194
Lovers' Cioppino, The, 179

M

Madeira Jelly, 217
Margaritaville Chicken, 87
Marietta's Anatra all'Arancio, 82
Martini Named Robert le Pur, 192
Marzipan Ice Cream, 212
Mayne Island Oyster Stew, 72
Meats, 101–129
  caribou, in True North Chili, Mark IV, 166
  Charentais Veal Stew, 152
  Baeckaoffa, 150
  Beef Tartare with Avocado, Papaya & Lime, 6
  Black Cat Lamb Roast, 110
  Cinnamon Roasted Pork Tenderloin with Pinot
    Gris Applesauce, 124
  Cuminized Garlic-Roast Round, 104
  Entrée de Tête Fromagée Maison, 8
  Lamb Chops with Chorizo & Garlic, 103
  Lapin aux Pommes, 122

Michael James's Espresso Marinated New
  Zealand Lamb, 108
muskox, in True North Chili, Mark IV, 166
Orange Beef Stew, 153
Passion Pâté, 9
Plymouth Martini'd Leg of Lamb with Jalapeño
  Olives, 118
Pork Loin in Tuna Sauce, 128
Portuguese Pork, Marinated with Garlic, 102
Real Man Bacon-Wrapped Anchovy Pâté
  Roasted Pork Steak, 107
Rummy Smoky Spicy Ribs, 120
Sauerkraut Soup, 28
Sausage in Bondage, 114
Tourtière, 126
Uccellini Scappati, 112
Ziti with Lamb, Ham & Greens, 56
Mexican-Style Chicken Salad, 22
Michael James's Espresso Marinated New Zealand
  Lamb, 108
Mincemeat, Blueberry, 36
Minestronska, 32
Morels & Morel Butter, with Roasted Prawns, 76
Moroccan Chicken Stew, 163

N

Niku-Miso, 12
Noodles, Egg, with Gorgonzola & Pistachios, 50
Noodles, Far Out, 51

O

Oceanwood Gimlet, The, 193
Old-Fashioned Chicken & Corn Stew, 162
Orange Beef Stew, 153
Oysters
  Angels in E-Types (Scrumpied Oysters), 71
  Mayne Island Oyster Stew, 72
  Sherried, Chilied Oysters, 66
  TVG Paella, 156
Oysters, Sherried, Chilied, 66

P

Paella, TVG, 156
Pappardelle with Tuna in Basil & Mint Sauce, 78
Passion Pâté, 9
Passion Poulet à la DiscDrive, 92
Pastas, 47–63
Pasta with Kale & Feta Cheese, 62
Pears with Chocolate, 221
Pears with Pepper & Honey, 227
Penne with Fresh Vegetables, 58
Peppers, Roasted Red, Antipasto, 10
Perfect Risotto, with Asparagus, The, 59
Philippe Jeanty's Raspberry Milkshake in a
  Chocolate Bag, 182
Piggies in the Middle, 44
Piña Colada Coffee Cake, 230

Pizza, Potato & Rosemary-Garlic, 140
Plymouth Martini'd Leg of Lamb with Jalapeño
    Olives, 118
Poire au Chocolat, 221
Pork
    Baeckaoffa, 150
    boar, bacon, picnic shoulder, in True North
        Chili, Mark IV, 166
    Canadian Choucroute, 158
    chili, David Lopez's Anti-Extravaganza, 172
    Cinnamon Roasted Tenderloin with Pinot Gris
        Applesauce, 124
    Entrée de Tête Fromagée Maison, 8
    Loin in Tuna Sauce, 128
    Niku-Miso, 12
    Piggies in the Middle, 44
    Portuguese, Marinated with Garlic, 102
    Rummy Smoky Spicy Ribs, 120
    Steak, Real Man Bacon-Wrapped Anchovy Pâté
        Roasted, 107
    Tourtière, 126
    Uccellini Scappati, 112
Pork Loin in Tuna Sauce, 128
Portuguese Pork, Marinated with Garlic, 102
Potato & Rosemary-Garlic Pizza, 140
Potatoes
    Baked Cholesterol (Goat Cheese 'n' Cream
        Potatoes) 138
    Freedom Fries, 146
    Hasselbacks with Fresh Bay Leaves, 139
    Janssen's Temptation, 70
    Potato & Rosemary-Garlic Pizza, 140
PPPPPPPPPasta, 52
Prawn & Peanut Soup with Lime & Coconut, 15
Prawns
    Fiery, in Orange Juice, 4
    Prawns & Okra over Spinach with Lemon, 67
    Prawn & Peanut Soup with Lime & Coconut, 15
    Prawns with Sugar Snap Peas & Garlic, 2
    Roasted, with Morels & Morel Butter, 76
    TVG Paella, 156
Pudding, Lancashire Sticky Toffee, 228
Pumpkin
    Buttermilk Cornbread with Pine Nuts, Pumpkin
        & Oka, 39
    Pumpkin Number, The, 176

R

Rabbit, Lapin aux Pommes, 122
Raspberry Crab Salad, 20
Raspberry Milkshake in a Chocolate Bag, Philippe
    Jeanty's, 182
Real Man Bacon-Wrapped Anchovy Pâté Roasted
    Pork Steak, 107
Ribollita, 30
Rice
    Perfect Risotto, with Asparagus, 59

TVG Paella, 156
Risotto, with Asparagus, The Perfect, 59
Roasted Prawns with Morels & Morel Butter, 76
Roy's Concord Grape Tart, 222
Rummy Smoky Spicy Ribs, 120

S

Salads
    Fennel & Orange, with Black Olives, 17
    Jicama & Green Papaya Slaw with Water
        Chestnuts, 24
    Mexican-Style Chicken, 22
    Raspberry Crab, 20
    Sharon's Caesar, & Diane's State-of-the-Art
        Croutons, 18
Salmon, Drambuie, 79
Sardines, Chili & Capers, with Linguine, 63
Sauces
    Almond Caramel, 21
    Anglaise, 214
    Basil & Mint, with Pappardelle & Tuna, 78
    Brown Sugar, 228
    Butter, with a Rumour of Tomatoes, 136
    Butterless Béarnaise, 41
    Cilantro Pesto, 73
    Ginger-Cream, with Scallop Fettucine, 60
    Joe Muer's De Johnge Butter, 43
    Morel Butter, 76
    Mint, Celery Braised with, 135
    Pinot Gris Applesauce, 124
    Tropical Tartar, 68
    Tuna, 128
Sauerkraut Soup, 28
sauerkraut, Canadian Choucroute, 158
Sauerkraut, Cornish Game Hens with, 88
Sausage in Bondage, 114
Sausage
    Canadian Choucroute, 158
    Chorizo & Garlic, with Lamb Chops, 103
    In Bondage, 114
    Italian Sausage, Eggplant & Dill Winter Soup, 25
    Piggies in the Middle, 44
    Portuguese, in Caldo Verde, 14
Sautéed Grapes with Espresso & Red Wine, 37
Scallops
    Boba Seafood Cakes with Tropical Tartar Sauce, 68
    Fettuccini with Ginger-Cream Sauce, 60
    With Mushrooms & Lime, in Parchment, 74
Sharon's Caesar Salad & Diane's Croutons, 18
Sharpish Cheddar Thins, 42
Sherried, Chilied Oysters, 66
Shredded Brussels Sprouts with Pine Nuts &
    Prosciutto, 141
Shrimp
    Boba Seafood Cakes with Tropical Tartar Sauce,
        68
    Shrimp & Mango Ceviche, 5

Soups
    Caldo Verde, 14
    Escarole & Tomato, with Lemon & Mint, 16
    Italian Sausage, Eggplant & Dill Winter, 25
    Minestronska, 32
    Prawn & Peanut, with Lime & Coconut, 15
    Ribollita, 30
    Sauerkraut, 28
    Spicy Sweet Potato, Roasted Corn & Chipotle
      Bisque, 29
    Uncle John's Nostalgic Carrot Bisque & Sweet
      Variation, 26
Spaghetti with Sage & Celery, 54
Sparkling Jell-O with Moscato d'Asti, 210
Spicy Sweet Potato, Roasted Corn & Chipotle
  Bisque, 29
Spicy Thai & Luscious Basil Chicken, 94
Stews, 149–63
Strawberries in Pepper Foam, 212
Sweet Potato, Roasted Corn & Chipotle Bisque,
  Spicy, 29
Syrup, Sugar, 214

T

Tagine of Beef with Prunes & Almonds, 160
Tea by Two: Erika's Austrian Jägertee, 191
Three-Alarm Black Bean "Caviar," 11
Tiramisù, 220
Tito's Texas Tenderloin, 106
Toffee Pudding, Lancashire Sticky, 228
Tonno con Cilantro Pesto, 73
Tourtière, 126
Tower of Pisa, 173
True North Chili, Mark IV, 166
Tuna
    Fettuccine with Rosemary & Tuna, 48
    Pappardelle with Tuna in Basil & Mint Sauce, 78
    Pork Loin in Tuna Sauce, 128
    Tonno con Cilantro Pesto, 73
    Tuna, with Fettuccine & Rosemary, 48
TVG Paella, 156

U

Uccellini Scappati—Those Little Disappearing
  Birds, 112
Uncle John's Nostalgic Carrot Bisque & Sweet
  Variation, 26

V

Veal
    Charentais Veal Stew, 152
    Entrée de Tête Fromagée Maison, 8
    Tourtière, 126
Vegetables 131–47
    Artichokes, Fresh, with Sherry, 38
    Asparagus, Festive, 147
    Asparagus, White, Ragout with Morels, 40

Asparagus, with The Perfect Risotto, 5
Beans & Escarole, 145
beans, broad, in Fresh Artichokes with Sherry, 38
beans, lima and edamame, in La-La Succotash, 134
beans, lima, in West Coast Scafata, 137
Black Bean "Caviar," Three-Alarm 11
Brussels Sprouts, Shredded, with Pine Nuts &
  Prosciutto, 141
Carrot Bisque, Uncle John's Nostalgic, & Sweet
  Variation, 26
Celery, Braised with Mint Sauce, 135
Corn, Confetti (La-La Succotash) 134
Escarole & Tomato Soup with Lemon & Mint, 16
Escarole & Beans, 145
kale soup, Caldo Verde, 14
Giardiniera Marietta, 132
Mushrooms with Scallops & Lime, in
  Parchment, 74
Penne with Fresh Vegetables, 58
Potato & Rosemary-Garlic Pizza, 140
potatoes, Hasselbacks with Fresh Bay Leaves, 139
potatoes, Freedom Fries, 146
potatoes, Janssen's Temptation, 70
Potatoes, with Goat Cheese 'n' Cream, 138
pumpkin, in Buttermilk Cornbread with Pine
  Nuts, Pumpkin & Oka, 39
Red Peppers, Roasted, Antipasto of, 10
Spinach, Prawns & Okra over, with Lemon, 67
Spaghetti with Sage & Celery, 54
Spicy Sweet Potato, Roasted Corn & Chipotle
  Bisque, 29
Vegetarian
    Baked Cholesterol (Goat Cheese 'n' Cream
      Potatoes) 138
    Blueberry Mincemeat, 36
    Braised Celery with Mint Sauce, 135
    Brussels Sprouts With Pine Nuts & Sage Cream,
      144
    Butter Sauce with a Rumour of Tomatoes, 136
    Buttermilk Cornbread with Pine Nuts, Pumpkin
      & Oka, 39
    DiscDrive Tends-to-Get-Spicy Veggie Chili, 154
    Egg Noodles with Gorgonzola & Pistachios, 50
    Escarole & Beans, 145
    Fennel & Orange Salad with Black Olives, 17
    Festive Asparagus, 147
    Freedom Fries, 146
    Giardiniera Marietta, 132
    Hasselbacks with Fresh Bay Leaves, 139
    Japanese Eggplant Baked with Apricots, 3
    Jicama & Green Papaya Slaw with Water
      Chestnuts, 24
    Joe Muer's De Johnge Butter Sauce, 43
    Katzenthaler Fusilli, 49
    Les Amis' Pecan Cheese Shortbread, 216
    Pasta with Kale & Feta Cheese, 62
    Perfect Risotto, with Asparagus, 59

Perfect Risotto, with Asparagus, 59
Penne with Fresh Vegetables, 58
Potato & Rosemary-Garlic Pizza, 140
Sautéed Grapes with Espresso & Red Wine, 37
Sharpish Cheddar Thins, 42
Spicy Sweet Potato, Roasted Corn & Chipotle
    Bisque, 29
Three-Alarm Black Bean "Caviar," 11
Uncle John's Nostalgic Carrot Bisque & Sweet
    Variation, 26
White Asparagus Ragout with Morels, 40
Veljacic, David, 116–17

W

Wassail & Other Hotties, 198
West Coast Scafata, 137
Whisky Mac, 202
White Asparagus Ragout with Morels, 40

Y

Yard of Flannel, 200

Z

Ziti with Lamb, Ham & Greens, 56

Jurgen Gothe
began writing
about wine and
food in grade two.

About the Author

Jurgen Gothe began writing about wine and food in grade two.

There simply wasn't room in this current collection for his incisive essay on the fate of three empties—water, medicine and wine bottles—that met in a post-World War II landfill in Berlin and ruminated on their adventures. The wine bottle (no surprise there) got all the best lines. Perhaps there's a movie in there somewhere, or the nucleus of a subsequent volume.

He began his broadcasting career shortly thereafter—he was by now in grade three—as a "sporadic" (as opposed to a regular) on the program "Die Sonntagskinder," which aired on Sundays, as the name would suggest, on RIAS (Radio in the American Sector) in his hometown.

It seemed inevitable he'd eventually combine the two activities. Fast forward to the fall of 2005 and the 20th anniversary of CBC Radio 2's popular afternoon drive program, "DiscDrive." In the driver's seat, Jurgen Gothe, still entertaining his sizeable audience (there are actually more of you in Michigan, Ohio, New York and Vermont than in all of Canada, and thank you) with a mix of music and ruminations on the good things in life—food, wine, cats (sometimes dogs), films, books, CDs, restaurants, the lot. Here—on CBC Radio 2—he remains the only network host in the 70-year history of the Corporation to have won three gold medals at the New York International Radio Festival for his work, the most recent, for Best Network Radio Personality, in June 2005.

As well as driving the discs daily, five days a week, 52 weeks a year, he's the Food & Wine Editor of *NUVO* magazine, the wine columnist for Vancouver's *Georgia Straight* entertainment weekly, and the host of "Vancouver Flavours," a daily feature on CKBD 600 AM.

Jurgen Gothe is frequently featured in all media, electronic and print, having spent four seasons as co-host of a national wine and food program—"Simply Wine & Cheese/A Taste of Home." He wrote the complete first season of the popular Food Network series "New Classics with Chef Rob Feenie." He's also a frequent contributor to *Western*

Living magazine, with annual food/recipe features and his annual Hit List, a roundup of the best CDs of the year.

He was for many years a *Vancouver Sun* columnist, with his popular "Carte Blanche" column, and did several seasons as the *Globe and Mail's* Vancouver restaurant correspondent. He has appeared in more than 200 different national and international publications over nearly five decades as a journalist.

He has judged food and wine on every continent except Antarctica, including such unlikely locations as Beirut, Snowbird, Utah and a Canadian naval destroyer, albeit in harbour.

Jurgen Gothe heads QGITV, a television production group. He spent seven consecutive springs hosting a cooking class at Villa Delia in Tuscany. He has appeared with dozens of performing arts ensembles, orchestras, clubs and professional organizations as host, auctioneer, wine tasting tutor, et cetera.

He appears in the role of the Journalist (originally voiced by Richard Burton in the London production) in Jeff Wayne's musical *The War of the Worlds* at the H.R. MacMillan Planetarium in Vancouver, in October and November 2005.

He also holds executive positions in a corporate communications consultancy, a company currently focused on interesting food and drink from around the world, and a group planning to produce organic sea salt products.

He has published three previous books and released four CDs. He divides his time between Vancouver and Mayne Island, British Columbia, Ripoli di Lari, Italy, and any other place where there may be good things to eat, drink and hear.